**VOICES OF CHANGE**

**PITT LATIN AMERICAN SERIES**

JOHN CHARLES CHASTEEN & CATHERINE M. CONAGHAN, EDITORS

# VOICES of CHANGE in CUBA

## FROM THE NONSTATE SECTOR

**CARMELO MESA-LAGO**

IN COLLABORATION WITH ROBERTO VEIGA GONZÁLEZ,
LENIER GONZÁLEZ MEDEROS, SOFÍA VERA ROJAS, & ANÍBAL PÉREZ-LIÑÁN

University of Pittsburgh Press

Published by the University of Pittsburgh Press, Pittsburgh, Pa., 15260
Copyright © 2018, University of Pittsburgh Press
All rights reserved
Manufactured in the United States of America
Printed on acid-free paper
10 9 8 7 6 5 4 3 2 1

Cataloging-in-Publication data is available from the Library of Congress

ISBN 13: 978-0-8229-6509-1
ISBN 10: 0-8229-6509-7

COVER ART: From top to bottom: photo by Torontonian / Alamy Stock Photo; *Vendor pushing his bike to sell his wares on Varadero beach in Cuba* by Flickr user skypilot2005 (CC BY-SA 2.0); photo by Javier Ignacio Acuña Ditzel via Flickr (CC BY 2.0)
COVER DESIGN: Joel W. Coggins

EDITIONS IN SPANISH:
*Voces de Cambio en el Sector No-Estatal Cubano*
(Madrid: Editorial Iberoamericana Vervuert), 2016
*Voces de Cambio en el Emergente Sector no Estatal en Cuba*
(Havana: Cuba Posible), 2017

Translation from Spanish by Kenya C. Dworkin, associate professor of Hispanic studies, Department of Modern Languages at Carnegie Mellon University, revised by Carmelo Mesa-Lago

The authors sincerely hope this study will be useful, promote an enriching discussion, and elicit important scientific surveys on Cuba's nonstate sector.

Allow free reign to the fertile imagination we Cubans are exhibiting, which should be done unhindered and unrestricted; the government should facilitate that flow, not obstruct it, and control only what must be controlled.

—Self-employed worker

The current way of thinking must be changed, not only among us but by our leaders. They have to give us more freedom to grow and keep cooperating.

—Member of cooperative

If the state wants us to produce more and better, it should help us do so . . . and give Cuban small farmers a greater chance to cultivate the land.

—Usufruct farmer

I would like that those who govern us think more on how to make citizens' lives simpler, and less about how to preserve ideas that have been demonstrated to bring nothing more than destitution.

—Home seller

# CONTENTS

Acknowledgments  ix

List of Abbreviations  xi

1  The Emerging Nonstate Sector and Its Importance  1
2  Self-Employed Workers  12
3  Usufruct Farmers  45
4  Members of Nonagricultural and Service Cooperatives  69
5  Buying and Selling Dwellings  87
6  Comparisons, Conclusions, and Suggestions  117

Notes  143

Appendices  149

Bibliography  159

About the Authors  165

Index  167

# ACKNOWLEDGMENTS

THE AUTHORS are solely responsible for this study but appreciate the support given by various people and entities. Mitchell Seligson, endowed professor of political science and sociology and principal advisor for the Latin American Public Opinion Project, Vanderbilt University, granted funds for the interviewers' work, transportation, and materials. The Center for Latin American Studies at the University of Pittsburgh, whose director is associate professor of political science Scott Morgenstern, provided research funds for the interviews' tabulation, and the staff administered the project's funds. Alejandro de la Fuente, distinguished professor of Latin American history and economics at Harvard University, organized a 2016 workshop at which the study's results were first presented and discussed. William Bello Sánchez served as a field assistant during the interviews; he resides in Cuba and has undergraduate and master's degrees in geography. Jorge Pérez-López, a renowned expert on Cuba economy and the informal sector, revised the entire manuscript and made numerous useful comments and suggestions. Finally, we appreciate the valuable recommendations from two anonymous readers for the University of Pittsburgh Press.

# ABBREVIATIONS

| | |
|---|---|
| ANAP | National Association of Small [Private] Farmers (Asociación Nacional de Agricultores Pequeños) |
| ANPP | National Assembly of People's Power (Asamblea Nacional del Poder Popular) |
| CCS | Credit and Services Cooperatives (Cooperativas de Crédito y Servicios) |
| CNA | nonagricultural production and service cooperatives (cooperativas de producción no agrícola y de servicios) |
| CPA | agro-livestock production cooperatives (cooperativas de producción agropecuaria) |
| CUC | convertible Cuban peso (peso cubano convertible) |
| CUP | Cuban national peso (peso cubano nacional); 25 CUP = 1 CUC = US $1 |
| GDP | gross domestic product |
| IPF | Institute of Physical Planning (Instituto de Planificación Física) |
| MINCIN | Ministry of Domestic Trade (Ministerio de Comercio Interior) |
| MINCON | Ministry of Construction (Ministerio de Construcción) |
| MINTUR | Ministry of Tourism (Ministerio de Turismo) |

| | |
|---|---|
| MTSS | Ministry of Labor and Social Security (Ministerio de Trabajo y Seguridad Social) |
| NSS | nonstate sector |
| ONAT | National Office of Tax Administration (Oficina Nacional de Administración Tributaria) |
| ONEI | National Office of Statistics and Information (Oficina Nacional de Estadísticas e Información) |
| PCC | Cuban Communist Party (Partido Comunista de Cuba) |
| TRD | state hard-currency shops ("shoppings," as Cubans call them) |
| UBPC | basic units of cooperative agricultural production (unidades básicas de producción cooperativa) |

**VOICES OF CHANGE IN CUBA FROM THE NONSTATE SECTOR**

# 1

# THE EMERGING NONSTATE SECTOR & ITS IMPORTANCE

THIS BOOK examines the "nonstate" sector in Cuba (NSS), whose importance is increasing and has the potential to transform the predominant state economy (71 percent of the labor force), which is in a precarious situation. In this chapter, we quantify the nonstate sector and identify four principal groups: self-employed workers, usufruct farmers, members of new cooperatives, and buyers and sellers of private dwellings. In the chapters that follow, we will explain each group's antecedents based on all available information: characteristics, sizes and trends, achievements, obstacles, and impacts. The most innovative element is the results of our analysis of 80 intensive interviews conducted in Cuba, in 2014–15, to collect the NSS's "voices." The book's main objective is to offer key otherwise unavailable information about the NSS: (a) its characteristics (age, sex, race, and level of education), (b) important economic aspects (e.g., level of satisfaction, occupation, profits, investment, contracted employees, receipt of remittances, microcredit and other assistance, competition, advertising, expansion plans), and (c) their perception regarding the challenges they face and what they would like to see improve or change. We compare these aspects or perceptions among the four groups, explore associations between their characteristics and a series of the groups' responses to similar questions, and extrapolate suggestions made by the "voices" about improving the sector and further contributing to the country's economic and social development.

## WHAT IS THE EMERGING "NONSTATE" SECTOR?

In August 2006, Raúl Castro took his brother, Fidel's, place as the leader of the Cuban government, due to the latter's illness; in 2008, Raúl formally became the president of the State Council and Council of Ministers. Since 2007, approximately, Raúl has implemented numerous reforms, the most important of which he qualified as "structural" (July 27, 2007) because they modify aspects of the current economic system in both diverse and impactful ways.[1]

One of the most important structural reforms has been the reduction in the size of the state sector and the corresponding expansion of the NSS, which had never before occurred in revolutionary Cuba. In 2010, the government announced that there was a vast surplus or unnecessary number of state employees that had to be dismissed to save resources, improve productivity, and increase salaries; 500,000 employees would be fired between October 2010 and March 2011. Another million would be dismissed in December of that same year. It was later estimated that 1.8 million positions would be eliminated by 2015. Those dismissed would find employment in the NSS, which is amply divided into two parts, "private"[2] and cooperative, both with differences regarding how long they've been in existence, property rights, their relationship with the state, the market's role, their size, and growing or shrinking trends (see Mesa-Lago 2013).

The "private" subsector includes four groups:

1. Owners of small parcels of land ("small farmers") that began with the 1959 agrarian reform and continue, although their numbers have been reduced by half; they own the land but have certain obligations to the state—among them, the sale of part of their harvest to the state at a price fixed by the government below the market price (procurement quota: *acopio*), which limits the sale of their products at market prices, although reforms have loosened that up a bit.

2. Self-employed workers who have experienced ups and downs since they started in the 1970s but have been experiencing significant growth since 2011 (operating in 201 state-determined occupations); most are owners of small businesses or are involved in individual economic activities (they can also be lessees of a business the government has ceded them); their products and services are sold at market price.

3. Usufruct farmers on state-owned idle lands who receive the land in order to work it, according to legal rules (including *acopio*). They began in the 1980s but have really taken off since 2008; they do not own the parcels but cultivate them and appropriate what they produce; once they have fulfilled *acopio*, they can sell whatever is left over at market price.

4. Workers hired by the three aforementioned groups; they are not owners or lessees, but salaried employees.

The cooperative subsector that occupies a midpoint between private and state property comprises three groups:

1. Agricultural production cooperatives, including the basic units of cooperative production (UBPC)—created in 1994 by the transformation of large state farms—and Agro-Livestock Production Cooperatives (CPA). Neither of the two owns the land but work it in a collective manner (the state keeps the property and authorizes indefinite leasing contracts to members). Both are the cooperatives most dependent upon the state and have decreased in number and members; the majority of their production goes to the state, which sets prices.[3]
2. Credit and Services Cooperatives (CCS) in which private farmers join forces to obtain credit, purchase input wholesale, and share some equipment; they are the most independent and are increasing in number and membership.
3. Nonagricultural production and service cooperatives (CNA), which include, for example, barbershops created in 2013, and which have expanded, although the membership is still low; they lease from the state, which holds on to property, but sell their products and services at market prices, which government officials say are more independent than agricultural production cooperatives.

The emerging NSS also includes the purchase and sale of dwellings at prices determined by supply and demand; this started in 2011 and has been expanding, as has the construction of new, private dwellings by individuals (which is known as "population's effort").

The Seventh Congress of the Cuban Communist Party (PCC) held in Havana in April 2016 prepared two documents: the conceptualization of the economic model and the development plan through 2030. The former recognizes the existence of heterogeneous forms of ownership and management of the means of production, properly intertwined, such as private and cooperative property; it also accepts the role of the market[4] within a model that gives predominance to central planning and the state enterprise. The government concentrates its action on the economy, its regulation, the conduction and control of the development process, and the management of the fundamental means of production.[5]

Private ownership of specific means of production plays a "supplementary" role to the state; the latter gets detached from the direct administration of activities that need a high degree of independence and autonomy, which in turn contribute to socioeconomic development, efficiency, job creation, and welfare. This "provokes the growth of the nonstate sector of the economy" (NSS) and frees scarce resources; nevertheless, the management of nonstate forms of property does not imply their "privatization or alienation." Furthermore, "the concentration of property and wealth by natural or legal persons are not permitted"; finally, "the state regulates the NSS, as well as the private appropriation of the results of another person's labor and the profits from their businesses" (PCC 2016a: 7–9).

The Congress's two documents specify two types of private entrepreneurialship (*emprendimiento*): small businesses mainly performed by the worker and his/her family, recognized as natural persons (individuals); and micro-, small-, and medium-private enterprises, recognized as legal persons. In addition, "the types of cooperatives accepted by the model are part of the socialist ownership system" and have legal personality, through the collective ownership of the means of production (PCC 2016a: 10). The above constitutes the official legitimacy of the NSS but, paradoxically, stills rejects privatization; even more, the NSS is only conceived in a subordinate manner to the state and with additional restrictions, for instance, in the 2011 party guidelines, concentration of property was banned, and the Guidelines of the 2016 Congress added concentration of wealth (PCC 2016b).

The Congress announced a law of enterprises to regulate the NSS but it had not yet been enacted by December 2016.[6] After stressing the relevance of the recognition of the private enterprise in Cuba's economic system, Monreal (2016: 1–2) pinpoints the slow follow-up to legalize and regulate private enterprise and asks "whether this issue has lost its initial steam." He adds that the educational stage of the process, key for its implementation stage, "has almost not been visible in the national communication media."

## QUANTIFICATION OF THE NONSTATE SECTOR

It is difficult to calculate the number of people in the NSS due to the lack of a figure that integrates the distribution of everyone in the sector. For several years, the *Anuario Estadístico de Cuba* (Cuban Statistical Yearbook) (ONEI) has published a table (7.2 in 2015) containing the distribution of those "employed in the economy according to their job situation," which divides them into cooperative members (until 2012 only the UBPC, CPA, and CCS, and also the CNA since 2013), self-employed workers, and "private" employees. This last category is comprised of salaried employees in mixed enterprises with foreign capital, private owners of land, and the self-employed, until 2010. Since 2011, employees of the self-employed are included in the total number of the latter, which largely explains the huge 167 percent increase that year (table 1). It is probable that the "other private" in the table are being counted twice. Another table in the Yearbook (9.4) shows "land tenants by

Table 1. Employed Labor Force by Employment Situation, 2005–15 (in thousands and percentages)

| Years | Employed labor force | State sector | | Nonstate sector[a] | | | | | | |
|---|---|---|---|---|---|---|---|---|---|---|
| | | | | Cooperatives[b] | | Self-employed | | Other private[d] | | Total[e] |
| Dec. | | | | | | | | | | |
| 2005 | 4,723 | 3,786 | 80.2 | 271 | 5.7 | 169 | 3.6 | 496 | 10.5 | 936 | 19.8 |
| 2006 | 4,755 | 3,889 | 81.8 | 257 | 5.4 | 153 | 3.2 | 456 | 9.6 | 866 | 18.2 |
| 2007 | 4,868 | 4,036 | 82.9 | 242 | 5.0 | 138 | 2.8 | 453 | 9.3 | 834 | 17.1 |
| 2008 | 4,948 | 4,112 | 83.1 | 234 | 4.7 | 142 | 2.9 | 460 | 9.3 | 836 | 16.9 |
| 2009 | 5,072 | 4,249 | 83.8 | 232 | 4.6 | 144 | 2.8 | 448 | 8.8 | 823 | 16.2 |
| 2010 | 4,984 | 4,178 | 83.8 | 217 | 4.4 | 147 | 2.9 | 442 | 8.9 | 806 | 16.2 |
| 2011 | 5,010 | 3,873 | 77.3 | 209 | 4.2 | 392 | 7.8 | 537 | 10.7 | 1,137 | 22.7 |
| 2012 | 4,902 | 3,684 | 75.2 | 217 | 4.4 | 405 | 8.3 | 600 | 12.2 | 1,222 | 24.9 |
| 2013 | 4,919 | 3,629 | 73.8 | 227 | 4.6 | 424 | 8.6 | 639 | 13.0 | 1,290 | 26.2 |
| 2014 | 4,970 | 3,592 | 72.3 | 231 | 4.6 | 483 | 9.7 | 664 | 13.4 | 1,378 | 27.7 |
| 2015 | 4,864 | 3,460 | 71.2 | 215 | 4.4 | 499 | 10.3 | 687 | 14.1 | 1,400 | 28.8 |

Notes: [a] This excludes usufruct farmers, small private farmers, and land lessees (see table 2).
[b] In 2005–10, figures are limited to members of agricultural cooperatives; beginning in 2011, they include nonagricultural and service cooperative members (2,300 in 2013; 7,700 in 2015).
[c] Since 2011, they include contracted, salaried employees.
[d] In 2005–10, they included salaried employees at mixed enterprises, self-employed workers, and small private farmers; since 2011, those contracted by self-employed workers appear in the "self-employed" column.
[e] Total of cooperatives, self-employed workers, and other private activities.

Source: Absolute figures from ONEI 2010, 2012, 2013a, 2014, 2015, 2016a; based on those sources, we have calculated the absolute numbers that correspond to the state, to others in the private sector, and to the total nonstate sector, as well as all the percentages.

TABLE 2. Estimated number of people in the nonstate sector, 2014

| Categories | Total | Percentages of | | Percentages of Women[d] | |
|---|---|---|---|---|---|
| | | Subtotal | Labor force | Number | Percent |
| Self-employed [a] | 483,400 | 41.4 | 9.5 | 142,500 | 29.4 |
| Usufruct farmers [b] | 312,296 | 26.7 | 6.1 | | |
| Landowners | 99,500 | 8.5 | 1.9 | | |
| Cooperative members | | | | | |
|   UBPC, CPA, CCS | 231,500 | 19.8 | 4.5 | 31,600 | 13.6 |
|   CNA | 5,500 | 0.5 | 0.1 | 1,200 | 21.8 |
| Peasants | 32,000 | 2.8 | 0.6 | | |
| Lessees | 2,843 | 0.2 | 0.1 | | |
| 1. Subtotal | 1,167,911 | 100.0 | 22.8 | | |
| Private jobs [c] | 663,600 | | | | |
| 2. Total | 1,831,511 | | | | |
| 3. Labor force | 5,105,500 | | | | |
| Percentages | | | | | |
| 4. One-third nonstate | 22.8 | | | | |
|   State | 77.2 | | | | |
|   Total | 100.0 | | | | |
| 5. Two-thirds nonstate | 35.8 | | | | |
|   State | 64.2 | | | | |
|   Total | 100.0 | | | | |

*Notes:* [a] This includes owners (402,185) and salaried employees (81,125).
[b] This includes 142,862 approved in the 1970s, and 169,434 since 2008.
[c] This category is not defined; it could include salaried employees working for mixed enterprises with foreign investment, owners of parcels, and cooperative members' employees.
[d] These percentage distributions exclude salaried employees.

*Source*: Calculated by authors based on ONEI, 2015.

natural persons," which separates out usufruct farmers, private owners, lessees, and dispersed peasants. Nevertheless, data on this table has only been available since 2013, so it was not possible to include this group in table 2.[7]

The size of the employed labor force peaked in 2009 but afterward exhibited a downward trend (save for 2012) and in 2015 was 4 percent below the peak; this was caused by population aging and the government attempt to dismiss 1.8 million surplus state employees (36 percent of the labor force). In 2010 the firing of such employees began and by 2015, the state sector had shrunk by 718,000 workers, 40 percent of the target.[8] State employment went down from 83.8 percent of the labor force in 2010 to 71.2 percent in 2015, 12.6 percentage points less, while the NSS grew from 19.8 percent in 2005 to 28.8

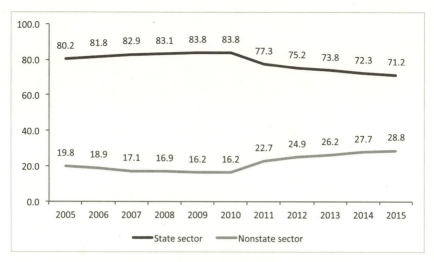

Figure 1. Evolution of state and nonstate sector, 2005–14.

percent in 2015, and this is not counting landowners, lessees, and dispersed peasants (fig. 1). Despite this notable growth, the state sector shrank less than planned because the NSS expanded at a slower rate (see Mesa-Lago 2014: chaps. 2–5).

In table 2, we bring together these diverse figures to calculate the number of people in the NSS and calculate their proportion of the labor force. In addition, we estimate the percentage of women in the three available categories. Due to previously explained problems regarding the "others private" category, we decided to calculate the state sector, both in absolute numbers and as percentage of the labor force, with and without the "others private." Respectively, the absolute figures are 1,167,911 and 1,831,511 (the 663,000 difference represents "others private"), while the NSS percentages relative to the labor force are 22.8 percent and 35.8 percent, respectively.

A serious problem with the previous figures is that when the total number of NSS persons in 2014, including "others private" (1,831,511), is added to the number of employees in the state sector (3,592,000), the total, 5,423,511 equals 106 percent of the employed labor force, which confirms that there is a double counting, probably in "others private." If the latter are included, the target of 1.8 million people in the NSS in 2015 appears to have been met but, in reality, it has not, as there were already one million people in this sector in 2010. Thus, the cipher that was truly added was less than 800,000, or 44 percent of the target.

Women are a minority in the three NSS categories: 29.4 percent in self-employment, 21.8 percent in CNA, and 13.6 percent in agricultural production cooperatives (we will contrast that with the interview sample); no distri-

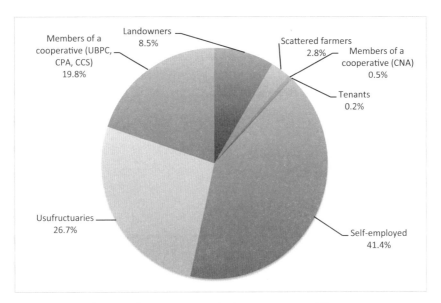

FIGURE 2. Distribution of nonstate sector by its components, 2014.

bution by gender is available in the remaining categories (table 2). A review of the licenses authorized to the self-employed in 2010–13 reveals that women had an average of 34 percent of the total. In addition, a general trend was observed: the number of males getting licenses increased, even in categories such as home decoration, music instruction, and hairdressing, while there was also a raise in the percentage of jobs traditionally assigned to women, for example, clothing pressers (Díaz and Echevarría 2015).

The distribution of people by group in the NSS (excluding "others private") is as follows: 41.4 percent self-employed workers, 26.7 percent usufruct farmers, 19.8 percent agricultural production cooperatives, 8.5 percent small landowners, 2.8 percent diverse-dispersed peasants, 0.5 percent CNA members, and 0.2 percent lessees (fig. 2). We lack data about the last three groups. The sum of self-employed workers and usufruct farmers totals 68 percent, which makes these two groups crucial for the interviews. There are very few CNA members compared to the number of agricultural-livestock cooperative members, but the latter numbers are declining, whereas in 2013 the CNA began to increase their membership. As a new type of cooperative and part of the structural reforms, the government considers CNA to be important and gives them benefits that self-employed workers and usufruct farmers lack. This is why we decided to include CNA in our interviews. Table 2 excludes buying and selling of private dwellings because there is little data, but this private activity plays an important role in the reforms. It is estimated that there were 133,000 transactions in 2011–14, another reason to include them.

There are no statistics about the proportion of Cuba's gross domestic product (GDP) generated by the NSS; in 2011 it was projected that it would reach 35 percent of GDP in 2015, but no figure was given in that year.

Participants in the emerging NSS are primary players in the reforms and have the potential of substantially changing Cuba's economy and society in the medium term. We lack adequate information about perceptions on important issues from the four identified NSS groups: the degree of satisfaction in each group regarding their work and earnings; the number of employees they hire and their salaries; the taxes they pay; net profits they make and how they are allocated between investment and consumption; the potential reception of foreign remittances, government micro-credit and/or assistance from family in Cuba or abroad; the sources to buy their inputs; competition or the lack thereof; publicity channels; challenges they face; and improvements and changes they would like to see implemented.

## STUDY METHODOLOGY AND BOOK STRUCTURE

The ideal way to obtain the NSS data would be a scientific survey done throughout all of Cuba. However, only the government and the party (PCC) conduct regular opinion polls, and their results are not published. The ONEI (2015) cites the "Survey of Self-Employed Workers" as the source of some statistics, but we were not able to access it. Cuban social scientists need to be authorized to conduct surveys.[9] Therefore, it was impossible to conduct a national survey as it would have been quite difficult to get state permission and carry it out free of risk.

A viable alternative was to conduct interviews in one geographic area. The self-employed have been the subject of several interviews with a diverse number of interviewees, dates, activities, and locations: 60 in 1999–2001 (half of them were re-interviewed in 2002–9 and an undefined number in 2011), targeted on *paladares*, taxi drivers, and private lodging in Havana, by two North American experts (Ritter and Henken 2015); an undetermined number were interviewed in 2007–8 by a U.S. anthropologist (Armengol 2013); 35 in 2010, about gender, in Havana (Díaz and Echevarría 2015); 72 in 2011, by three Cuban academics (Díaz, Pastori, and Piñeiro 2012); 25 in 2012, by a U.S. economist (Feinberg 2013); 419 in 2013–14 in 57 self-employed activities, mostly in Old Havana, which asked a large number of important questions (Pañellas, Torralbas, and Caballero 2015); and a survey done in January–April 2014, conducted with 746 self-employed workers, based on a stratified, national sample, which provided multiple choice answers (Padilla Pérez 2015).[10] Most of the interviews did not publish the questionnaires and tabulated responses, and five of them were carried out before the expansion of self-employment or just as it was starting. In 2014, a Cuban sociologist conducted interviews in 29 CNA in the province of Havana and analyzed their results (Piñeiro 2014). To the best of our knowledge, there have not been interviews with usufruct farmers and dwelling buyers and sellers.[11]

To conclude, despite notable advances made on the self-employed, there is no overarching, integrated, and recent study using detailed methodology to generate systematic and adequate information that captures the perceptions among the four selected groups about their work and desires, and their views on the reforms. To fill the existing void and give voice to the protagonists, standardized interviews were conducted in a number of municipalities mainly in Havana province, which was where the greatest number of these groups' members were concentrated. It would have been much more difficult and costly to conduct them in other provinces. The interviews were done by two Cuban social scientists living on the island and trained in social communication, sociology, and political science.

A total of 80 interviews were conducted between September 2014 and December 2015, 25 each with self-employed workers, usufruct farmers, and dwelling buyers, sellers, and realtors. Only five were done with CNA members due to difficulties getting authorization to carry out the interviews with CNA transferred from state enterprises, which is the majority. As much as possible, a certain degree of diversity was sought with regard to age, gender, race, education, occupation, and location. Interviewees were selected using nonprobabilistic methods. The sample was chosen by the interviewers based on their contact with interviewees, who took them to other people, producing a snowball effect; therefore, the sample is not representative and the results cannot be generalized to the universe and should be considered as indicative.

The interviewees were informed that the interview was anonymous and for an independent, scientific study. They also were told that they did not have to answer a question if they didn't want to, so some questions remained unanswered and no one insisted otherwise. In some cases, such as regarding profits, interviewees did not provide quantities. Each questionnaire had about 20 questions, some common, for the purpose of comparison, and other specific ones adjusted to the characteristics of the group. Most questions were open-ended, and none offered specific options prior to the responses. Thus, interviewees had complete freedom to speak out during the interview period that took between one-and-a-half to two hours. No interviewee refused to participate and very few questions remained unanswered, although there were times when answers were imprecise, probably due to apprehension. Appendix 1 contains the full questionnaires for each one of the four groups. A pilot with the questions was carried out to be sure that they worked well and some adjustments were made to them thereafter.[12]

This study offers comprehensive, concrete, and empirical information regarding the structural reforms in Cuba as seen through their principal protagonists; it should be useful to anyone interested in Cuba: scholars, policy makers, foundations, and others.

For this English edition, statistics, information, and leaders' important speeches were updated to November 9, 2016, which included key events such as the Seventh Congress of the Communist Party held in April 2016, the National Assembly of People's Power (ANPP) meeting in July 2016, the Five-Year Plan (2012–16) Guidelines released in August 2016, the Long-Term Plan through 2030, and so forth. In addition, we included whatever data was available from ONEI Statistical Yearbook 2015 at the time this study was completed.

The book is organized in six chapters. After this introduction, there are four chapters that examine in a similar manner the four chosen groups. It offers antecedents (size and trends, characteristics, progress, obstacles, and impact) and then presents and analyzes the tabulated interview results, with examples of the most relevant and interesting answers (Vera Rojas and Pérez-Liñán 2015). Chapter 6 offers the conclusions, the results of comparing interviewee characteristics among the four groups with common responses, and the voices of change: problems, desires, and suggestions. Information in the antecedents is current to November 9, 2016.

# 2
# SELF-EMPLOYED WORKERS

## ANTECEDENTS

Self-employed workers are "those who being or not owners of the means of production, do not have a labor contract with legal entities and are not paid wages" (ONEI 2015; see Cobo 2016). They must be Cubans or foreign permanent residents, over age 17, work in authorized occupations, register as contributors at the National Office of Tax Administration (ONAT), obtain a license, pay all taxes punctually, enroll in social security pensions and pay their contributions, and fulfill any other obligation (*Juventud Rebelde*, Oct. 1, 2013).

### Size and trends

The number of self-employed workers diminished from 169,000 in 2005 to 147,000 in 2010. With 18 new occupations authorized (the number grew from 183 to 201), as well as a plan to reduce the state labor surplus, self-employment increased 167 percent to 391,000 in 2011; this leap was also the result of including salaried employees hired by self-employed owners who had appeared previously in the category of "others private." The rate of annual growth decelerated to 3.3 percent in 2012, grew to 4.7 percent in 2013, and 13.9 percent in 2014, and then decelerated again to 2.6 percent in 2015. In fact, there was a decrease in self-employment in 2015. According to the Ministry of Labor and Social Security (MTSS), between May and October 2015, the number of self-employed workers dwindled by 2,213, from 504,613 to 502,400; later on,

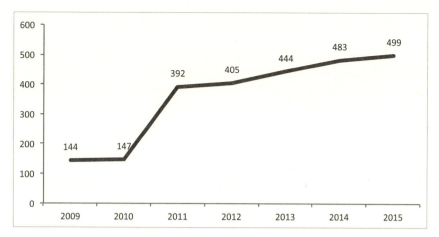

FIGURE 3. Evolution of number of self-employed, 2009–15. *Source*: Elaboration based on ONEI 2011, 2013, 2015, 2016a.

a new drop was reported, from 504,613 to 496,400, a decline of 1.6 percent in December compared to the peak in May 2015. Finally, in March 2016, the MTSS announced an increase to 505,342 ("Expectativas" 2014; MTSS 2015; *Trabajadores,* Nov. 1, 2016; *EFE,* Apr. 29, 2016; see fig. 3).

The impetus in 2013–14 was due to the approval of new occupations, dwelling rentals, relations between state tourist companies and the self-employed, and the transfer to the latter of gastronomical state enterprises (food, restaurants, etc.), and personal or technical services. However, the 2015 deceleration was caused by the suppression of various occupations with no new ones approved, the closure of small businesses, the reinforcement of tax payment controls, and the increase of inspections and fines due to legal infringements (see the section titled "Obstacles" below).

In 2010, there were 147,000 self-employed owners that in 2015 rose to 382,400 (not counting their 114,000 employees), which means the net increase was 235,400, a jump of 60 percent when compared to the 147,000 in 2010 (based on table 1 and *Trabajadores,* Jan. 11, 2015). The target for 2012 was 695,300, which, based on the total of 499,000 (owners and employees) at the end of 2015 (three years later), means that only 72 percent of the target was met. In 2015, "the number of new businesses does not compensate for the closed number, that is, that net growth is negative" (Cuba Standard 2015: 6).

## Characteristics

In 2013, only 16 percent of the self-employed had been previously fired from state jobs; in 2014, 69 percent of self-employed had no prior labor ties (they were probably informal workers who became legalized). These characteristics have not been published again. According to the MTSS, in December

2015, 17 percent of the self-employed also had a state job. These figures suggest that very few self-employed workers had been dismissed from their state positions and also explains why the dismissal plan is so far behind. Conversely, 30 percent were women (a slight increase from 2014), similar to the 29.4 percent calculated in table 2. Another 30 percent were young people, a stable percentage since 2013.[1] An additional 22 percent were salaried employees, a decline of 11 percentage points since 2013. The great majority worked in food and transportation jobs. In addition, 12 percent were retirees, a proportion similar to others published previously. Principal labor activities toward the end of 2015 were the following: 11 percent food preparation, 10 percent cargo and passenger transport, 6 percent rental of dwellings or rooms, and 5 percent communication agents; 68 percent were not specified, which indicates an enormous variety of occupations, which have been confirmed by our interviews. Regarding their location, 65 percent of self-employed workers were concentrated in the provinces of Havana, Matanzas, Villa Clara, Camagüey, Holguín, and Santiago de Cuba (*Juventud Rebelde*, Aug. 16, 2013; *Trabajadores*, Aug. 25, 2014 and Jan. 11, 2016; MTSS 2015). Very little information is available on age, sex, race, education, earnings, and location of self-employed workers; the interviews will be useful in this regard.

## Advances

We have seen that the Seventh Congress of the party legalized self-employment and acknowledged the workers' contributions to job creation, efficiency, and production (see chapter 1). Recently an official campaign in the national media shows in a positive light the rise and consolidation of the "private" sector in the country and portrays it as more efficient than the state sector, including interviews with owners of small businesses (Amuchástegui 2016).

The expansion of self-employed work has had a very positive impact, which is reflected in the diverse offering of services (mostly) and products, as well as in the improvement in quality. An example of this is the proliferation of *paladares* (small private restaurants), some of which have very high standards. Self-employment has also given Cubans the hope of improving their income and having a better future. Generally, self-employed workers are owners of the micro-enterprises (except when they lease from state companies), and they fix market prices for the sales of their products or services. In addition to family members, they can also contract a limitless number of salaried employees, although with previous authorization; they can also open bank accounts. Finally, by paying a contribution, the self-employed have a right to monetary benefits for maternity leave and social security pensions for old age, disability, and death. Self-employed previously paid contributions (set with a minimum) as state employees are counted toward their pensions (MTSS 2014).

Since mid-2014, 12,988 state food establishments (69 percent of the total) and personal or technical services (31 percent) are being gradually transferred to self-employed workers and nonagricultural production and service cooperatives (CNA). Until October 2014, 27 percent of all state establishments had been transferred, as well as 12 percent of their 134,402 workers. Marino Murillo, vice president of the Council of Ministers, minister of economics and planning until mid-2016, and the chief of the commission to implement the reforms, has said, "Up until now, the state units that have become nonstate business have garnered favorable results; the workers have increased their income, refurbished buildings, and expanded service hours; while rising the prices at which they sell to the public, they have improved the quality and assortment of their offerings" (*Granma*, June 23, 2014). These businesses' property and transportation assets remain in the hands of the state, which rents them out through ten-year (renewable) contracts under the control of the Ministry of Domestic Trade (MINCIN) at tax rates established by the government according to the size and location of buildings, whereas state equipment, tools, and supplies are rented or sold. The cost of electricity, water, and telephone, purchase of inputs, and maintenance and repairs are defrayed by these new forms of management ("Más de 12.000 unidades" 2014). In May 2016 the government started bidding on the remaining inactive state enterprises in commerce gastronomy and services, which were leasing to those who offered the highest leases and better quality and professionalism (Resolution 61, 2016).

*Granma* has reported that private taxis, which previously belonged to the state company Cubataxi, have been a notable success because the state "traditional system had not been able to resolve service irregularities, theft of receipts, excessively large payrolls, and an aged vehicle stock," which caused a "loss of quality in service." Since 2014, taxis have been rented to previous drivers or self-employed workers, who cover gas, maintenance, and a portion of repairs with their earnings (the state pays the other portion), on par with them paying taxes. The new system was extended throughout the country in 2014; this resulted in a "substantial increase in productivity," "considerable decrease in client wait time," and an appropriate use of taximeters, which increase earnings. After a year, the average state income per taxi rose 30 times, which allows for replacement of 60 percent of the existing taxi stock (Puig 2014: 3).

In 2014, two-year contracts between the state travel company Cubanacán and self-employed workers that handled lodgings and *paladares* were approved for the purpose of ensuring the places necessary for foreign tourists and better quality in services; payments are made in CUC. State entities sell packages to 50 European agencies that include some private services ("Turismo . . . ," 2015). In addition, the Ministry of Tourism authorized self-employed workers and CNA to set contractual relations with state tourist establishments. In 2015, 40 activities were permitted to receive payment not only in Cuban national pesos (CUP), but also in convertible pesos (CUC), via bank transfers, not in cash. This norm seeks to guarantee the procurement of a service or product of higher quality and under better conditions than those offered by state entities and mixed enterprises (MINTUR 2015).

In 2013, two taxes on self-employment were exempted for three months for those getting started in their activities, and for the tax on the labor force for those who had five or fewer salaried employees. In addition, a 5 percent discount was granted to those who punctually paid their annual personal income tax as well as a simplified tax payment to 56 percent on all activities with lower earnings (*Juventud Rebelde,* October 2, 2013). Deductible expenses from income taxes were expanded by 10 percent at the December 2015 meeting of the National Assembly of People's Power (ANPP) (Pedraza 2015). In 2016, ONAT added the possibility of sending taxpayers the income declaration form via email, which could speed up their receipt. The 2016 guidelines of the party stipulated that it would continue the provision of fiscal incentives to promote the "orderly" development of the nonstate sector (NSS) (PCC 2016b: 3).

In terms of training, the Catholic Church's Centro Padre Félix Varela pioneered a program entitled "Cuba Emprende," which in three years has graduated 2,000 micro-businessmen and helped 1,300 with their businesses. The program offers free, one-month workshops that include courses in marketing and management, accounting and finances, sales and client services, and human development; upon completing the workshop, participants must elaborate a business plan based on a proposal developed in the workshop. After completing the program, advisors are assigned to help the graduates with business management and problem solving (Cuba Emprende 2016). The Santa Clara District Center of Training Felicia Pérez, a Catholic nonprofit, cultural organization, has joined the effort (*Cubaeconomía,* July 9, 2015). The minister of education, in coordination with the MTSS, offers free training to self-employed workers on taxes, economics, marketing, communication techniques, and electronics. Other courses are given to those associated with tourism agencies; the National Association of Economists and Accountants also offers courses to those who apply for bank credit ("Mas de 12.000 unidades" 2014; "Turismo . . . ," 2015; Fong and Rosabel,2015; "Nuevos cursos" 2016).[2]

Decree-Law 289 of 2012 authorized granting credit to the NSS; in 2013, none was given and in 2014 only 2 percent of all self-employed workers, usufruct farmers, and CNA members received credit ("En la reunión" 2014). The amount of the micro-loans increased in 2015; it is reported that the process was made more flexible and that "the paperwork is not cumbersome," that borrowers are offered advice through business consultants, and that interest is low. The sum of loans granted in January–July 2015 quadrupled those awarded in all of 2014. In 2015, Peoples Saving Bank increased the average credit amount from 10,000 to 20,000 CUP (from US $400 to US $800), without requiring real estate or other collateral guarantees, and with less cumbersome documentation, which is expected to facilitate credit approval in three days. In addition, the grace period and the rate of amortization were extended from five to ten years (*EFE*, Sept. 8, 2015; *Granma*, Oct. 6, 2015; Fong and Rosabel 2015).

Over the past two years, progress has been made on publicity. Posters on building façades,[3] flyers, announcements on light posts, and on Revolico.com are still being used. New avenues include the telephone book's yellow pages, tourist guidebooks, the so-called Weekly Package (*Paquete Semanal*: an external memory drive with TV programs, games, Revolico, etc.),[4] and monthly *ofertas* (ads) from the National Information Agency, which publishes 60,000 copies and sells them at a price of 3 CUC, although only one of the 16 pages contains classified ads. New telecommunications agents devote their time to promotions and small-scale sales of products and services, including Internet access, although it continues to be limited due to the little access the population has to it and the high cost (2.25 CUC/hour). Start-ups like AlaMesa, Conoce Cuba, and Isladentro are rapidly gaining ground: they contact potential clients among self-employed workers and put them on the digital map. Apps are provided to the public free of charge via cell phones and charge small businesses 5 CUC to include them (*Juventud Rebelde*, March 26, 2015; Henken 2015).

## Obstacles

According to *Granma* (Jan. 31, 2014), the principal problems that self-employed workers face are: shortage of raw materials and inputs due to the lack of a wholesale market, the mistrust of state managers who do not sell to and buy from them, and the unprofessionalism of inspectors. Another source adds that self-employed workers have to finance themselves with their savings or family loans, while high taxes increase a micro-business's start-up price (CSG 2015). A survey taken among 120 small businesses in Cuba identified the following obstacles: 75 percent lack of inputs, 47 percent high taxes, 41 percent excessive regulations, 17 percent absence of financing; only 4 percent said they had no obstacles (Vidal 2016b). Our interviews show similar results.

The 2011 guidelines ordered the creation of wholesale markets, which began in 2013 with El Trigal, but there were complaints of its insufficient sale of inputs. The magazine *Bohemia* (Apr. 1, 2015) argued that if there were a wholesale market it would put an end to the theft (*desviación*) of state resources, make fiscal declarations more transparent, and foment the necessary climate of legality. The absence of such a market and the impossibility of importing inputs,[5] force self-employed workers to buy at hard-currency state stores (TRD, called "shoppings" by Cubans) that charge a 240 percent or more margin of profit, and at the black markets, also at high prices; such buying may cause problems when the time comes to prove the legal origin of inputs. El Trigal was closed in May 2016. Nevertheless, the same month Resolution 62 was enacted to regulate the wholesale market. Furthermore, in July, an experimental warehouse market (Zona+) was opened in the Miramar neighborhood of Havana offering food and personal hygiene products for the self-employed; it was said that Zona+ is better stocked that the TRD but only a handful of goods are available for buying in bulk at a 20 percent discount ("State firm" 2016). The administrator of the gastronomic CNA Casa Potín stated, "we had great illusions with Zona+ but, in reality, there is no difference in its prices with those of other markets" (Mata 2016b).

The vast majority of occupations that the self-employed are authorized to work at are very specific and generally unskilled (clowns, magicians, fortune tellers, water carriers, produce cart sellers, night watchmen, public bathroom caretakers, street flower vendors); the minority are skilled (real estate, insurance, and telecommunications agents, bookkeepers, refrigeration equipment mechanics, translators, language professors (see Ritter and Henken 2015). Occupations are concentrated in the area of services; small businesses are still not permitted in industry, except for a few marginal ones. University graduates cannot be self-employed; an architect is forbidden from practicing his or her profession privately, which would considerably help in private construction (it is reported that many do so illegally), but they can be taxi drivers. These restrictions waste Cuba's great investment in education and obstruct both dismissing professionals who are state employees and expanding the NSS. There are rules that strictly control all occupations, sometimes very specific ones, like those for bathroom caretakers. It is not logical to define in a detailed manner the activities that the state approves; it would be much better to create a list of activities banned and leave the rest to free initiative (Pérez Villanueva and Torres Pérez 2016 has the same opinion).

In 2013, three resolutions authorizing ten new occupations and revising rules concerning self-employment were enacted. They reiterated proving the legal origin of raw materials and inputs; taking responsibility for the quality of products or services; protecting urban decor, the environment, and hygiene; and facilitating controls by inspectors. Among these new rules are the following: street vendors must follow itineraries determined by municipal councils and are only allowed to spend a few minutes in one spot; the sale of merchandise acquired on the retail network or imported is prohibited;[6] cafeterias can sell beer but no other alcoholic beverages; a food and soda vendor cannot use kiosks or similar installations; and new licenses to make or sell soap, shoe polish, and dyes were suspended (*Resoluciones* 353, 41, and 42, 2013; *Juventud Rebelde* Oct. 2, 2013). About this, President Castro said, "Each step we take should be concomitant with the establishment of a sense of order. . . . Inadequate controls by government entities regarding illegal activities carried out by private businesses were not resolved at the appropriate time, which created an environment of impunity and accelerated the increase of activities that were never authorized." He went on to add that when problems arise, "we must act immediately and without hesitation when the activities are small and isolated, which is always preferable than waiting for the problems to take root" (AP, Dec. 20, 2013).

Taxes are designed to control the growth of self-employment and avoid the concentration of wealth, one of the guidelines' objectives.[7] There are two payment categories: (1) a *simplified plan* for activities that generate low income, which represent 56 percent of self-employed workers; these contribute a monthly rate from 20 to 150 CUP, plus the social security contribution, which is 25 percent of the income level declared and fluctuates between 88 and 500 CUP, and (2) a *general plan*, which includes four taxes: (a) 10 percent tax on sales; (b) social security, as in the simplified plan; (c) on the labor force, which was 10 percent in 2015[8] but increases progressively with the number of contracted employees: it is exempted for five or fewer employees, 6 to 10 employees pay 436 CUP, 11 to 15 employees pay 1,017 CUP, and more than 16 employees pay 1,191 CUP for each additional one, which penalizes self-employed workers that generate more jobs and conspires against the official goal of dismissing unnecessary state personnel; and (d) personal income tax, which is also progressive, and includes a monthly payment that fluctuates between 30 and 700 CUP according to labor activity, and a scaled annual payment (the first 10,000 CUP are exempt) that increases from 15 percent per 10,000 to 20,000 CUP up to 50 percent for over 50,000 CUP;[9] if the annual total is greater than the sum of monthly taxes, the difference must be paid via an affidavit.[10] It is possible for the tax burden to exceed net profit.

It is estimated that in 2015 Cuba's tax burden generally took 37 percent of income, twice the Latin American average; the top 50 percent tax on personal income can be compared to 27 percent for the region, and the few countries that tax the labor force do so at a much lower rate (Pérez 2015; Ritter and Henken 2015). This prompts evasion, underdeclaration of income, and high selling prices. A report to the ANPP in June 2014, based on a sample of 30,000 self-employed workers, revealed that 95 percent underdeclared their income in 2013; furthermore, ONAT lacks the resources to verify self-employed workers' income and their deductible expenses. Finally, there is an incentive to contract salaried employees illegally; thus, in 2015 there was only an average of 0.3 percent employees per each self-employed owner (see the subsection "6. Employees" in the section titled "Results and Analysis of Interviews" below).

A 2014 Decree-Law stipulates the imposition of fines up to 1,500 CUP; withdrawal of license; and confiscation of equipment, tools, and raw materials for self-employed workers who infringe the law. Supervisors in provincial and municipal districts, state inspectors, and the police are responsible for imposing sanctions; their decisions can be appealed before the director of the corresponding unit, who serves as judge and has a conflict of interest (Decree-Law 315, 2014). Sanctions are imposed for legal violations, such as using more tables, chairs, or other things higher than the number set; employing a worker without having the needed authorization; or creating cooperatives that are not expressly authorized.

In January–June 2015, 2,482 self-employed workers applied for loans— only 0.6 percent of all self-employed; a tiny 0.06 percent of Havana self-employed workers had been granted credit at the end of 2014. The applicant must fill out a form, present his or her ID card, authorization for the proper activity, the ONAT registration and last tax payment receipt, a copy of the financial statement, evidence of liquidity outflow (which is very complex for inexpert applicants, who often have to hire help), and other documents. Instead of the alleged three days for making a decision, it takes from seven to twenty days after all documents are processed; one applicant claimed that it took him six months. Before granting the loan, the bank undertakes a rigorous analysis of the micro-business's feasibility, its chances for success, and the applicant's record; afterward, the bank oversees the loan every three months to check how it is being invested. Even though there are assurances that no collateral guarantee is needed, borrowers must have a bank account in which the very income the business generates serves as the guarantee, which frequently takes from 48 to 50 percent of such income. In contradiction to the affirmation that interest rates are low, it actually depends on the credit period: rates oscillate between 2.5 percent and 3.5 percent for three months but increase to between 8 percent and 10 percent for two years. All this ends up being excessive for a maximum loan of US $800. Finally, only 35 percent of the loans granted to the NSS in 2012–15 were assigned to self-employed workers, small farmers, and CNA members. Moreover, in 2014, 99 percent of loans went to private farmers (Fong and Rosabel 2015; *EFE*, Sept. 8, 2015; *Granma*, Oct. 6, 2015; León and Pajón 2015). León and Pajón conclude that the credit policy has been incapable of expanding the potential of productive forces.

The 2014 law regarding foreign investment excludes the self-employed from receiving such investments or creating mixed enterprises. Neither can they have credit cards like MasterCard, which started being used in 2015, hence an obstacle for U.S. visitors (Havana Consulting Group, Jan. 27, 2015).

Self-employment was successively permitted, reduced, and reauthorized; that uncertainty worsened due to the following government actions taken in 2013–16: the closure of hundreds of micro-businesses located in Havana building arcades; the imposition of high taxes on the sale of imported clothes and shoes, and their later prohibition, which affected 20,000 self-employed workers (their competition took sales away from TRD, which enjoys profits of 240 percent or more); the shutdown of small movie theaters exhibiting 3-D films that state theaters do not show, as well as of video game galleries; the removal of hundreds of self-employed from the ground floor of a former department store; and the cancellation of licenses to leasers of rooms to tourists in Pinar del Río because they built swimming pools for their guests. Public teachers that tutor students (*repasadores*) on the side to supplement their meager salaries have been accused of performing unethical, illegal activities. In October 2016, Havana's city government suspended licensing *paladares*, warned existing ones to strictly obey regulations, and called to meetings the most important *paladar* owners to hear the regulatory violations some of them had committed; a wave of inspections followed (*Reuters*, Nov. 22, 2013; Ravsberg 2015; *Juventud Rebelde*, Oct. 4, 2015; *Havana Times*, May 25, 2016; Mata 2016a; Frank 2016).

The problems above are a disincentive to self-employment. The magazine *Bohemia* (March 9, 2014) has revealed various cases of disinterest in their contracts with state enterprises: the latter delay paying the self-employed and use checks with a commission—and to cash them requires standing in long lines, for hours, at banks that also pay out pensions and salaries. There have been cases in which the contracting enterprise lacks the checks to pay. Those who work in transport prefer negotiating directly with tourists and fixing their prices, free of these trappings. Despite the fact that 1,000 gastronomical establishments had been transferred to self-employed workers toward the end of 2014, still 40 percent of them were managed by the state (*Havana Times*, Sept. 22, 2014).

In 2014, *Granma* criticized the "savage self-employment" that generated a spiraling effect on prices, but rejected the notion that high prices were due to the heavy tax burden and the expensive inputs, already analyzed. At the ANPP meeting at the end of 2015, a delegate criticized the high price of agricultural products (blaming the middle men and free markets), and proposed capping them to prevent excessive profits and a worsening of already devalued wages. Slating the growing concentration in the distribution and sale of agricultural products, Raúl asked for a provisional solution because said situation could not go on, and hence it was necessary "to confront a group of crooks that is getting richer day by day," although he did not know what would work (*Granma*, Dec. 20, 2015). In January 2016, the government capped prices in state markets, returned to *acopio* (in chapter 3, see the subsection titled "Advances" in the section titled "Antecedents") for buying and distributing produce, and reduced some prices at the TRD.[11]

Two Cuban economists criticized the return to *acopio* and capped prices, which for decades have proven to be a failure. Pérez Villanueva (2016) warned, "we've already done this and the long-term results are not the expected ones." Vidal (2016a: 1–2) said that "the worst outcome [of the Seventh Congress] for the Cuban economy is the decision to curb the experiment of agricultural distribution in the provinces of Havana, Artemisa and Mayabeque." He added that middlemen are not the cause of higher agricultural prices but, rather, the increment in the demand (due to expanding tourists and *paladares*) and the excessive prices of inputs caused by the lack of a wholesale market; he foresaw adverse effects.[12] Carmelo Mesa-Lago predicted that the new policies would not be financially sustainable in the long run (cited by Gámez 2016). Until November 2016, there had been no interventions on private market stalls nor had their prices been capped, but the government was competing with the middlemen cutting prices in its own markets and the TRD.[13]

In the first quarter of 2016 the output of all agricultural products fell, except for citrus, which stagnated; although the production of milk and eggs rose, the number of cattle heads diminished (ONEI 2016g). In the same quarter, the sale value of agricultural goods dwindled: 12 percent in free agricultural markets, 6.5 percent in selling stalls, and 1 percent in state markets, whereas in tons the decreases were, respectively, 22 percent, 20 percent, and 15 percent (ONEI 2016h). In July, Raúl reported that the economy had grown only 1 percent in the first six months of the year, half of the annual target of 2 percent, which was already low. In November 2016, the minister of foreign trade said that there would be no growth that year (Castro 2016b; Malmierca 2016). Murillo reported that price cuts in state markets had led to a strong increase in domestic sales (43 percent in rice, 118 percent in oil, 249 percent in chicken meat), hence forcing the "importation of additional food to be able to support the new policies," this happening in the midst of economic difficulties that provoked cuts in expenses and some salaries (Murillo 2016b: 7–8).

Concerning cuts in TRD prices, in May 2016, out of 53 products examined, 79 percent had the same prices, only 19 percent had been reduced, and one had increased. It was also estimated that, between 2014 and 2016, the monthly cost of food and some basic needs for a family of four persons had declined from 5,708 CUP to 5,494 CUP (US $228 and US $220, respectively), hence a monthly saving of 214 CUP or US $8 (Foresight Cuba 2016). Conversely, the mean monthly salary in the state sector in 2015 was 687 CUP or US $27 (ONEI 2016f). If in a family of four there are two working members, the mean family income would be 1,340 CUP or US $55, tantamount to one-fourth of the estimated cost of food and some basic needs after the small price reduction explained.

A debate at the ANPP in July 2016 concluded that the explained policies had the support of citizens, especially of the poorest, but had caused some adverse effects: agricultural free markets "kept high prices but have quality products and stability in the assortment supply, which are normally scarce in state markets." Small state units that sell produce in CUC lack "a strategy of steady supply [to] confront shortage of some products," and it is not clearly known which are the products with price cuts ("many times the people go to a market and ignore what is its type thus don't see the change in price"). There are doubts about price formation and the index calculation; therefore, it's difficult to control them. Most state-store weights are not certified or are broken, transportation means are neither sufficient nor in a good state, and refrigeration equipment in some TRD is absent or deteriorated. Unpaid bills in Mayabeque have affected the supply of inputs, and it is questioned "how to attain the sustainability of the new policies without fluctuations in prices or dearth of products." Facing these troubles, Minister of Finances and Prices Lina Pedraza stated, "It would not be responsible right now to take other measures, without having secured the needed supplies" (Figueredo, Domínguez, and Pérez 2016).

## Impact

There is no statistical tracking of the reforms, which makes it very difficult to evaluate their effects. Information is very scarce on the self-employment economic impact. Its contribution to employment creation grew from 2.9 percent of the labor force in 2010 to 9.7 percent in 2014, that is, 6.8 percentage points at an annual rate of 1.4 points, which is noteworthy. Yet, according to a Cuban economist, self-employed work only generated 5 percent of GDP in 2014, about one-half of its proportion of the labor force (Pons 2015), which is probably due to its low skills and productivity. Self-employment tax contributions to the state budget rose 18 percent in 2010–13; in 2011–13, they averaged 2 percent of tax revenue—more recent data are not available ("Más que un asunto" 2013; *Bohemia*, Jan. 3, 2014). The contribution of the self-employment market to final household consumption (at 1997 constant prices) increased from 5 percent to 7.5 percent in 2009–14, while the state-market share declined from 80 percent to 75.5 percent (ONEI 2015). Finally, out of the total value of sales of agricultural produce in January–September 2015, self-employment accounted for 30 percent in sale stands, and for 24.4 percent by street cart sellers (54.4 percent combined), compared to 33 percent in state markets, 7.7 percent in agricultural free markets, 3.3 percent in CNA markets, and 1.6 percent in leased agricultural markets (ONEI 2015). If the number of self-employed workers and their skills were to increase, their contribution to GDP, the state budget, sales of agricultural products, home consumption, and job creation would raise in tandem.

## RESULTS AND ANALYSIS OF INTERVIEWS

Twenty-five interviews consisting of 19 questions were conducted between September and October 2014 in 13 districts of the Province of Havana (see Questionnaire in appendix 1).

Interviewees' ages ranged from 22 to 64 years and 80 percent of them were under 40, younger than the age average of 42 in the labor force (ONEI 2015). Concerning gender, 56 percent were men and 44 percent women; the latter is higher than the 30 percent given by the MTSS and the 29.4 percent calculated in table 2. It is also higher than the 37 percent of women employed in the labor force (ONEI 2016a), but lower than the proportion in Latin America, where the majority of self-employed workers are women (ECLAC 2014). As for race, 72 percent are white and 28 percent black or mulatto (Afro-Cubans): this last number is lower than the 36 percent given in the 2012 population census.

Regarding educational level, 48 percent have a university degree (twice the 22 percent average in the labor force), 28 percent have precollege, and 24 percent have technical training, which reflects the population's very high degree of education. In addition, 68 percent are professionals (but not employed in their own profession—because it is not permitted—and instead are involved in other activity) and 32 percent have a craft.[14] In terms of how long they have been self-employed, 80 percent have had a business for four years or fewer, and 64 percent for two years or fewer, due to the fact that the expansion of self-employment only began in 2011 (four years prior to the questionnaire being administered).

What follows are the tabulated results and analysis of the interviewee answers. The numbers correspond to the 19 questions on the questionnaire. When there is an additional question, it is discussed in the same number.

### 1. Satisfaction with occupation and earnings

The interviewees ranked by themselves (without any help from the interviewer) on their degree of satisfaction between 1 (very unsatisfied) and 10 (very satisfied). Figure 4 presents the distribution: 72 percent (18 interviewees) were in the top three levels of satisfaction (8 to 10), 20 percent (five) in

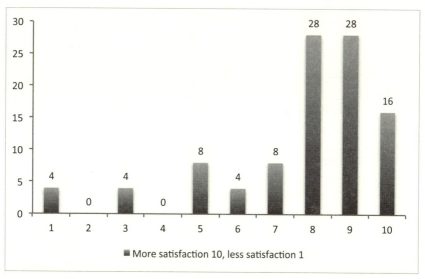

FIGURE 4. Self-employed: Are you satisfied with what you do and earn?

the four intermediate levels (4 to 7), and only 8 percent (two) in the three lowest levels (1 to 3). This is surprising, when considering the obstacles faced by the self-employed, described above, and is a testament to Cuban's entrepreneurial spirit.

Some voices: "I am already on top"; "I really like what I do and the income from the business is comfortable"; "my work helps me develop professionally and personally"; "I am satisfied with what I do, but not with what I earn" (four responses); "I think I could achieve more"; "it's not the best, but it is better than before"; "it is much better than working for the state, but I am not meeting my expectations, I want to improve them."

## 2. Previous occupation

The vast majority (76 percent) was employed by the state before being self-employed, which does not match the information from MTSS that very few came from the state sector; none kept their state jobs while being self-employed (17 percent, according to official figures). Of the rest, 12 percent were students, 8 percent were unemployed, and 4 percent constituted "others." Those that came from the state sector and gave up their occupations were accountants or auditors (three), computer science university professors (two, one a career under-director); manager of a large business, doctor, topographer, schoolteacher, carpenter, and gas-station operator (one in each category).

Relevant voices: "I had 50 workers under my command [in the state sector], they were doing outrageous things, and I was responsible for all that"; "I

TABLE 3. Self-employed: Current activity

| Occupation | Number of interviewees | Percentage |
|---|---|---|
| Food preparation | 5 | 20 |
| Bookkeeper | 4 | 16 |
| Designer and decorator | 4 | 16 |
| Leasing of rooms to tourists | 3 | 12 |
| Other | 9 | 36 |
| Total | 25 | 100 |

had one of the best positions at that time and requested dismissal in order to be self-employed"; "I was a doctor and decided to leave it primarily because it did not pay me enough to cover my necessities"; "I kept trying some way to get started as an entrepreneur until I came across this possibility, which was real and viable."

## 3. Description of current employment

The most common activities are: food preparation, 20 percent (also the top occupation according to official data), as in cafeterias, pastry shops, and hamburger and shake places; bookkeeping, 16 percent; design or decoration, 16 percent; and dwelling or room leasing to foreigners, 12 percent (table 3). The most important category was that of "others," with 36 percent and a great variety of activities, as was noted in the Antecedents: organizer of receptions, weddings, and sweet fifteenth birthday parties; chauffeur of a 1955 Cadillac convertible for tourists, and leaser of this vehicle for weddings and sweet fifteenth parties; organizer of a simulated combat game; hairdresser, manicurist, masseur; crafter and seller of soaps; vendor of Afro-Cuban religious articles (*santería*); computer scientist for businesses; clothing manufacturer; and photographer and printer.

Note that with two exceptions—clothing and soap crafting (artisanal activities), all are in the area of service and all except one (technology), involve low skills, which confirms information provided in the Antecedents (see subsection "Obstacles" in the section titled "Antecedents" above).

## 4. Procurement and payment of license

To practice any of the authorized occupations it is necessary to obtain a license or permission, which requires official stamps bought at banks. With the license, the self-employed register at the ONAT and obtain an ID card or certificate that allows him or her to work as self-employed. The total cost of the official stamps is not fixed; it varies according to the activity's importance.

TABLE 4. Monthly tax payment in CUP and CUC

| Monthly tax | Number of Interviewees | Percentage |
|---|---|---|
| CUP 120–200 | 7 | 28 |
| CUP 217–387 | 7 | 28 |
| CUP 1,450–2,170 | 4 | 16 |
| CUC 30–135 | 3 | 12 |
| Didn't say or was imprecise | 4 | 16 |
| Total | 25 | 100 |

Interviews yielded a range of 5–100 CUP (500 CUP for a driver of tourists), but 100 CUC was cited in two cases (lessors of dwellings or rooms to foreigners). Seventy-two percent of the interviewees confirmed they had paid for a license; the remaining 28 percent did not recall.

## 5. Taxes

As was explained in the Antecedents, there are two payment categories for self-employed workers, the simplified one (a monthly tax on income, plus social security), and the general one (the two aforementioned ones plus taxes on sales and on the labor force, and an annual tax when the sum of monthly payments exceeds the pre-established sum). Eighty-eight percent of the interviewees paid the simplified rate and only 12 percent (three) paid the general one, indicating that the immense majority of interviewees had incomes under 10,000 CUP per year after deductions. The three who earned more per year than this sum were two leasers of rooms to foreigners and the owner of a cafeteria. Seventy-two percent of the taxes were paid in CUP and only 12 percent in CUC (room leasing to foreigners and party organizer). Sixteen percent did not answer or specify.

The taxes on monthly income in table 4 show the percentage distribution of the tax paid in CUP or CUC. The lowest payments were for less skilled and remunerated activities such as street vendor (150 CUP), while the highest ones were for high-income activities like leasing rooms to foreigners (2,170 CUP), selling hamburgers, shakes, and food at a cafeteria (2,000 CUP), and owning and driving a Cadillac for tourists. Payments in CUC were from lessors and agencies that organize parties. The interviewees that paid higher taxes were the three who did so at the general rate.

Only three interviewees paid the annual tax set for those who earn more than 10,000 net CUP (after deducting authorized costs): the two lessors (between 300 and 400 CUC) and the cafeteria owner (950 CUP). Unfortunately, the sample did not include a *paladar* owner, which is one of the most lucrative occupations and pays high taxes. The highest tax payment among the interviewees, after adding up the monthly payments and the annual one, was US $1,800, for the biggest lessor of rooms, which is equivalent to six times the mean yearly salary in the state sector. It is probable that some underdeclared their income, as mentioned in the Antecedents.

The contribution paid to social security is always 88 CUP monthly (1,056 yearly), exactly the minimum established by law on a monthly income of 352 CUP chosen by the self-employed person (obviously less than what he or she really earns), in order to reduce the payment, even if this yields a smaller pension, because such a benefit is quite low anyway. Another tax, paid to the city historian by those who lease rooms in Old Havana's reconstructed area, goes up to 300 CUC. There is also a tax of 120 CUP for hanging a poster on the façade of the business building.

## 6. Employees

Table 5 shows that 80 percent of the interviewees either don't have employees (32 percent) or have fewer than five (48 percent), confirming that the sample concentrated on small-scale self-employed workers who are exempted from paying the labor force tax. This is the usual, as it was already mentioned that the national ratio was only 0.3 employees per each self-employed. Notwithstanding, it is possible that self-employed owners underdeclare employees, as one of them insinuated: "officially, I don't have any."

The three self-employed workers that hired more than five employees (8, 12, and 25) were the room lessors and party organizers. Of the 15 interviewees that had employees, 29 percent said that they were relatives or friends, and 71 percent said that they don't have a relationship with them. Two hired temporary employees when there was more activity, such as a fair.

The interviewee who had 12 employees said, "among family members, my father is the true owner of the business. The rest are people I've met with the passage of time; I began to work with very close friends who helped me, but the ones I have now are workers." An interviewee who has an employee explained, "she works with me at closings; processing all the information . . . and I do the analysis."

## 7. Payment methods

First, the frequency with which employees are paid is analyzed and then the method by which it is done. Table 6 shows the distribution among the 15 self-employed workers with hired employees plus two who did not respond about their number of employees but did about the payment method (the eight who do not have employees are excluded): 35.3 percent paid daily, 17.6 percent weekly, 35.3 percent monthly, and 11.8 percent some other way.

TABLE 5. Number of contracted employees

| Do you have employees? | Number of interviewees | Percentage |
| --- | --- | --- |
| Yes | 15 | 60 |
| More than five | 3 | 12 |
| Five or fewer | 12 | 48 |
| No | 8 | 32 |
| Doesn't say or imprecise | 2 | 8 |
| Total | 25 | 100 |

TABLE 6. Frequency of Payment to Employees

| Frequency of payment | Number of interviewees | Percentage |
| --- | --- | --- |
| Daily | 6 | 35.3 |
| Weekly | 3 | 17.6 |
| Monthly | 6 | 35.3 |
| Other | 2 | 11.8 |
| Total | 17 | 100.0 |

TABLE 7. Form of payment to employees

| Payment method | Number of mentions | Percentage |
| --- | --- | --- |
| Fixed salary | 11 | 52.4 |
| Salary plus incentive | 2 | 9.5 |
| Commission per sale or piece | 7 | 33.3 |
| Doesn't say or is imprecise | 1 | 4.8 |
| Total | 21[a] | 100.0 |

Note: [a] Over 21 mentions because categories are not exclusive

The payment method is shown in table 7. Excluding the eight interviewees who don't have employees, the remaining categories are not exclusive: 52.4 percent paid a fix salary; 9.5 percent paid a salary plus an incentive; 33.3 percent got a commission per sale or piece (piecework), the greater the complexity, the greater the pay; and 4.8 percent did not specify. Incentives are varied, for instance, between 10 percent and 20 percent of the profit, and a fix sum when sales are high.

It is impossible to uniformly quantify the total amount of the taxes paid because of the large variety of paying periods and methods, for instance: 50 CUP per day (one interviewee also provided 10 CUP for meals); a fixed 80 CUC monthly and a percentage of the profits; 3 CUC per day; from 8 to 15

TABLE 8. Types of problems with employees

| Types of problems | Number of interviewees | Percentage |
|---|---|---|
| Firing due to theft or damage | 2 | 33 |
| Lack of motivation or care | 2 | 33 |
| Low-level training | 1 | 17 |
| Shortage of manpower | 1 | 17 |
| Total | 6 | 100 |

TABLE 9. Profits

| Profits | Number of interviewees | Percentage |
|---|---|---|
| Yes | 24 | 96 |
| Provided no details | 18 | 72 |
| Little profit | 5 | 20 |
| A lot of profit | 1 | 4 |
| No | 1 | 4 |
| Total | 25 | 100 |

CUC weekly, depending on the pieces completed. The highest pay was for a bookkeeper and it went up to 100 CUC per month for four days of work (25 CUC per day); this salary is equivalent to 2,500 CUP, more than four times the mean salary for state employees (584 CUP), while the others are approximately two or three times greater.

## 8. Problems with employees

Among the 19 self-employed workers with employees, 68 percent said they had no problems and 32 percent had various kinds. The first percentage is high and could be due to two reasons: the high pay they give their employees in comparison with a mean state salary or the self-employed owners are very strict. A bookkeeper explained that he had no problems with his employees "because they have a relatively high salary and the demands on them are not too high. In addition, I am always appealing to their conscience . . . and tell them if things aren't working out they have to leave . . . if the quality of the work is not adequate I pointed out to them and they ask me to discount their salaries," which might be because they are afraid of losing their jobs.

A minority of six (only one-fourth of the total) attributed the problems with employees to the following: 33 percent theft of or damage to equipment; 33 percent lack of motivation or care; 17 percent personnel's low level of training; and 17 percent shortage of trained workers (table 8). One self-employed worker in textiles and one in clothing manufacturing offered the following example: "The employee might be a great seamstress, but doesn't take care of the sewing machine, and after calling her on it several times, continues without understanding, ruins the machine, and leaves." The gardener said, "given what I'm doing, it is very hard to find people who want to work; it is hard job, under the sun, and people don't like it." The party organizer explained: "it's a lot of people, and some of them are complicated. It is difficult to constantly maintain professionalism among 25 employees. I had to take some of them off the payroll, but the people I have now are very good, as they've been through the filter." The interviewee who provides computer technical services to businesses expressed, "finding trained personnel in order to be able to offer these services is tough because our training standards are pretty high."

## 9. Profits and their use for investment and/or consumption

Of the total number of interviewees, 96 percent had profits after paying taxes and only 4 percent (one) had none; this is a remarkable sign of success given the hurdles analyzed in the Antecedents. No one specified a profit amount, possibly due to apprehension; 72 percent of those that reported profits gave no details. Among the most explicit, 20 percent said profits were small and only 4 percent (one) answered they were plentiful (table 9). Several described their profits as "minimum" or "very small"; but one explained: "if I had no profits, I would not have been working at this for so long"; a bookkeeper made "lots and lots" of profits.

Among those that made profits (24), 50 percent invested them, 29 percent mixed investment and personal use (consumption), 4 percent (1) spent them only on personal use, and 17 percent (4) did not answer or contradicted themselves (fig. 5).

Investment was used to "expand or grow the business," repair the building, buy office materials, a computer, printer, raw materials or tools, and maintain or improve the room that is leased. Personal investment was for "subsisting," constructing a dwelling and purchasing furniture, or saving. One interviewee recounted: "we are already thinking about reinvesting in technology, because we have a bottleneck when demand goes up, and hinders the process; investing in technology in this country is very complicated; one must import the equipment from private companies."

## 10. Time to recover investment

Of the total number of interviewees, five invested little or nothing (20 percent); of them, three said that the investment was small because one already had a computer and bought a printer, which he paid off in a month; another

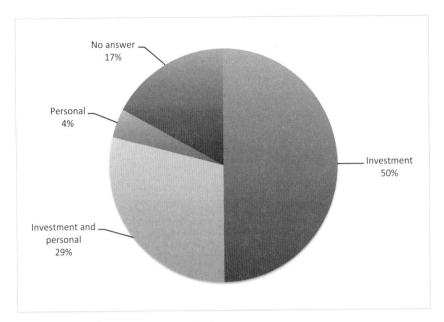

FIGURE 5. How do you use your profits?

only needed a computer and cell phone; and the third began renting an apartment with old furnishings and began to replace them little by little. Another three did not respond or were not precise (32 percent). Of the 17 who invested (68 percent of the total), 29 percent took less than a year to recover their investment; 18 percent took from a year and half to two, and 53 percent between two and four years (table 10). The Kellogg study of nine self-employed workers found that seven had the *potential* to recover their investments in less than a year (78 percent), but this is not the reality of the interviewees in our study, and the Kellogg self-employed were in the *Cuba Emprende* training program and must have had more training (CSG 2015).

## 11. Foreign remittances

It is surprising that 88 percent of the interviewees said they did not get remittances and only 12 percent (three) received them—compared to an estimated 65 percent of the population—those who received remittances partially or totally invested them in the business. The very low proportion receiving remittances might be explained as being from fear since there is no legal authorization to invest them (although many do so). One interviewee said that remittances ended when he began his business; another argued that he didn't need them because he was now solvent after being in business for three years. The unlimited total for family remittances from the United States, approved in 2015, could increase the percentage of self-employed workers that receive and invest them.

TABLE 10. Time to recover investment

| Recovery of investment | Number of interviewees | Percentage |
|---|---|---|
| Less than 1 year | 5 | 29 |
| 1 year to less than 2 years | 3 | 18 |
| 2–4 years | 9 | 53 |
| Total | 17 | 100 |

TABLE 11. Government credits or bank loans

| Credit or bank loans | Number of interviewees | Percentage |
|---|---|---|
| Didn't get one (didn't explain reason) | 9 | 36 |
| Doesn't want one | 8 | 32 |
| Doesn't need one | 5 | 20 |
| Was denied one | 3 | 12 |
| Total | 25 | 100 |

## 12. Government credits or bank loans

None of the interviewees received government credit or small loans from state banks, which is understandable given the small sum assigned to self-employed workers and the cumbersome process involved. Table 11 divides the responses garnered into four categories: 36 percent did not receive it, without explaining why; 32 percent did not want one; 20 percent didn't need one, and 12 percent requested one but did not get it.

Frequently repeated answers: "I began the process but abandoned it because it did not move forward," "I tried and by the third week I regret it because there is so much bureaucracy"; "that doesn't really help me and would be one more paper work"; "that would complicate things for me"; "leave the state over there and me here."

## 13. Other sources of assistance

Eighty-four percent received assistance from other sources and only 16 percent did not get any, which might be another reason for the very low percentage of self-employed receiving remittances. Of those who received assistance, the majority, 44 percent, was from family, 20 percent from friends, and 12 percent from both, while 8 percent did not indicate from whom (table 12). Sixty-two percent did not specify if the help was domestic or external; of the remaining 38 percent, half said it was domestic, 38 percent said both domestic and external, and 12 percent said external only. This indicates that there is an extensive domestic, assistance network that supports self-employed workers.

TABLE 12. Other sources of assistance

| Source of assistance | Number of interviewees | Percentage |
|---|---|---|
| Did receive | 21 | 84 |
| Family | 11 | 44 |
| Friends | 5 | 20 |
| Both | 3 | 12 |
| Didn't indicate | 2 | 8 |
| Did not receive | 4 | 16 |
| Total | 25 | 100 |

TABLE 13. Pricing policy

| Reduction in prices? | Number of interviewees | Percentage |
|---|---|---|
| No | 16 | 64 |
| No details given | 6 | 24 |
| Superior quality | 8 | 32 |
| Has no competition | 2 | 8 |
| Yes | 9 | 36 |
| Total | 25 | 100 |

Of helping family members, those mentioned were parents, siblings, spouses, and children. Assistance was varied: a loan of 500 CUC to start a microbusiness, contact with businesses and clients, purchase of materials, shipment of inputs from abroad, organizational help, and moral support.

## 14. Competition

Eighty-four percent of the interviewees said they had competition from other self-employed workers and 16 percent said they had not. The degree of competition was expressed as "yes, a lot," 32 percent (eight); a lot but "it doesn't affect me," 24 percent (six); "yes," there is competition but it was not specified, 28 percent (seven); and "no" or "little," 16 percent (four) (see fig. 6). This suggests that in addition to the obstacles it faces, self-employment is competitive.

Explanations of why the competition does not affect a fourth of the interviewees were: "bookkeepers abound, but very few, hardly any, who are competent and responsible"; "there are lots of people selling, but when the client identifies your product . . . [he] looks for you . . . , we sell to an institution that appreciates . . . the product's quality and it contracts us"; "there are many who rent, but my competition is not on guesthouse rooms that cost 15 CUP;

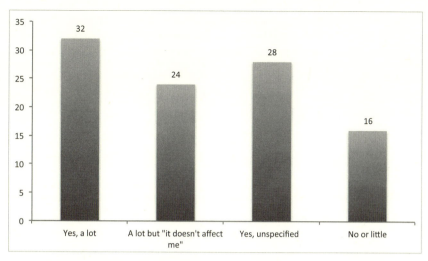

FIGURE 6. Do you have competition?

I offer something different." Some self-employed workers revealed difficulties in negotiating with state enterprises in authorized areas: "Competition is from the state enterprises themselves because we offer state service; those enterprises rely on state computer tech companies, but they don't have the level of quality that our services offer"; "more than competition, I face state bureaucratic obstacles; there are lot of hurdles when negotiating with them, because they reject us, fundamentally, they want to do business with state enterprises and not private ones."

When asking the interviewees if they would reduce their prices to attract clients, the vast majority (64 percent) said no, and only a minority (36 percent) answered yes. Among those that reduced their prices, 24 percent failed to give a reason, 32 percent explained that it was because the quality of their products or services was superior to that of their competitors; and 8 percent didn't cut prices because they had little competition (table 13).

Those who offer discounts (36 percent) explain how they do so: "I give my new clients three months with a 50 percent discount for them to try the service and then decide if they want to pay the regular tariff"; "I have some prices below the rest of the kiosks, and there are other products that I charge higher prices because the other kiosks don't have them"; "I offer a discount at the end of the month or on Students' Day, to increase sales." The most elaborate response was the following: "there are products that are sold cheaper and others that are exclusive are sold for a higher profit, but we always negotiate with the client: for how much do you think I can sell you this so you will buy it?; we order small lots, and if the product sells well ... we buy more, but with an agreed understanding that my product is sold."

TABLE 14. Comparison of products/services with those of competitors

| Comparison with competitors | Number of interviewees | Percentage |
|---|---|---|
| Better | 15 | 60 |
| Different | 4 | 16 |
| The same | 3 | 12 |
| Imprecise | 3 | 12 |
| Total | 25 | 100 |

There is a certain contradiction in the last analysis, first because 84 percent of those interviewed said that there was a lot of competition, and second, 64 percent asserted that they did not reduce prices, although the majority offered as a reason the superior quality of their product or service when compared to their competitors. This is an important point, in view of the debate that began in late 2015 about the high price of agricultural products, and the imposition, in January 2016, of price caps in state markets (see subsection "Obstacles" in the section titled "Antecedents" above). But these events took place after the interviews were finished.

### 15. Comparison of product or service with that of competitors

In order to delve deeper into the issue of competition, the interviewees were asked if they believed that their product or service was superior to that of their competitors, and if their answer was yes, they were asked to explain why. Sixty percent responded that their product or service was better than that of their competitors, 16 percent that it was different (but better, which increases the total to 76 percent); 12 percent said it was the same, and 12 percent were not precise (table 14).

Those who answered that their product or service was better based on its quality gave specific reasons: "professionalism, the integral way we organize our events [weddings, receptions]; we do it all and well"; "the seriousness with which we work"; "the complete integrity of the service; not only do we take care of the accounting, but we also constantly follow up on the business, both on the tax side as well as the legal one; in addition, we issue periodic reports on the state of our business"; "due to our training and organization, which . . . allows us to know which service is better for each client"; "our product is more attractive . . . because of its new shape and fragrance; we use natural components that are healthier for the skin"; "I take good care of clients, explain things to them . . . , advise them on what they want to purchase." Those who said their product was different implied that it was better for that very reason: it is different "because I guarantee security, cleaning, and treat-

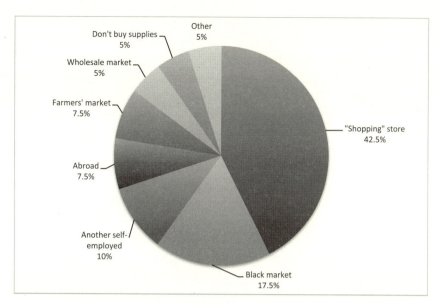

FIGURE 7. Where do you obtain your inputs?

ing the clients well"; "we must ensure that the product be different from the rest with regard to its image and price . . . we manufacture many varieties of bedspreads, because even if you wanted to make two alike, they wouldn't be" (also see responses in 14).

## 16. Sources of inputs

Answers are not exclusive because there were interviewees who gave more than one source (there were 40 mentions): 42.5 percent (17 interviewees) purchased inputs with CUC at "shopping" stores (TRD), despite their high prices, because it was the only place where they were available;[15] 17.5 percent (seven) acquired them on the black market at the risk of confiscation (because one must prove the legal source of the inputs); 10 percent (four) bought from other self-employed workers (indicating that links between them are being forged); 7.5 percent (three) from abroad (this is doubtful since imports are rarely allowed; it is probably through "mules" that buy merchandise abroad and sell them to self-employed workers in Cuba; see below); 7.5 percent (three) on the cooperative agricultural market; 5 percent (two) in the wholesale market; 5 percent buy no inputs; and 5 percent purchase them other ways (fig. 7).

Some relevant voices: "The prices are very expensive at the [shopping] store; sometimes I have to wait for seconds" [lower quality products that have not sold]; "there are hairdressing products at all shopping stores but at very high prices, so the final product becomes more expensive"; "some products are costly, like machinery and tools; sometimes the state 'shopping' store sells them, but usually they are Chinese, and I don't like them"; "I buy detergent at state stores because generally that's the only place that sells it"; "I buy tires, spare parts . . . and sometimes gasoline on the black market, secretly"; "sometimes the black market has better prices than the state stores, and vice versa"; "I get them at a kiosk or private stall that has a license, just like me, but they sell at wholesale prices; they bring in herbs from the countryside, remove bones from the cemetery (seller of articles for *santería*)"; "one must get most things from abroad, with someone who travels, since they are cheaper that way"; "I import some raw material, like fragrances"; "the only wholesale market that works is El Trigal, where I buy tubers and vegetables; there is no other wholesale market" (El Trigal was closed in 2016).

Among the few in the minority that don't buy inputs: "I have friends who work at publishing houses and they give me some leftover material, like recovered paper sheets"; "I do all my work digitally . . . , if I have something to print I do it with another self-employed worker." Other purchase sources: "I often buy them from people who close their businesses and have leftover products"; "I craft equipment and scenery from recycled materials from enterprises that don't use them, and I modify them."

## 17. Advertising

There were 52 mentions, as categories are not exclusive. The most popular form of advertising is word-of-mouth (29 percent), which is followed by fliers (19 percent), Internet (15 percent), business cards (15 percent), posters (8 percent), some other method (10 percent), and there are those who do not advertise (4 percent). Traditional forms of advertising amount to 73 percent, while the Internet, which predominates in many countries today, is only used by 15 percent, due to scarce Internet access in Cuba, although it is increasing (fig. 8).

Advertising is expensive and there is scarce access to Internet (Revolico), radio, and TV (which only one of the interviewees used). One of them observed, "I have not placed ads in the telephone yellow pages, not so much due to its cost, but because often one must be prudent, and avoid a lot of publicity." Other methods used are tastings, samples, fairs, social gatherings, visits to businesses, personal interviews, telephone book, and classified ads in the *Paquete Semanal*. The two interviewees who didn't advertise voiced their reasons: "I already went through that phase; it has to be something very attractive for me to attract a client"; "virtually, everyone in Havana has known me for 20 years."

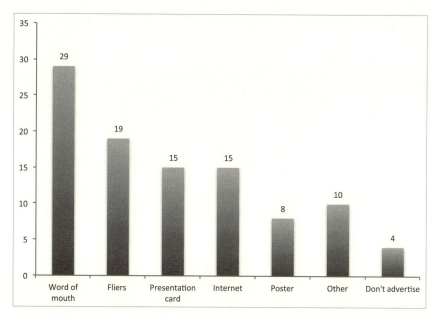

FIGURE 8. How do you advertise your business?

## 18. Small-business expansion

Proof of the Cuban entrepreneurial spirit is found in the fact that 92 percent of the interviewees plan to expand their businesses, and only 8 percent have no immediate plans. Among this latter group, one gave a rational reason: "the low profile of this activity is important because if I expanded, I'd have to contract workers, my license would shift to the general tax rate, I would have to file an affidavit, and given my level of income, taxes would take a large portion of my profits."

Among the 92 percent (23 interviewees) who plan to expand, 44 percent (11) wanted to do it geographically, 16 percent (4) by hiring employees, and 32 percent (8) in order to do something else, such as rehabilitating another room to lease it, finding more educated clients who can pay more, procuring orders from a state store (fig. 9). Of the 44 percent who plan to expand geographically, 16 percent expect to do it in Havana, 8 percent in other provinces, 8 percent abroad, and 18 percent some other way, like generating new products/services, having more cars for driving tourists, doing consulting, and buying houses with rooms for lease.

Entrepreneurial aspirations are voiced by many self-employed workers: "I want to dominate the market in Havana; anyone who wants to have a wedding or a sweet fifteen party, should consider what I offer first; afterwards I'd like to establish a branch in Cienfuegos"; "I plan to expand our service . . . to

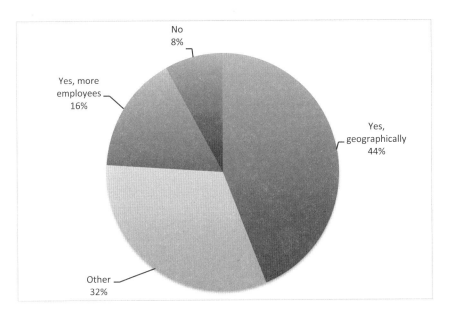

FIGURE 9. Do you plan to expand your business?

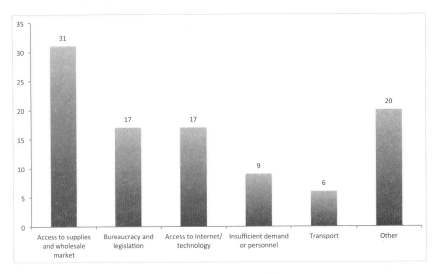

FIGURE 10. What are the most serious problems you face?

the entire capital ... in a period of five to ten years"; I would like to have ... a virtual office on the Internet so I could sell my services abroad"; "I envision a container leaving for the Caribbean. Why wouldn't we be able to sell in the Bahamas or the Cayman Islands?"

## 19. Principal problems faced and changes desired

These are the two questions about which the interviewees went into more detail; their responses are consistent with the obstacles analyzed in the

TABLE 15. Principal problems faced

| Principal problems faced | Number of mentions | Percentage |
|---|---|---|
| Access to inputs and wholesale market | 11 | 31 |
| Bureaucracy and legislation | 6 | 17 |
| Access to Internet/technology | 6 | 17 |
| Insufficient demand or personnel | 3 | 9 |
| Transportation | 2 | 6 |
| Others | 7 | 20 |
| Total | 35[a] | 100 |

Note: [a] 35 mentions because categories are not exclusive.

Antecedents (see subsection "Obstacles" in the section titled "Antecedents" above). These answers are not exclusive as various interviewees identified more than one problem.

a. Principal problems faced

The two principal problems identified were: access to inputs and the need for a wholesale market (30 percent), followed by the bureaucracy and restrictive legislation (17 percent); access to the Internet and technology (17 percent), insufficient demand or personnel (9 percent), transportation (6 percent), and others (20 percent) (table 15 and fig. 10).

Among "others," the obstacles are: "to be associated with Cuban state tourist agencies . . . an experiment is on the way on this but a serious thing has not been done yet"; "to improve my computer"; "to expand my business space, which is very small and hence does not allow me to hire more employees"; "to have new forms that compete, such as the cooperatives [to whom the state give preference over self-employment]."

The interviewees voiced their difficulties: "One has to walk a great deal to buy things, two days to buy a plumbing elbow"; "today I ran more than 30 kilometers searching for *malta* [a nonalcoholic, malted beverage] but did not find any; there are no colas or lemon sodas"; "if you don't buy on the spot, there isn't any later"; "the prices at the shopping [state stores] are very high, which reduces profits"; "we need a wholesale market; [if we had it] our prices wouldn't be so high"; "legislation is always changing; every month there are two or three resolutions; if one is not able to keep up, one is lost"; "the bureaucracy . . . does not allow things to flow"; "legislation greatly limits the possibility of offering some other, broader kind of service"; "they don't see us yet as a small business capable of supplying their products"; "I would like selling things that are not [specifically] within our activities, and hence are prohibited"; "that our right . . . to export and import products is acknowledged"; "they prohibit you from going to the airports and hotels to

Table 16. Desired changes or improvements

| Desired changes or improvements | Number of mentions | Percentage |
|---|---|---|
| More freedom, fewer regulations | 9 | 30 |
| Better access, lower prices for inputs | 9 | 30 |
| Reduction in taxes | 3 | 10 |
| Greater access to the Internet | 3 | 10 |
| Others | 6 | 20 |
| Total | 30[a] | 100 |

Note: [a] 30 mentions because categories are not exclusive.

seek clients"; "there is very little access to the Internet, since few people see it"; "I would like that all my clients had email, consult my Facebook page"; "personnel at state businesses have been working with obsolete systems for a long time, and don't see the benefit of our service for their work." Only one interviewee did not find a serious problem: "[there are] always complications, but one solves them along the way."

b. Desired changes

This question is essential for hearing the voices of self-employed workers and publicizing them so they are heard. Their desire for change is concomitant with the problems they identified (except for wanting a reduction in high taxes, which was not mentioned among the problems). The two most important changes are "more freedom and fewer regulations" and "better access to inputs and lower prices" (each 30 percent); these are followed by a reduction in taxes (10 percent), better Internet access (10 percent), and others (20 percent) (table 16 and fig. 11).

In what follows, we select voices for the most relevant desired changes for each question, starting with more freedom and less regulation: "Allow free rein to the fertile imagination we Cubans are exhibiting, which should be done unhindered and unrestricted; the government should facilitate that flow, not obstruct it, and control only what must be controlled"; "more freedom for private businesses to do other things"; "more freedom to work directly with foreign clients . . . we have to rely on an intermediary to reach clients and they are the ones who control the prices [making them more expensive]"; "more freedom to negotiate with Cuban state agencies"; "much clearer and permissive regulations regarding what the private sector can do"; "open up a broader range of possibilities for offering services to professionals . . . that would be very useful for the development of entrepreneurs and small- and medium-sized businesses in Cuba." We conclude with this voice: "First

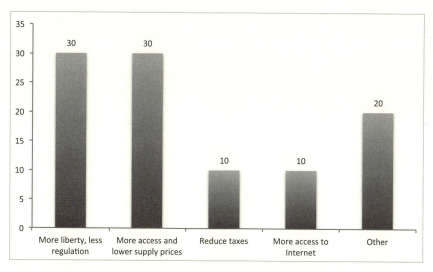

FIGURE 11. What would you like to see change or improve?

of all, we'd have to change the form of government. . . . Our way of thinking must change, not only ours, but that of those who govern us; they must give us more freedom to be able to grow, to keep collaborating . . . when these things have taken place, I too, will change."

Concerning better access to inputs and lower prices: "Everything is very expensive, tires, spare parts, gasoline; I wish they were cheaper"; "[allow] imports, to reduce the cost of equipment"; "an easier time to acquire raw material"; "there is competition among buyers but not among providers, because they don't exist"; "what I would most like is not to waste so much time looking for the littlest thing"; "that there be a wholesale market so that things are easier to find"; "to be able to buy without having to worry afterward about justifying where things came from."

On tax reductions: "Taxes are very high . . . they're abusive; a foreigner who is going to invest millions and recover them, of course, is receiving up to eight years of no taxes on profits, and a self-employed worker who is trying to survive has to pay taxes of up to 59 percent on his or her profits"; "the taxes we pay to the state should result in some benefit for us, [for example] guaranteed maintenance of building façades; we pay a tax for these things and they are not visible: each day that goes by, Old Havana is deteriorating more, and I fear that soon it will cease being a world heritage site."

Regarding Internet access: "May everyone have access to the Internet."

Among "other" desires, the following deserves attention: "We are affiliated to [official] unions; it would be better for self-employed workers . . . to create their own groups among themselves, establish an agency within the territorial government in charge of authorizing licenses . . . to create consensus among them, interact, get feedback on what is happening, and recommend what the territory needs. The taxes we pay to ONAT should revert in some benefit to our territory so it would be cleaner, more beautiful, better . . . ; if my business is dressmaking, I want my street to be clean and repaired to [attract clients]. If there were a timeframe for us to systematically get together . . . , I am certain that we could offer more and better [services and products]."

# 3

# USUFRUCT FARMERS

## ANTECEDENTS

Usufruct farmers are not defined in the ONEI (2015) yearbook's chapter on agriculture. Under usufruct, the owner (the state) keeps ownership of the property and cedes the land to the farmer for his use and appropriation of its yield.[1] In Cuba, authorization is through ten-year contracts extendable for another ten, provided that the usufruct farmer fulfills all his or her obligations. Usufruct started in 1995 during the economic crisis but was stagnant until 2009 when the government began to distribute "idle" state lands—mainly to individuals but also to co-ops and state entities. Two laws, in 2008 and 2012, regulate usufruct, the second more flexible than the first (Decree-Laws 259 of 2008 and 300 of 2012). Usufruct is the key aspect of Raúl Castro's agrarian reform and a modest step toward the market. According to Nova (2013), the essential issues that need to be solved in agriculture are real ownership of the land (the right to decide what to grow, to whom to sell the produce, and to set their own price); recognition of the key role of the market; abolition of monopolies and diversification of distribution with autonomous co-ops; and freedom to contract workers.

## Size and trends

By the end of 2012, 1.5 million hectares of idle state land (2,471,054 acres) had been distributed to 174,271 usufruct farmers (natural persons) and 2,700 to legal persons (*Juventud Rebelde*, Nov. 10, 2013). In 2015, Murillo informed the ANPP that there were more than 200,000 usufruct farmers to whom 1.7 million hectares (4,200,791 acres) had been turned over since 2008 (Martín 2015; "Cuba entrega" 2015). Conversely, ONEI statistics show 300,810 usufruct farmers in 2012, 157,948 of whom were governed by the 2008 usufruct law; 142,862 received their authorization in 1995–2000 and were under the 2012 law. The total number of usufruct farmers increased to 312,752 in 2013, but slightly decreased to 312,296 in 2014; no breakdown was given for usufruct farmers in the 1995–2000 period and since 2009, but it continues to be doubtful that there are more than 200,000 in the latter group (table 17).

Table 18 shows the changes between 2007 (before the enactment of the first usufruct law) and 2014, in thousands of hectares, relative to agricultural lands, cultivated or not, by type of ownership: state, basic units of cooperative agricultural production (UPBC) and agro-livestock production cooperatives (CPA), and credit and services cooperatives (CCS) plus the private sector. There is a notable decrease in total agricultural lands, especially cultivated ones, with the greatest declines being in the UBPC/CPA lands followed by state lands, while the CCS/private lands show a strong increase. The ONEI does not publish disaggregated statistics on usufruct farmers, who neither own their land nor are necessarily CCS members, although they should be in the CCS/private sector, given that were usufruct farmers who primarily received state lands. In 2007–14, state participation in total agricultural lands declined by 4.9 percentage points, and by 4.6 points in cultivated lands; the decline in UBPC/CPA was even greater, 12.3 and 9.1 percentage points, respectively. Conversely, participation of the CCS/private sector increased by 17.2 percentage points relative to agricultural lands, and 13.8 points concerning cultivated lands; this was probably due to usufruct farming.[2] However, table 18 shows that the agricultural land in the CCS/private sector increased by only 1,014,000 hectares (2,505,649 acres) in 2007–14, much less than the 1.7 million hectares (4,200,791 acres) than were supposed to be granted to usufruct farmers in 2008–14.

Noncultivated lands are natural pastures and idle lands.[3] Table 19 estimates the percentage of idle lands relative to both total agricultural lands and noncultivated lands in 2007, 2013, and 2014. Data is only for these three years because no statistics were published in 2008–11, and the 2012 figures were incorrect.[4] In 2007–14, idle land fell from 18.6 percent to 15.3 percent with respect to total agricultural land, while it decreased from 34 percent to 26.6 percent for noncultivated land, which is positive. Yet, total agricultural land decreased by 5 percent, cultivated land decreased by 10.7 percent, and noncultivated land stagnated. There is no official explanation for these trends.

To summarize, the total number of usufruct farmers in 2012 and 2015 was higher than official statistics. There is no breakdown of usufruct farmers

TABLE 17. Number of usufruct farmers and land turned over to them, 2012–14

| Usufruct farmers | 2012 | 2013 | 2014 |
|---|---|---|---|
| Total | 300,810 | 312,752 | 312,296 |
| 1995–2000 | 142,682 | | |
| Since 2009 | 157,948 | | |
| Lands delivered[a] | 1.5 | 1.6 | 1.7 |

Note: [a] Million of hectares distributed in usufruct.
Source: Our own calculations based on ONEI 2013, 2014, 2015; Martín, 2015.

TABLE 18. Distribution of agricultural, cultivated and noncultivated farm lands, by type of tenure, 2007–14 (in thousands of hectares and percentages)

| Years and categories | Total | State | Nonstate | |
|---|---|---|---|---|
| | | | UBPC/CPA | CCS/private |
| Area (1,000 hectares) | | | | |
| 2007 | | | | |
| Agricultural | 6,619 | 2,371 | 3,034 | 1,214 |
| Cultivated | 2,988 | 694 | 1,495 | 799 |
| Not cultivated | 3,631 | 1,677 | 1,539 | 415 |
| 2014 | | | | |
| Agricultural | 6,279 | 1,943 | 2,108 | 2,228 |
| Cultivated | 2,668 | 497 | 1,092 | 1,079 |
| Not cultivated | 3,611 | 1,446 | 1,016 | 1,149 |
| Change 2007/2014 | | | | |
| Agricultural | -340 | -428 | -926 | 1,014 |
| Cultivated | -320 | -197 | -403 | 280 |
| Not cultivated | -20 | -231 | -523 | 734 |
| Distribution (%) | | | | |
| 2007 | | | | |
| Agricultural | 100.0 | 35.8 | 45.9 | 18.3 |
| Cultivated | 100.0 | 23.2 | 50.0 | 26.7 |
| Not cultivated | 100.0 | 46.3 | 42.4 | 11.4 |
| 2014 | | | | |
| Agricultural | 100.0 | 30.9 | 33.6 | 35.5 |
| Cultivated | 100.0 | 18.6 | 40.9 | 40.5 |
| Not cultivated | 100.0 | 40.1 | 28.1 | 31.8 |

Source: Our own calculations based on data in ONEI 2012, 2015.

TABLE 19. Idle lands, 2007, 2013, and 2014

| Year | Lands (1,000 hectares = 2,471 acres) | | | | Percentages | |
|---|---|---|---|---|---|---|
| | 1. Agricultural | 2. Cultivated | 3. Noncultivated | 4. Idle | 4/1 | 4/3 |
| 2007 | 6,620 | 2,988 | 3,631 | 1,233 | 18.6 | 34.0 |
| 2013 | 6,342 | 2,646 | 3,697 | 1,046 | 16.5 | 28.2 |
| 2014 | 6,279 | 2,668 | 3,610 | 962 | 15.3 | 26.6 |

*Source*: ONEI 2011, 2014, 2015; percentages by authors.

authorized in the 1995–2000 period or of those approved since 2009, but the total number fell 0.14 percent in 2014 vis-á-vis 2013, which indicates that no more lands have been given in usufruct. In 2007–14, the amounts of agricultural and cultivated land decreased for UBPC/CPA but increased notably for CCS/private sector; the amount under usufruct farmers is not identified but one can assume that the aforementioned growth is due to the transfer of idle state lands to usufruct farmers since 2009. In 2007–14, agricultural lands, cultivated and idle, dwindled, and cultivated lands stagnated (fig. 12). Idle lands sank from 34 percent to 27 percent relative to noncultivated lands, but there was also a decrease in cultivated lands. Agricultural land expansion in 2007–14 was 60 percent of what was reported as having been distributed to usufruct farmers.

## Characteristics

Unlike self-employment, there is no official information about the characteristics of usufruct farmers, for example, their age, sex, race, level of education, location, and so on. The interviews partly fill this void.

## Advances

The 2012 usufruct law brought about important improvements when compared to the 2008 law, which was quite restrictive and did not produce results. The size of the parcel went up from 13.4 to 67.1 hectares (33 to 166 acres, respectively), provided that the usufruct farmer was associated with a state or cooperative farm. The contract's duration (ten years) has not been modified for individuals,[5] although it has been extended from 20 to 25 years for cooperatives and state entities. Despite the advantages granted to the last two forms, 98 percent of the usufruct land has been assigned to individuals. The usufruct farmer can construct dwellings (more than one if there are family members who work the land) and stables on the parcel, and can plant orchards; all these activities used to be prohibited.

If the contract is not renewed, the government must assess the investment

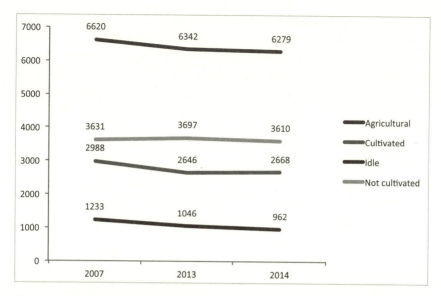

FIGURE 12. Evolution of agricultural land, cultivated, noncultivated, and idle, 2007–14. *Note*: 1,000 hectares = 2,471 acres.

in improvements made in the parcel and pay the corresponding reimbursements to the usufruct farmer. In case of a usufruct farmer's death or disability, the family members who work the land inherit both the usufruct land and the investment.

The 2013 tax reform authorized usufruct farmers a two-year exemption on their personal income tax payments (5 percent), the tax on the land's value, and the hiring of contracted workers. The income tax exemption can be extended for up to four years if the land is cleared of *marabú* (spiny brush that is difficult to eradicate). The ANPP ratified this last exemption at the end of 2015. In addition, that year affidavits and annual income taxes were not required of non–sugar-growing usufruct farmers. Furthermore, the sales tax (5 percent) was not applied to agricultural produce in Artemisa, Mayabeque, and Havana. The tax on inactive lands in usufruct was also suspended for a year (Law No. 113, 2012; *Bohemia,* Jan. 3, 2014; Pedraza 2015). Eighty-eight percent of interviewed usufruct farmers said they did not pay income and sales taxes (see subsection "Taxes" in the section title "Results" below).

In 2007–14, cultivated agricultural lands decreased considerably for UBPC/CPA and state farms, while it rose substantially for CCS/private sector, where one should assume usufruct is being practiced, although it is not disaggregated. Idle lands also decreased relative to both total agricultural land and noncultivated land (tables 18 and 19).

Beginning in 2011, the government offered micro-credit to usufruct farmers, and allowed them to open bank accounts. In 2015, the directors of the state-owned banks Ahorro Popular, Metropolitano, and Crédito y Comercio reported on the availability of small loans to the agricultural sector, including usufruct farmers, to whom they offered a preferential interest rate for two years (*Granma*, Nov. 30, 2015).

All agricultural producers, including usufruct farmers, can sell more on the market (47 percent in 2012), and since 2013, they can sell directly to state tourist agencies free of intermediation by cooperatives (Murillo 2013; Reuters, June 30, 2013). Decree-Law 318 (2013) reformed the *acopio* system, put an end to the state monopoly on distribution in three provinces, allowed competition, and setting market prices for chicken, pork, greens, eggs, and noncitrus fruits. This resulted in "a discreet increase in supply and diversification of produce, but still the insufficient production keeps high prices" (*Granma*, June 23, 2014).

The press reported that the first wholesale market selling agricultural products was created in Pinar del Río, in 2014 (Reuters, June 1, 2014). An announcement in 2015 stated that prices for inputs like insecticides, seeds, equipment, and veterinary medicines would be reduced by 40 percent to 60 percent ("Cuba entrega" 2015); legal regulations were enacted later.

## Obstacles

The 2012 law introduced greater flexibility but is still restrictive and generates uncertainty. The usufruct contract's term lasts ten years, but Sino-Vietnamese contracts are for an indefinite time or for 50 years, and farmers decide what to plant, who they should sell to, and fix market prices—there is no *acopio*—Nova's recommendations, as cited above. Contracts in Cuba can be terminated or not renewed due to infringement of usufruct farmers' obligations: (a) for "not using the land in a rational manner," which is left to the government's interpretation; (b) for failing to sell obligatorily to the state approximately 70 percent of the harvest at official fixed prices below the market price (*acopio*, with the 2013 explained modification); (c) for contracting a higher number of workers without state authorization; and (d) for selling the investment in the parcel or making investments without state permission. In addition, the state may cancel the contract for public need or social interest. In 2015, Murillo reported that the contracts of 43,000 usufruct farmers had been canceled because they did not use the land correctly (Martín González 2015).

El Trigal was the only wholesale market, but it failed to meet demand and was closed in May 2016 (in chapter 2, see subsection "Obstacles" in the section titled "Antecedents"). Furthermore, we cannot confirm the functioning of the agricultural inputs market. The answers usufruct farmers gave to the question on where they obtained their inputs never mentioned the wholesale market (see subsection "Input" in section titled "Results" below). In order to obtain inputs or services and distribute their products, usufruct farmers must be associated with a state farm or cooperative, a UBPC,[6] preferably, or CPA, which are the ones that have the least level of autonomy and inefficient forms of production.[7] But, in practice, usufruct farmers resort to CCS to sell their products because it is easier for them due to their scarce production (see subsection "Ties to cooperatives" in section titled "Results" below). It would be more convenient to authorize voluntary usufruct cooperatives.

In the face of the contractual freedom suggested by Nova, usufruct farmers can only hire family members or seasonal workers as long as they are self-employed or members of a cooperative. The area of investment cannot be larger than 1 percent of the parcel's size. The official reason for these disincentives is to avoid the concentration of wealth. Nearly 77 percent of usufruct farmers lack agricultural experience (*Juventud Rebelde*, Nov. 10, 2013, but see subsection "Advances" in the section titled "Antecedents"); the government offers training but has not given specific data on the number of usufruct farmers that have been trained.

The government fixes *acopio* prices lower than the market price, although it has increased this price in the last two years; it has also said that *acopio* will disappear, but, as we explained, in January 2016 the government partially returned to *acopio*, distributing and selling agricultural products at capped prices in state markets (in chapter 2, see subsection "Obstacles" in the section titled "Antecedents"). A weekly publication of the PCC in Tunas expressed its skepticism about the possibility of intervening in market prices by decree: "The tempting idea sells very well in public opinion polls, but in the last two decades... the government has not been successful in telling private vendors how much it should charge for their merchandise... because such prices would once again be infringed since they require actions that will affect the objective conditions that push prices higher [see subsection "*Acopio*" in section titled "Results and Analysis"]. To what extent do they reproduce the profits of 200 percent and 300 percent the state gets in part of its retail market? To try to impose prices... would only fuel the black market and its surrounding corruption" (Ojeda 2016).

Usufruct farmers' access to state micro-credit and bank accounts is minimal; it is said that 4,000 potential usufruct farmers received credits, about 1.3 percent of the total (*Granma*, Nov. 30, 2015). *Marabú* covers half of all the usufruct land and should be cleared to be able to start production, but state micro-credit cannot be used for this purpose; tax exemptions are not given until *marabú* is eradicated.

Procedures for requesting usufruct land, signing and extending a contract, and getting approval for investment (including the construction of a house) are cumbersome. Getting the parcel measured can take up to two months because of deficiencies at public registries, and thousands of applications suffer delays due to negligence or a lack of skilled personnel. The comptroller general, Gladys Bejarano, said that audits done in 2013, targeted on the distribution and use of usufruct land, revealed that the change of mindset needed to increase food production and people's standard of living had not yet happened. Irregularities and violations were found: 63 percent of the audited entities were graded as bad or so-so because of failing to deliver the parcel in a set period of time, delays in procedures, and disarray regarding idle lands (*Granma*, March 3, 2014; Fonticoba 2014; "Presentan Informe" 2014).

Decree-Law No. 318 (2013) prohibits the sale of beef, dairy by-products, coffee, cacao, and honey, and also keeps rice, beans, corn, potatoes, sweet potatoes, taro root, and grapefruit within the *acopio* system, which means that the most important agricultural products are excluded from the free market.

The official statistics indicate that the total number of usufruct farmers declined for the first time in 2014, possibly due to the obstacles analyzed above; it is probable that such a decline was among the CAN that have been authorized since 2009 (table 17). In the Seventh PCC Congress in 2016, Raúl asked to impose limits on the NSS, and Murillo gave as an example "the establishment of limits on the amount of hectares that anybody can have" (Castro 2016a; Murillo 2016a).

## Impact

As with the case of the self-employed workers, there is very little information about the impact of usufruct farming in agriculture. Figures on production are provided by the state and nonstate sectors, and include all the cooperatives and peasants who own their own land. Usufruct farmers should be included here as well but are not identified, so it is very difficult to determine if usufruct has had an effect on agricultural output. The GDP generated by agriculture and livestock diminished from 5.7 percent in 2007 to 3.9 percent in 2009, and 3.7 percent in 2014–16. The annual rate of agricultural growth averaged 1.8 percent in 2008–15 (ONEI 2010, 2014, 2015; Martín 2015; Murillo 2015a). This forces the importation of more than two billion dollars' worth of food to cover 80 percent of domestic consumption, 60 percent of which could be produced in the country ("Cuba entrega" 2015). In 2014, the minister of foreign commerce reported that usufruct farmers, agricultural cooperatives, and private peasant farmers generated 83 percent of agricultural production, while state farms and businesses produced only 17 percent (Malmierca 2014; "Presentan Informe" 2014). This data is not available for 2015, but the share of the CCS/private sector (which should include usufruct) in the output of the most important nonsugar agricultural products oscillated between 61 and 86 percent, much higher than the corresponding shares of the state and UBPC/CPA, except for citrus, in which the state had a majority (ONEI 2016e). In 2014, the existing 312,752 usufruct farmers equaled 6.1 percent of the labor force (ONEI 2015).

## RESULTS AND ANALYSIS OF INTERVIEWS

Twenty-five usufruct farmers were interviewed with 21 questions. The interviews were conducted in April–June 2015 in the provinces of Artemisa, Mayabeque, and Havana, including six municipalities in Havana province.

Interviewees were between 26 and 75 years of age, and averaged 51 years; only 25 percent were younger than 40, 44 percent were from 41 to 60, and 28 percent over age 60. Thus, it was a more aged population than that of the self-employed, and also older than the labor force (ONEI 2015), despite the fact that agricultural work is tough. One hundred percent were men, precisely due to the hard work it demands, and also 100 percent were white, compared to the much more diverse self-employed population. The level of education was much lower: only 48 percent had completed between sixth and ninth grades, 28 percent a technical middle school, 16 percent precollege, and only 8 percent had gone to a university. Fifty-six percent were peasants or cowboys, while only 44 percent had a profession, four of them related to farm work, like animal husbandry, veterinary, and plant health; this also contrasts with the self-employed population, the majority professional. Out of total usufruct farmers, 80 percent said they had previous agricultural experience.

In the next section, we offer the tabulated results and analysis of the answers. The numbers correspond to the 21 questions on the questionnaire; when there is an additional question, it is discussed under the same number (see appendix 1).

### 1. Satisfaction with occupation and earnings

The level of satisfaction among the interviewees oscillates between 1 (very unsatisfied) and 10 (very satisfied). No one said they were very unsatisfied. Figure 13 shows the distribution by percentages: 64 percent (16 interviewees) were concentrated in the three highest levels of the distribution (8 to 10), 24 percent (6) in the intermediate levels (4 to 7), and 12 percent (3) in the three lowest levels (1 to 4); 40 percent were in level 8 and zero in levels 1 and 2. The degree of satisfaction based on the highest three levels was less than that among self-employed workers, but it is still surprising given the obstacles that usufruct farmers face.

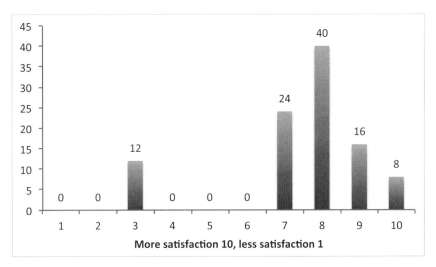

FIGURE 13. Usufruct farmers: Are you satisfied with what you do and earn?

## 2. Previous agricultural experience

Eighty-four percent of interviewees said they had previous agricultural experience and only 16 percent said they didn't; this is the reverse of the figure given by *Juventud Rebelde* in 2013, which had 77 percent without previous agricultural experience, but one must remember that the sample is not necessarily representative of the whole. The four usufruct farmers who said they didn't have agricultural experience noted that they had not been trained by the state or other entity.

## 3. Size of parcel

Parcel sizes varied between 6 and 20 hectares (15–49 acres); 40 percent had between 6 and 10 hectares (15–25 acres); 44 percent had between 12 and 20 hectares (30–49 acres); 16 percent had 26 hectares (64 acres). Sixty-eight percent had 13.4 or fewer hectares (33 acres), the maximum established by the 2008 law, and none come close to having the 67 hectares (166 acres) fixed by the 2012 law; the average is 13.8 hectares (34 acres) (table 20). All of this indicates that parcels are relatively small, although this cannot be compared to the national average because that number is not available.

## 4. Clearing of *marabú*

The parcel of land is given by the state, and 56 percent of those interviewed said they cleared *marabú*, while 44 percent answered that there was no *marabú* ("they gave me a good little parcel"). These percentages coincide with the official figure of 50 percent of land having *marabú*. Of the 56 percent that cleared it, 32 percent did it by hand (hatchet, machete, and shovel), 16 per-

TABLE 20. Usufruct farmers: Size of parcel

| Hectares | Number of interviewees | Percentage |
|---|---|---|
| 6–10 | 10 | 40 |
| 12–20 | 11 | 44 |
| 26 | 4 | 16 |
| Total | 25 | 100 |

TABLE 21. Removal of marabú

| Did you clear the marabú? | Number of interviewees | Percentage |
|---|---|---|
| Yes | 14 | 56 |
| By hand (hatchet, machete, shovel) | 8 | 32 |
| By hand and tractor | 4 | 16 |
| Bulldozer | 2 | 8 |
| No | 11 | 44 |
| Total | 25 | 100 |

cent by hand and a tractor, and 8 percent with a bulldozer (table 21). Those who used equipment had between 16 and 26 hectares (40–64 acres) of land; one person who used a tractor said that it was "*por la izquierda*," or doing it illegally, to avoid the government finding out. The answers revealed the hard work required to clean the *marabú,* and that a third paid for the use of equipment, which means a substantial investment to be able to start producing, and there was no micro-credit for doing this kind of work (see subsection "Obstacles" in the section titled "Antecedents" above).

## 5. Construction of a house or barn

No interviewee had built a house or barn on his parcel; one built a palm-roofed watering trough for livestock, which confirms that they are small usufruct farmers. Only ten explained why they had not built a home and the categories are nonexclusive: 36 percent have a house near the land, 29 percent find it too difficult or think it takes too much time, 21 percent need the land for a grove or livestock, and 14 percent didn't need a house—without explanation (table 22). There is no national data on how much has been built by usufruct farmers, which is a key indicator of the investment made by them.

## 6. Crops or livestock

Thirty-two percent of usufruct farmers devoted their parcels to the raising of cattle for milk because selling meat is prohibited, whereas 68 percent worked

TABLE 22. Reason for not having built a house

| Why haven't you constructed a house? | Number of mentions | Percentage |
| --- | --- | --- |
| Has a house nearby | 5 | 36 |
| Costs too much or takes too much time | 4 | 29 |
| Needs the land for a grove or pasture | 3 | 21 |
| Doesn't need one | 2 | 14 |
| Total | 14[a] | 100 |

Note: [a] 14 mentions because the categories are nonexclusive.

TABLE 23. Crops

| Crops | Number of mentions | Percentage |
| --- | --- | --- |
| Taro | 6 | 15 |
| Beans | 6 | 15 |
| Bananas | 5 | 12 |
| Onions | 4 | 10 |
| Corn | 3 | 7 |
| Tomatoes | 3 | 7 |
| Cassava root | 3 | 7 |
| Others | 11 | 27 |
| Total | 41[a] | 100 |

Note: [a] 41 mentions because the categories are nonexclusive.

on diverse crops. This last group is nonexclusive and the crops are quite varied: 15 percent taro, 15 percent beans, 12 percent bananas, 10 percent onions, 7 percent each of corn, tomatoes, and cassava root, and 27 percent others, such as garlic, flowers, potatoes, rice, lemons, avocados, other fruits (table 23).

## 7. Fruit tree planting

Eighty percent of interviewees had not planted fruit trees (avocado, banana, mango); only 20 percent had done so because it requires time, effort, and capital, and the short-term contract is a disincentive. There is no relationship between parcel size and the planting of trees.

## 8. Taxes

Taxes are only annual, and paid in CUP. Eighty-eight percent paid taxes and only 12 percent didn't pay because they had recently planted and still had no harvest. Among those who paid, 40 percent did, from 200 to 1,000 CUP, 36 percent from 1,001 to 4,000 CUP, and only 12 percent (three) from 5,000 and

TABLE 24. Tax payments

| Annual tax payment (CUP) | Number of interviewees | Percentage |
|---|---|---|
| Paid | 22 | 88 |
| 200–1,000 | 10 | 40 |
| 1,001–4,000 | 9 | 36 |
| 5,000–20,000 | 3 | 12 |
| Don't pay | 3 | 12 |
| Total | 25 | 100 |

TABLE 25. Type of taxes paid

| Type of tax paid | Number of interviewees | Percentage |
|---|---|---|
| 5% on sales | 16 | 73 |
| 5% of profits | 4 | 18 |
| Doesn't know or imprecise | 2 | 9 |
| Total | 22 | 100 |

TABLE 26. Contracted employees

| Do you have employees? | Number of interviewees | Percentage |
|---|---|---|
| Yes | 11 | 44 |
| More than five (6–10) | 3 | 12 |
| Five or fewer | 8 | 32 |
| No | 14 | 56 |
| Total | 25 | 100 |

20,000 CUP; one paid 5,200, another 15,000, and a third 20,000 CUP (table 24). The latter is exceptional, as he had 26 hectares (64 acres)—among the three largest parcels—two tractors, a jeep, and ten employees, meaning he must have earned a very high income.[8] Conversely, 79 percent of the interviewees either didn't pay taxes or paid less than 4,000 CUP per year, which equals US $239, another confirmation that this is a relatively low-income group, although they earned much more than the mean salary in the state sector.

The type of tax paid by 22 of the interviewees (excluding the three who did not pay) was: 73 percent on sales and 18 percent on profits; 9 percent (two) did not know or did not specify (table 25). These answers contradict the earlier mentioned tax exemptions (see subsection "Advances" in the section titled "Antecedents" above).

TABLE 27. Form of payment to employees

| Methods | Number of interviewees | Percentage |
|---|---|---|
| Fixed salary | 7 | 28 |
| Salary plus stimulus | 4 | 16 |
| Has no employees | 14 | 56 |
| Total | 25 | 100 |

## 9. Employees

Fifty-six percent of those interviewed didn't hire employees (some had family members) and 44 percent did; among these, 32 percent contracted from two to five employees and 12 percent from six to ten. The vast majority of employees were occasional workers, but three had permanent workers and contracted seasonally for the harvest (table 26). Usufruct farmers hire fewer employees than self-employed workers (44 percent vis-à-vis 60 percent); hence, the former were either involved in individual work or had fewer resources than the latter.

## 10. Payment methods

Among those who had employees, 28 percent paid a fix salary per day ("morning": from 6:00 AM to 2:00 PM), whereas 16 percent were paid a fixed monthly salary plus a stimulus, which depended on the workers' effort; incentives could have been a given share of the harvest or being allowed to take home some of what has been produced (table 27).

The total remuneration varied: the daily wage ("morning," eight hours) fluctuated from 40 to 50 CUP, tantamount to between 960 and 1,200 CUP monthly, if one worked six days a week. The lower number is 50 percent higher than the mean state salary (640 CUP), and the higher number almost twice as much. One interviewee paid about 2,000 CUP per month or three times the mean state salary. The monthly wage paid to permanent employees was about 600 CUP plus a stimulus. It is very difficult to compare salary totals between usufruct farmers and self-employed workers because of their diversity; notwithstanding, some in the latter group were paid in CUC, which is not the case with the former.

## 11. Problems with employees

Of the 11 interviewees who had employees (44 percent), 36 percent of them had no problems with them because they paid well and "there are always people to work"; 8 percent (two interviewees) did have problems; one said, "people don't like farm work." Usufruct farmers seemed to have fewer problems with their employees than did the self-employed workers.

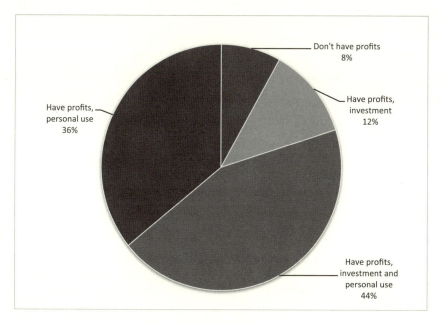

FIGURE 14. How do you use your profits?

## 12. Profits and their use for investment and/or consumption

Ninety-two percent of those interviewed said they had net profits and only 8 percent (two) said they didn't, which is similar to results for the self-employed. Usufruct farmers were even less explicit about the amount of profits; only two said that they were meager; none said he earned a lot. Of those with profits, 36 percent (nine) said that they were for personal use only (consumption), only 12 percent (3) for investing, and 44 percent (11) for both uses (fig. 14). Self-employed workers invested much more, which might be because they owned their micro-businesses, while usufruct farmers did not own the land and had only ten-year contracts, both disincentives for investing.

The few usufruct farmers that specified what they invested in listed land, groves, orchards, and animal replacement. Three interviewees said they saved some. The question on how long it took to recover investment was not asked, given the very small number who did.

## 13. Ties to cooperatives

All the interviewees were tied to a CCS (the most independent co-ops from the state), with one exception, which was with a UBPC; none was tied to a CPA or state farm. Benefits they gained from being tied to CCS were: 48 percent said it was because the CCS commercializes what is produced, "which is more efficient, since they don't produce enough for them to directly sell the produce"; 12 percent said it was because they give them fertilizer; 28 percent

Table 28. Benefits of being tied to a cooperative

| Benefits | Number of interviewees | Percentage |
| --- | --- | --- |
| Commercializes the product | 12 | 48 |
| Provides fertilizer | 3 | 12 |
| Others | 7 | 28 |
| Not much | 3 | 12 |
| Total | 25 | 100 |

Table 29. Would you prefer to be independent?

| Would you prefer to be independent? | Number of interviewees | Percentage |
| --- | --- | --- |
| No | 21 | 84 |
| Doesn't make a difference | 2 | 8 |
| It's not possible | 1 | 4 |
| Doesn't know | 1 | 4 |
| Total | 25 | 100 |

Table 30. Reasons for not requesting credit or loans

| Why you did not request credit or loan? | Number of interviewees | Percentage |
| --- | --- | --- |
| Doesn't need it | 4 | 16 |
| Too complex | 4 | 16 |
| Others | 2 | 8 |
| Total | 10 | 40 |

Table 31. Other sources of assistance

| Source of assistance | Number of interviewees | Percentage |
| --- | --- | --- |
| Did receive | 13 | 52 |
| Family | 10 | 40 |
| Friends | 2 | 8 |
| State | 1 | 4 |
| Did not receive | 12 | 48 |
| Total | 25 | 100 |

listed other reasons, such as providing water or wire (which they could not otherwise obtain); 12 percent said that the tie to CCS didn't give them much (table 28). One of them clarified: "here, one must be tied"; three in the "others" category added: "if I am not tied, working the land gets complicated"; "many are the things that otherwise would not flow," and "it's easier."

When asked if they would prefer to be independent (not to be tied to co-ops), 84 percent answered no, 8 percent said it didn't make a difference, and 4 percent (one) said, "it is not possible" (table 29).

The answers above suggest that usufruct farmers do not want to be tied with the state's most dependent cooperatives (UBPC and CPA), nor to state farms because both are notoriously inefficient; they are inclined to link to CCS because in return they receive some benefits, although various interviewees expressed reserve regarding these. And yet, the majority did not want to be independent because there are things they could not obtain on their own, such as the sale of their products, fertilizers, and fence wiring. One, in all honesty, voiced: "it is not possible" to be untied or independent.

## 14. Foreign remittances

Sixty-eight percent of the interviewees did not receive remittances and only 32 percent did—a somewhat higher proportion than among the self-employed. Among those who received remittances, none of them invested it in land; it was for personal consumption and for the family.

## 15. Government credits or bank loans

None of the interviewees received credits or loans, just like the self-employed (table 30). Only 40 percent (10) gave a reason: 16 percent didn't need them; 16 percent said it was too complex ("too much paperwork," "a big mess"), whereas 8 percent gave other explanations: "one shouldn't get involved with that," "if I ask for a loan and the crop doesn't pay off, how do I pay the bank?"

## 16. Other sources of assistance

Fifty-two percent received assistance from other sources and 48 percent did not receive any—three times the proportion among the self-employed. Among those who did receive assistance, 40 percent said it came from family, 8 percent said it was from friends, and 4 percent (one) said it came from the state (consulting on exotic fruit production) (table 31). Among the family members, those mentioned were siblings, parents, and a grandfather. As with other indicators, the usufruct farmer group had fewer resources and less assistance than the self-employed.

## 17. *Acopio*

Fifty-six percent of interviewees (14) sold part of their harvest to the state *acopio* at a price fixed by the government under the market price (fig. 15): 40 percent (10) sold between 51 and 100 percent of their crop and 16 percent (4) between 20 and 50 percent; 44 percent (11) didn't sell at all (the 56 percent who sold to *acopio* was lower than the 70 percent previously cited, see subsection "Obstacles" in the section titled "Antecedents" above). One-third of

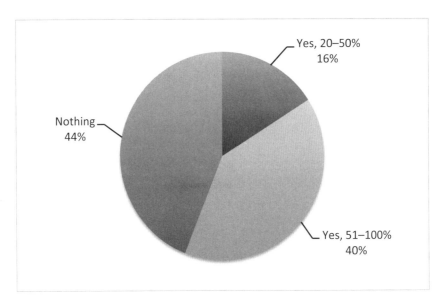

FIGURE 15. What portion of your production do you sell to state *acopio*?

usufruct farmers raised milk cows; the milk could not be sold to anyone else but the state dairy enterprise, so virtually all of it went to the *acopio* (families could consume a small portion of it). Three interviewees grew beans, potatoes, and corn, and it all went to the *acopio* too. Among the 44 percent who didn't sell to the *acopio*, a few had small crops and others delivered their produce to the CCS, which sold them.

Usufruct farmers sold their production to different buyers: 52 percent to the state (*acopio*), 24 percent directly to markets, and 21 percent through CCS; one interviewee was ambiguous and several resorted to a combination of these methods (e.g., state and CCS, state and direct, state and cooperative), frequently depending upon the price paid by the buyer (table 32).

Those who sold to the state (or to CCS) gave various reasons: they had to do it; it was easier because it bought all the crop at a fixed price; it took too much time to do it directly; the market for selling was far away; one said that the state paid well sometimes, but other times it didn't, so he preferred to sell it on his own. Those who sold directly often had a small crop; one said that sometimes the state made a commitment to buy and later didn't pick up the produce.

On the subject of pricing policies, specific answers indicate that almost all who said that they could lower prices of their products were confused, and that in reality they were referring to what would be needed for them to lower said prices. Thus, virtually all of them actually responded "no." Based on that interpretation, table 33 distinguishes between the two categories: 53 percent

TABLE 32. Production distribution methods

| To whom do you sell your product? | Number of mentions | Percentage |
|---|---|---|
| State | 15 | 52 |
| Directly | 7 | 24 |
| Cooperative (CCS) | 6 | 21 |
| Ambiguous | 1 | 3 |
| Total | 29[a] | 100 |

Note: [a] 29 mentions because the categories are nonexclusive.

TABLE 33. Possibility of lowering selling prices

| Do you or do you not lower prices, and why? | Number of interviewees | Percentage |
|---|---|---|
| Cannot be lowered | 13 | 52 |
| Too much work, I earn little, and inputs are costly | 3 | 12 |
| The state pays little/low sales prices | 3 | 12 |
| The prices are already low | 2 | 8 |
| Inputs are very costly (including TRD) | 2 | 8 |
| Product cannot be sold at market | 2 | 8 |
| Doesn't know | 1 | 4 |
| What is needed for lowering prices | 12 | 48 |
| Lower input prices | 6 | 24 |
| Lower price of transportation and pallets | 6 | 24 |
| Total | 25 | 100 |

said they could not lower prices and 48 percent specified what would have to be done for them to reduce their prices.

Although the debate about capping prices began in December 2015, when the interviews had already been finished, the above answers shed light on the question of whether or not usufruct farmers (as well as private peasants) are making good profits with high sale prices; the answers indicate that they are not. The reasons the usufruct farmers offered on why they cannot lower prices are: 12 percent said farm work is very hard and they earn very little or inputs are very costly; 12 percent felt the state paid little in *acopio*, or sales prices are low; 8 percent said the prices are already too low; 8 percent said that inputs are very costly ("prices at shopping stores are very high and the state does not lower them"; "fertilizer price is through the roof"; "state stores excessively inflate prices and so do pallet stall vendors . . . they should strive to earn more by selling more quantity and not from the price of each product; they let products rotten rather than sell them cheaper"); and 8 percent

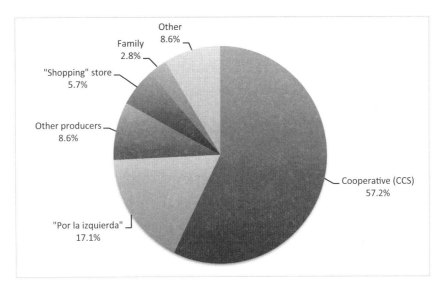

Figure 16. Where do you get your inputs?

said the product (milk) cannot be sold to the market. When asked what is necessary for price reduction, 24 percent suggested they lower the price of inputs (including state stores), and 24 percent said to reduce the price of transportation (truck drivers) and the price of those who sell the products at the market ("cart drivers," "pallet stall vendors"). A number of the interviewees reasoned: "farmers are not the ones who make the product expensive"; "if the TRD lower prices of ropes, hoes, carts, then we could lower our prices"; "farmers are not the ones who raise prices; they go up as soon as they hit the road"; "if I tell you what I earn for a string of garlic and what the guy who sells it in Havana charges for it, it would make you laugh."

## 18. Where do you obtain inputs?

Fifty-seven percent of the inputs were sold by the CCS (except in one case, by a UBPC); 17 percent obtained them "on the side," illegally (on the black market); 8.6 percent obtained them from other farmers; 5.7 percent came from state stores; 2.8 percent (one) were given by family, and 8.6 percent came from other sources, such as the domestic market, in CUP—or "wherever things can be found" (fig. 16). In many cases, there were various combined sources of supply. No one mentioned having bought any at the wholesale market.

## 19. Contract renewal

Fifty-two percent of interviewees were not worried about the renewal of their contracts after ten years, and 48 percent were worried. The reasons given

TABLE 34. Principal problems faced

| Principal problems | Number of mentions | Percentage |
|---|---|---|
| High price of inputs | 15 | 56 |
| Bureaucratic obstacles | 4 | 15 |
| Commercialization | 3 | 11 |
| Low sales prices | 2 | 7 |
| Short term of usufruct | 2 | 7 |
| Others | 1 | 4 |
| Total | 27[a] | 100 |

Note: [a] 27 mentions because the categories are nonexclusive.

for not being worried were: "I have another plot of land"; "I'll take my cows elsewhere"; "I haven't invested in the land"; "the land is no good, so what do I care?" Reasons from those who were worried: "10 years is too little time to invest in the land and I think this is a bit of a disincentive"; "they should make the contracts longer"; "orchards take time to grow; if grafted, a *mamey* tree takes 15 years to bear fruit and you don't see the results of your work"; "I am fencing the land for livestock, and would lose it."

## 20. Inheritance of usufruct

To find out how much the interviewees knew about their rights, we asked: "Do you know that when you die your family members who work the land with you can inherit the contract and investment made?"; 100 percent answered positively.

## 21. Principal problems and changes

Like the self-employed, these two questions about problems and changes elicited more information from the interviewees; their answers are consistent with the obstacles analyzed in the Antecedents (see subsection "Obstacles" in the section titled "Antecedents" above).

### a. Principal problems faced

Several interviewees pointed out more than one problem, so the responses are nonexclusive (table 34 and fig. 17). The most serious problem (56 percent) was that inputs are scarce, take too long to get, or are very expensive: "here, everything is difficult and costly"; there is a lack of "wire for fencing [and because of that] I can't change the animals... there is no seed, fertilizer, pesticide"; "with the exception of potatoes, inputs for other products take a long time to get."

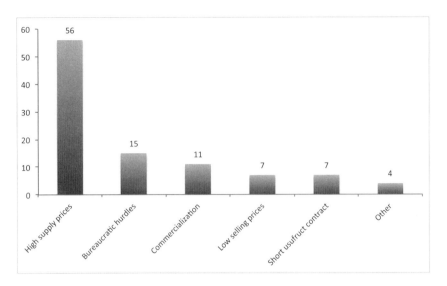

Figure 17. What are the most serious problems you face?

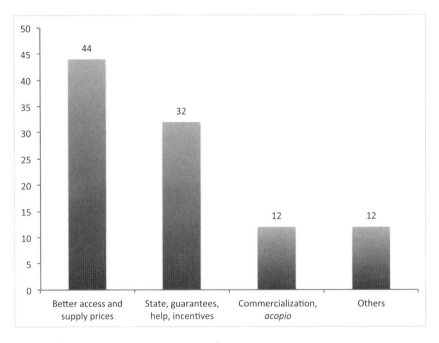

Figure 18. What would you like to see change or improve?

The next problem in order of importance was bureaucratic obstacles (15 percent): "they create a lot of hitches all over the place"; "let them not make things tougher, so we can make progress with the farm;" "the land is going to waste, and no one really cares." The first two problems jointly equal 71

TABLE 35. What would you like to see change or improve?

| Desire for change or improvement | Number of interviewees | Percentage |
|---|---|---|
| Greater access and lower prices for inputs | 11 | 44 |
| State guarantees, assistance, incentives | 8 | 32 |
| Commercialization, acopio | 3 | 12 |
| Others | 3 | 12 |
| Total | 25 | 100 |

percent, much higher than the 48 percent reported by the self-employed. Commercialization (distribution) was identified by 11 percent of the interviewees: "when one produces a lot of mangos, there is no industry for processing them, so they go to waste"; "the commercialization of tomatoes [is a drawback] . . . due to delays in delivering boxes for packaging." The fourth problem (7 percent) was the low prices paid to usufruct farmers (partly due to *acopio*); two said that "the price of milk is too low." The same proportion (7 percent) was blamed on the usufruct contract's short duration (ten years): "the term for usufruct is short"; "let them give us more time for the land." Finally, one interviewee complained, "I have no water on the land and have to sow almost everything on only rain-fed land."

### b. Changes they desire

The question on what the farmers would like to see improved upon is crucial to the study because it is a vehicle for listening to the usufruct farmers' voices and making them public so they can be tended to. It was difficult to completely separate the answers into categories, as we will explain. The first two answers add up to 76 percent, compared to 60 percent of self-employed workers: better access and lower prices for inputs (44 percent) and issues pertaining to the state, its guarantees, and the need for help (32 percent) (see table 35 and fig. 18). It appears that the order is inverted since, among the self-employed, freedom and fewer regulations were the most important, yet we will see it is not true when the usufruct farmers' answers are carefully analyzed.

For usufruct farmers who have fewer resources than self-employed workers, access to inputs and their price (as well as the price paid for *acopio*) are fundamental, which is what they demanded in the first place: "reduce prices of inputs, especially to us, who sell virtually everything to the state"; get supply inputs on time "since sometimes I finish production without them, hence produce and earn less;" "sell what we need and cheaper, so we can reduce our prices"; "price the fencing wire the same as what they pay for milk"; "pay more for goat milk"; "give us some fertilizer and resources for citrus, so we could improve our production, because it is badly needed."⁹ In virtually all of these answers, usufruct farmers are indirectly addressing the state, which is responsible for inputs and fixes their prices, as well as the prices it pays for *acopio*.

The second desire was for the state to provide guarantees, help, and incentives: "that one that has the land in production must be given guarantees that it will not be taken away"; "if the state wants us to produce more and better, it should help us to do so"; "the authorities should be more concerned in order for us to produce more and better"; "they should motivate more the people so they work the land"; "they should help the peasants to get tools to work, I don't mind to buy them, but I want to buy a tractor and where is it?, because I can't bring it in from abroad."

Commercialization/*acopio* was the third major concern (12 percent): "I don't want the *acopio* to buy everything I produce because it pockets all my produce," an obvious reference to the state. Among the "others" (12 percent): "allow us to change parcels"; "search for a cow appropriate for our climate and that produces both milk and beef"; "establish a tomato processing plant close to us in order to reduce the cost of transportation." Note that most of these claims are also addressed to the state without mentioning it.

If we totaled all the answers that directly or indirectly refer to a change in state attitude, we'd have at least 80 percent. Usufruct farmers did not identify other desires typical of the self-employed, such as greater access to the Internet, and that was true as well for the desire for unity so that they could better present their demands.

# 4

# MEMBERS OF NONAGRICULTURAL & SERVICE COOPERATIVES

## ANTECEDENTS

First-grade nonagricultural and service cooperatives (CNA) began tentatively in 2010; they were introduced nationally in an experimental manner in 2013, a status that still continued at the end of 2016; although CNA are expanding, their members are still small. CNA may be organized as a mandatory transfer from state enterprises or be voluntarily created privately by workers. In the latter case, members own everything, while in the former the state keeps ownership of the land and buildings concomitantly, allowing the cooperative's members the use and exploitation of the business via a ten-year, renewable lease contract with monthly payments. The purchase price for equipment from a former state enterprise should be negotiated with the CNA; once such equipment is bought it belongs to the cooperative. CNA should have a minimum of three partners who are over 17 years of age, be permanent residents, and be able to carry out their duties. Partners manage the activity, repair the locale, acquire inputs, pay utilities and gasoline bills, sell their products/services at market prices (in CUP or CUC), and receive profits to be distributed among the partners, usually in accordance with their contribution or effort. In addition, CNA should be self-financed, that is, their revenue must cover expenditures. These co-ops may be liquidated if they have sustained losses, insufficient capital to meet obligations, or negative results in audits. The CNA can't be sold or transmitted to other co-ops, nonstate sectors (NSS), or individuals. The cooperative is governed through

TABLE 36. Number of CNA and their members, 2013–15

| Years | Number of CNA | | Annual growth (%) | No. of members | Annual growth (%) |
|---|---|---|---|---|---|
| | Approved | Operating | | | |
| 2013 | 275 | 198 | - | 2,300 | - |
| 2014 | 498 | 345 | 71 | 5,500 | 139 |
| 2015 | 498 | 367 | 6 | 7,700 | 140 |

*Source*: Our own calculations based on ONEI 2015, 2016a; Piñeiro 2015.

by-laws approved by its partners. It is alleged that CNA are more independent than agricultural-production cooperatives (basic units of cooperative agricultural production [UBPC] and agro-livestock production cooperatives [CPA]). The government has expressed its preference to cooperatives, including CNA, over individual business efforts like self-employment and usufruct (see subsection "Advances" below). According to Murillo, CNA "are an example of how to transform ways of management, without changing the nature of property" (*Bohemia*, Aug. 29, 2013; PCC 2016b).[1]

"CNA take care of market segments that are not competitive for the state" ("Raúl: Lo que hacemos" 2015). The government decided that it would be better to transfer smaller activities, with low efficiency and high cost, to CNA; that way, "deviations" (thefts) would be avoided, as well as the cost of salaries, inputs, and public services. In addition, the state receives rent and tax payments from CNA.

## Size and trends

The National Office of Statistics and Information (ONEI) provides statistics on the number of CNA in operation as well as the number of members, but the history of the evolution is not precise and there are contradictions in the figures given in speeches and the media. CNA began as a pilot program in 2010, with barbers, hairdressers, and manicurists, and other activities were added in 2011 and 2012 (Mesa-Lago 2014). The Council of Ministers approved four groups of CNA: (1) 126 in April, (2) 71 in July, (3) 73 in October, all in 2013, and (4) 228 in March 2014, for a total of 498 (*Granma*, March 3, 2014). Table 46 shows that the number approved increased from 275 at the end of 2013 to 498 in 2014 and stagnated in 2015, while the CNA in operation rose 71 percent in 2013–14, but only by 6 percent in 2015. Conversely, the number of partners climbed from 2,300 to 5,500[2] in 2013–14, and to 7,700 in 2015; hence, the members have grown at a higher rate than the CNA ("Raúl: Lo que hacemos" 2015). A faster addition of CNA would significantly expand their membership (fig. 19).

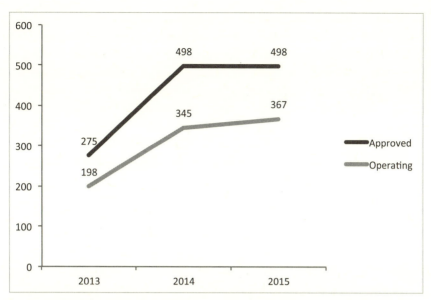

FIGURE 19. Number of (CNA) cooperatives approved and operational, 2013–15

We have seen that the number of self-employed workers decreased slightly in 2015, while that of usufruct farmers fell in 2014. Since March 2014, no more CNA have been approved due to obstacles in their establishment and operation; Raúl Castro (2016a) ratified at the Seventh Party Congress in April 2016 that no CNA had been created so far that year. And yet, 16 new CNA were created in the first quarter of 2016, raising the number in operation to 383; the number of members has not been disclosed (*Cuba Debate,* June 26, 2016). Pérez Villanueva (2016) considers that the process for creating cooperatives "is advancing very slowly . . . there are many that have presented their proposals, but require an excessively high level of approval . . . the fifth group of CNA, which everyone is expecting, has spent a year awaiting approval without receiving it." The 2016 guidelines announced a law regulating the CNA and the start of those of the second degree (cooperatives comprised of other CNA), announced five years ago at the Cuban Communist Party (PCC) Sixth Party Congress (PCC 2016b).

## Characteristics

Seventy-seven percent of the CNA in operation originated from transfers of state enterprises, whereas 33 percent were established by workers. Piñeiro (2015: 58) informs us that "the most successful cooperatives have been those that emerged from the initiative of a group of people who shared purpose and values." Eighty-eight percent of CNA are concentrated in three sectors: 59 percent in commerce, gastronomy, and technical and personal services;

19 percent in construction; 10 percent in small industry; 5 percent raising exotic birds; 4 percent recycling garbage, and 3 percent in transportation ("Raúl: Lo que hacemos" 2015). Fifty-two percent are located in Havana, 18 percent in Artemisa, 5 percent in Matanzas, and 4 percent in Mayabeque (ONEI 2016b). There is no information available on the key characteristics of CNA, such as production, sales, or profits, nor about their members' age, sex, race, or level of education. A state bank has asked to conduct interviews to collect this important data (see subsection "Obstacles" below). The small number of interviews with CNA (five) does not allow us to fill that void, as we do for other groups, but the anecdotal information is useful.

## Advances

Motivated by the goal to reduce costs and increase income and profits, CNA reportedly renovate locales, offer better services, improve labor discipline, meet schedules, decrease absenteeism, take good care of work tools, and save more resources; many have invested in improving equipment, and they earn an income three times the mean salary in the state sector (Piñeiro 2015). CNA can buy, sell, and lease from the state, and from tourist installations like hotels and restaurants. In addition, they can hire employees other than family members, open bank accounts, and receive micro-loans. Their products and services are sold to the state, cooperatives, private farmers, and self-employed workers (MINCIN 2013). Officials have asserted that CNA have obtained positive productive, economical, and financial results, can be sources for jobs, and have increased supply and the quality of products and services ("Raúl: Lo que hacemos" 2015).

In June 2013, the wholesale market was regulated, including contracts, competition, and free market prices (set by supply and demand). The only wholesale market was El Trigal; it belonged to Havana province, which leased it to a CNA, which in turn sublet 292 stalls (*tarimas*) to producers to sell their surplus after meeting *acopio*; the stalls were charged from 110 to 120 CUP independent of how often they were used. Private farmers supplied the most products, followed by CCS, CPA, UBPC, state farms, and wholesale vendors. Buyers were charged a 3 CUP (US $0.12) entry fee (*Granma*, Jan. 17, 2014).[3] El Trigal closed in 2016; the Zona+ storage sale market is mainly for self-employed workers; hence, usufruct farmers lack a wholesale market.

State enterprises can lease supply markets for agricultural products to CNA and CCS; in early 2014, there were 433 of said markets leased to 157 cooperatives (*Granma*, Apr. 17, 2014). State enterprises can also lease trucks to all retail producers and markets, to cooperatives, and to the self-employed, and also sign contracts for agricultural produce with all cooperatives that have direct contracts with consumers (Decree-Law No. 318, 2013).

There is a plan to transfer 9,000 state establishments to self-employed workers and CNA, 83 percent in gastronomy and the rest in personal and technical services, with 123,000 workers. In 2015, 11 of these CNA were established. In the construction sector, the sale price of state equipment to CNA is to be set by "mutual accord of the parties"; regarding national products, the sale price to co-ops is a minimum set by the MINCIN, with a discount of 20 percent, whereas imported products are charged 20 percent of the wholesale price (*Juventud Rebelde*, Aug. 18, 2014).

The state has expressed its preference for cooperatives because they are "a more social form of production than private business" (like self-employment) and so the government grants them a less burdensome tax treatment: (a) tax exemption on sales of agricultural products; (b) exemption on all taxes for six months after enrollment at the National Office of Tax Administration (ONAT) contributors' registry; (c) 20 percent fees to social security, compared to 25 percent to the self-employed; (d) increase in the scale of the profit tax from 10 percent on the first 10,000 CUP to 45 percent for over 50,000 CUP[4] (vis-à-vis 15 percent to 50 percent to the self-employed); (e) deductions to personal income tax are lower: they don't have to justify 40 percent of expenses, can deduct the sum that goes to the contingencies reserve and 50 percent of the cost of contracting third parties, and can deduct a sum equivalent to the mean salary in the province multiplied by the number of the CNA members; (f) they don't have to pay rent to the state when repairing the locale; (g) they receive a discount of 20 percent for buying inputs; (h) they are allowed to export and import through state entities; (i) professionals are permitted to be members of the CNA (prohibited to the self-employed). Finally, the Ministry of Finance and Prices has the power to grant CNA other exemptions and benefits (Law No. 113 [2012]; Resolution 427 [2012] and 124 [2016]).

A national budget fund has been established that supplies resources to banks so they can give small credits or loans to cooperative members; it is regulated by Decree-Law 289 (2012), and has been available since 2014 (in chapter 2, see subsection "Advances" in the section titled "Antecedents"). In 2015, Decree-Law 289 raised micro-loans from 10,000 to 20,000 CUP (US $400 and US $800); the grace and payment periods were extended, the process was simplified, and advice and courses were offered. The Metropolitan Bank lent start-up capital to 60 agricultural markets run by CNA in Havana, as well as gastronomical, construction, and bird-raising (Fong and Rosabel 2015).

There are reports of successful CNA like the Gold Pig (*Cerdo de Oro*), which is packed with consumers and has electronic scales, air-conditioning, and large refrigerators, as well as cleanliness and no flies, which is the opposite of state stores and agricultural markets (González 2014). In its first year, a textile-producing cooperative generated US $20,000, its members worked ten hours per day and on Saturdays if necessary, and salaries increased three times (Werner 2014). The Karabalí cabaret, which offers music on weekends, fills up with more than 100 clients; the salaries of the 21 members have tripled when compared to what they earned with the government, and they also receive some of the profits every three months; one of the partners says that there are no more thefts and that they earn according to the effort made by everyone (Frank and Valdés 2014).

One CNA textile manufacturer in Marianao has 53 members and has tripled salaries for seamstresses. Members arrive punctually, there are no absences, and people are not checked as they leave the factory (Chappi 2014). The Sazón Purita cooperative makes dehydrated products; in 2015, it produced 18 tons of peanuts, 1.4 tons of spices such as garlic, basil, onion, oregano, rosemary, and parsley, as well as nuts and bread crumbs; it obtained a 985,000 CUP loan equal to US $41,000 (Whitefield 2015).

In mid-2015, the Council of Ministers approved various changes to strengthen and improve CNA, expanded the contract term for nonfamily employees from a maximum of three months to a year, and extended the grace period for taxes—the latter already explained above ("Raúl: Lo que hacemos" 2015).

## Obstacles

Murillo has identified "negative aspects that have hindered good deeds" of CNA: (a) not everyone has understood the experimental nature of the process and the priority given to sectors that have a high impact on territorial development; (b) the procedure to establish cooperatives comes with a bureaucratic burden that generates delays; (c) the start of operations has been slow, principally due to the selection of locales, legalization at property registries, negotiation with cooperatives, and their approval and legal actions in the presence of a notary public and bank; (d) difficulties in accessing supplies, and (e) a tendency to increase prices, especially at agricultural markets and in gastronomy ("Raúl: Lo que hacemos" 2015).

The creation of a CNA is complex and prolonged, particularly if it's initiated by a group of people because it has more requirements than in the transfer of a state enterprise (Piñeiro 2014, 2015). The process begins with an application to the municipal administrative office that sends it to the provincial administration, which then takes it up to the State Central Administration, which submits it to the Permanent Commission for the Implementation of Reforms, which sends it, with an evaluation, to the Council of Ministers, which makes the final decision. There is no time limit to make this decision. If it is approved, a certificate of legal entity is issued and the CNA must be registered as a taxpayer at ONAT. After receiving authorization, there are 90 working days to go to a notary public with the proposed by-laws agreed upon by the group of members and initiate the process of its creation, which culminates with the inscription at the Mercantile Registry (Mesa 2015). If the CNA is transferred from a state enterprise, two of the above steps are skipped, but the enterprise must be inscribed in the Property Registry and there are delays in the completion of the Property Registries in Havana ("Raúl: Lo que hacemos" 2015).[5]

CNA face difficulties in entering into contracts with state enterprises, as well as with selling them products and services, for example, MINTUR hotels, transportation, mail services, telephone, Internet, food, and construction materials (Piñeiro 2014; see subsection "Principal problems faced and desired changes" in the section titled "Results and Analysis of Interviews"). The Central Bank grants a license for CNA bank accounts; in 2014, only one bank accepted these accounts, and it charged commissions for bank services and did not pay interest for deposits in such accounts (BCC 2014).

There are difficulties in buying inputs along with other restrictions. Agricultural markets are banned from selling livestock meat, fresh milk and its derivatives, coffee, cacao, and other state-subsidized products. There are complaints that the shortage of inputs increases prices. The latter is subject of controversy. On the one hand, prices at El Trigal were lower than at the agricultural markets (*Granma*, Jan. 17, 2014); on the other hand, El Trigal's prices were high and increased consumer prices while CNA had not augmented their prices (Piñeiro 2014, 2015). The director of the aforementioned textile CNA reported that fabric cost US $4.75 per meter, hence making it difficult to make profits (Chappi 2014). Members are supposed to receive a 20 percent discount on the price of inputs, but that is not always the case (Ritter and Henken 2015). Pérez Villanueva (2016) states that current rules allow imports, but only one CNA, which grows exotic birds, has been allowed to import fodder (see subsection "Principal problems faced and desired changes" in the section titled "Results and Analysis of Interviews").

Seeking to improve micro-loan efficiency, the Banco Popular de Ahorro took surveys to learn the number of CNA members and their activities and average income. The bank also dealt directly with cooperative members instead of waiting for them to come to the bank, and taught them the importance of loans and how to apply and use them. According to the Banco Metropolitano, there were 317 CNA in Havana province with thousands of members, but it had only granted 127 credits due to members' poor knowledge of them. One gastronomical CNA that received a loan reported that the application process was "long and tedious" with "obstacles, delays" and requested "a lot of information and the same paperwork, many times." To pay off the loan they had to give up 48 percent of the cooperative's income.

Of the total number of loans given in 2012–15, only 35 percent were granted to CNA members, self-employed workers, and usufruct farmers (Fong and Rosabel 2015).

The maximum term for contracting nonfamily workers is currently one year and cannot exceed 10 percent of the total hours worked by members. Start-up capital is funded only by members' monetary contributions and potential bank credits but excludes real estate property, furniture, and even work (Mesa 2015).

Lack of training is a serious problem. The National Association of Cuban Economists (ANEC) offers accounting courses for CNA members, but even in the best-case scenario the training is insufficient and worthless for most of them. In addition, CNA need information to learn from other cooperatives' experiences (Piñeiro 2015).

Several cooperatives that have leased agricultural markets found the installations in a "deplorable" physical state, which required a large initial investment (e.g., 35,000 CUP or US $1,400, a substantial sum in Cuba), as well as renovating roofs, walls, and doors. The same thing is said about transportation equipment, which demanded body work and repairs on brakes, steering, tires, and lights (*Bohemia*, Dec. 9, 2013; *Granma*, Jan. 17, 2014).

Internal control of expenditures and other management issues is insufficient. There are at least two cases in which the president of a cooperative stole substantial sums of money and left debts. Most CNA lack sales and purchase receipts. The National Auditing Office confirms that there is no registry for invoices or any monitoring of canceled bills (Piñeiro 2015).

It is not clear if CNA, particularly those of state origin, are independent from the state. The decision to transfer a state enterprise into a CNA is made by the government without consulting the workers (it is not voluntary, as in a CNA organized by a group of persons); if the employees refuse to join the CNA, they are fired (they have no other option); in some cooperatives, the election of board members was not by secret vote; in one case, the former director of the state enterprise became the president of the cooperative (Frank and Valdés 2014). The president of one CNA said, "Until we are entirely independent and can sign contracts with all suppliers, we will not make progress" (*Havana Times*, May 9, 2014). Pérez Villanueva (2016) argues that "it is not necessarily the case that the state enterprise that did not succeed will do so as a cooperative" because organizing a cooperative presupposes knowing how one works and having a vocation for that type of property: "Sometimes a group of workers in which the principal member is the one who seeks resources and pays the workers a salary with no clear criteria regarding distribution, is called a cooperative." Nor has it been proven that CNA set their prices according to supply and demand; there is evidence that prices of several products are centrally fixed. The 2016 guidelines stipulate "to keep centralized wholesale and retail prices of a group of essential products of services" (PCC 2016b).

At the eleventh National Association of Small [Private] Farmers (ANAP) Congress held in May 2015, the minister of agriculture, Gustavo Rodríguez, reported that the government's nonpayment to cooperatives continued, particularly in the provinces of Artemisa, Mayabeque, and Camagüey (Leiva 2015; International Press Service, May 21, 2015).

At the start of 2015, a journalist asked a state official if a movement from the self-employment way of doing business to a cooperative model would have an adverse effect on the self-employed. The functionary answered: "It is too early to evaluate the adverse impact on the self-employed. In any case, if such a movement were to occur, it would be beneficial" (*Juventud Rebelde*, Oct. 2, 2015).

In 2015, at a Council of Ministers meeting, Raúl Castro requested "not to encourage the spread of the creation of [first-level] cooperatives, the priority should be to consolidate the existing ones and make gradual progress, since not doing so would generalize the problems that come up.... Cooperatives are experimental in nature and although progress is being made in their implementation, we don't have any reason to accelerate the rate.... We have to keep pace with what's happening ... to correct errors before generalizing the experiments.... We ought to calculate the consequences of each step we take and foresee the future" ("Raúl: Lo que hacemos" 2015).[6]

## Impact

Among the three nonstate groups examined, the CNA continue to be "experimental" and are the most recently created,[7] which is said to have impeded the evaluation of their impact (*Juventud Rebelde*, Oct. 2, 2015). Notwithstanding, we gathered and calculated several figures. In 2015, sales at agricultural markets managed by CNA were 3.9 percent of the total value of sales in millions of CUP, and 4.1 percent of the total volume in tons, compared to 28 percent and 41 percent, respectively, for individual points of sale, as well as 38 percent and 45 percent, respectively, for state agricultural markets (ONEI 2015). In 2014, CNA contributed 87.7 million CUP (US $3.5 million) in taxes on sales and profits and in social security fees ("Raúl: Lo que hacemos" 2015), tantamount to 0.3 percent of the total budget's revenue from such taxes (ONEI 2015). CNA contribution to employment is even lower: 7,700 cooperative members in 2015 equal to 0.15 percent of the labor force (ONEI 2016a). There are no statistics on the contribution to GDP, but two Cuban experts affirm that the CNA "do not have a significant weight in the country's economic development" (León and Pajón 2015). In conclusion, CNA have the least impact among the three nonstate groups analyzed up to now.

## RESULTS AND ANALYSIS OF INTERVIEWS

It was not possible to conduct the 25 interviews planned for CNA because we had to obtain authorization from the cooperative president, and that was very difficult, especially in the CNA that have been transferred by state enterprises. We conducted only five interviews, four in CNA organized by people and only one of state origin because the latter's presidents psychologically continue functioning as administrators and fear giving an interview if their superiors have not authorized it. We could not interview the president of the only CNA of state origin, but we did interview a co-op member who lacked information on various key questions. In addition, we noticed more caution in the responses (even from the privately started CNA) compared to the two other groups. For example, they made no explicit or implicit mention of the purchase of inputs "illegally" or in the black market, and they were very brief in their responses regarding problems they face and changes they desire. In view of the tiny size of the sample, we decided not to tabulate the results, but compared the group's characteristics and used the answers as anecdotal information, with a comparative summary of the most important answers at the end.

The interviews were conducted in November–December 2015 and were the study's last. All the interviewees were founders of their cooperatives and their presidents, too, except in the state-origin CNA. All the interviews were done in four municipalities of the Province of Havana. The interviewees' ages varied between 36 and 63 years old. The sample included four men and one woman. The interviewers identified their skin color as white for three interviewees and mulatto for two. The female member of the state-origin cafeteria cooperative was the only woman and a mulatto; the bricklayer was also mulatto. Of the five interviewees, three had a university education (civil, industrial, and electrical engineering), and two had technical precollege (gastronomy and bricklaying). The activities were: one in gastronomy (cafeteria), one in technical services (energy), two in construction, and one in manufacturing production (condiments). These activities represent 88 percent of all CNA.

We asked 21 questions and the section numbers correspond to those in the questionnaire; when there is an additional question, it is discussed under the same number (see appendix 1).

### 1. Satisfaction with occupation and earnings

On a scale of 1 to 10, three interviewees responded they were satisfied (9, 8, and 7); respectively, they are in construction, cafeteria work, and construction-restoration; two responded that they were unsatisfied (4 and

2), respectively, in condiments and energy. Despite being one of the CNA with the most advanced equipment and the greatest volume of production in the country, the president of the condiments cooperative said he was unsatisfied, which does not square with other answers. In conversations with the president and several cooperative members, the low level of satisfaction was explained as being due to the enormous trouble they go through to complete any operation and the large number of barriers they have encountered, which impede them from taking advantage of their potential and, therefore, to increase their profits. They acknowledged some progress, but had to go through a torment of difficulties to subsist. These points of view were confirmed by the CNA answers.

## 2. Previous occupation

All the interviewees were previously employed by the state, but only one of them worked in a state enterprise that was transferred into a CNA; the other four left their state employment to start a personally organized cooperative. The proportions of 20 percent state origin and 80 percent private origin in the five CNA interviewed, dramatically differ from the official figures of 77 percent and 33 percent, respectively, due to the large obstacles we encountered trying to interview CNA of state origin. Three of the interviewees are engineers, one is in gastronomy, and one is a bricklayer.

## 3. CNA activity

The interviewed member who was an employee in a state cafeteria transferred to a CNA and continues in the same occupation. The bricklayer who worked in a construction brigade is president of the CNA specialized in restoration. The civil engineer, who left his state job to found a voluntary CNA, works in construction services, while the electrical engineer who abandoned his government job to start another personally initiated CNA offers energy services. The most interesting case is that of the industrial engineer, who is now president of the CNA he founded, among the most advanced in the country, and is devoted to the production of condiments or dehydrated spices such as garlic, basil, onion, peanut, and so on.

## 4. Number of members

The CNA in the renovation construction business has 40 members (it doubled its initial number), and it has the most members; the other construction CNA has 25 members (it lost two and two others joined). The one that produces dehydrated condiments has 20 members, more than three times the original number, which is a clear sign of its potential. The cafeteria has 15 members, and the smallest CNA, which offers energy services, has six members.

## 5. CNA advantages and disadvantages

We asked what the advantages and disadvantages of working in a CNA were compared to prior employment with the state. All interviewees emphasized the advantages and only one spoke about the disadvantages (contrary to the answers in the previous two groups), a difference that might be due to apprehension. Everybody mentioned that they are now their own bosses, make decisions together, and have greater participation than before, enjoying an autonomy they lacked, which allows for more flexibility in terms of change and adapting to the market, hence resulting in a better quality of products/services, greater efficiency, no more theft, suggestions for attracting new clients, and higher income.

"The advantages are greater than the disadvantages; we are the ones who make decisions, collegially, that are the most convenient for the cooperative's growth [not according to the criteria of only a few]; we can have tremendous dynamism for making changes and adapting to the market's needs or the advantages that a particular provider of raw material can offer us."

"The first thing is to achieve a level of autonomy that we didn't have before, be able to decide what contracts to sign, and organize our own time and resources, which increases efficiency and, with that, income."

"As we are all a part of the CNA and earn according to what we do, no one would ever think of taking anything [theft], which means that our work ends up being better than with the state. We want our work to be good, so we can rapidly be paid, and get recommended to other people, something that does not happen with the state."

Only one CNA (condiments) specified the disadvantages: "the one that most affects us is that for state enterprises or entities, we are not considered acceptable, despite public rhetoric; we cannot sell; they deny the possibility of buying inputs even when they are going bad. This is absurd."

The member interviewed in the state-origin cafeteria was vague: "In our case, we legalized what we had been doing all along. . . . As far as decisions, it is true that we participate more, but Carlos, who is now the president, has more of an eye for business." In the question about operating costs and taxes, this member added, "Carlos is the one who takes care of that; I am not up on that; I heard about it but I couldn't say, now." This suggests that the president plays a crucial role in decisions and that the members have little knowledge on key functions of the cooperative (also see subsection "Leasing from the state and its renewal" below). The following question offers guidelines concerning other disadvantages.

## 6. Limitations

One CNA member said that "in principle, no limitation affects what we do," while another confirmed that "in principle, the cooperative has no legal limits; in reality, there are other restrictions," but he did not elaborate.

Three interviewees referred to problems explained in the subsection "Obstacles" in the section titled "Antecedents" above "We have a tough time finding anything, even though this is a small cafeteria"; contradictorily, this is the same issue we asked before that was said to have been resolved (see question 17). The condiment CNA elaborated more on disadvantages: "It is still hard for us to insert ourselves as a legal entity and we cannot sell to industry, buy vessels from a factory, or sell at a state market." For another CNA its major problem was "contracting employees for a period of only three months [now a year]; hiring for a longer period is only feasible for members of another cooperative."

## 7. Public utilities and telephone costs, and taxes

Two CNA members said the electricity tariffs (combined with gas in one of them) were 2,000 CUP per month; another member said that his home was his office and that costs for public utilities were difficult to separate out. Two quoted the monthly cost of cell phones as 500 to 700 CUP and 40 CUC.

Annual taxes went up to 5,000 CUP in the condiments CNA and 10,000 CUP in the construction one. Two said they were new in business and had not yet paid taxes. The condiments CNA corroborated what was explained in the subsection "Advances" in the section titles "Antecedents" above: "We were able to justify much more than 60 percent of our expenditures. This is one of the advantages of a cooperative over self-employment, lower taxes . . . because you can deduct up to 100 percent of your expenses and one doesn't have to justify 40 percent; this is tremendous advantage."

No one mentioned the labor force tax, although three CNA have more than five employees.

## 8. Profits

Four CNA made a profit (none specified how much), and one did not. Although the sample was very small, the vast majority had profits, as in the case of self-employed workers and usufruct farmers. The four that earned profits invested them in the cooperative in differing degrees: "This is a growing business and a large part of the profits gets invested in the co-op"; "we reinvest almost all profits in equipment"; "first we establish a fund for the cooperative; we keep some to improve the locale, and the rest is distributed amongst us"; "we are already at the stage in which there is something left for us and our family . . . , although, if it is possible to improve the cooperative, we do it."

## 9. Distribution of profits

Three interviewees said they divided profits into equal parts; one explained, "the idea is to gradually return the initial contribution to each member as if it had been a loan to the cooperative." Two said they distributed profit according to the initial contribution and effort of each member: "we have a scale by which we assess members' contributions, the work they do, and their responsibilities at the cooperative"; "not everyone contributed the same and that has weighed in on the distribution of profits, but we have attenuated differences . . . in monthly salaries."

## 10. Improvements to the business

An official claim confirmed that four CNA made improvements and only one didn't because "it operates from home." The improvements are primarily in equipment, utensils, and tools, for example, "the capacity of the ovens to dehydrate and packaging systems." One renovated the building and another improved its office.

## 11. Employees

Three had employees and two did not because they are all members. The number of nonfamily employees varies: 10 (condiments), 20 (construction), and 25 (renovation construction).

## 12. Payment methods

In the four CNA that had employees, payments were weekly in three (one of them could also pay daily or monthly), and the other did not specify. Wages depended fundamentally on the worker's efforts and the type of activity (not all require the same effort), and whether a worker's shift was in the morning, afternoon, or evening (construction).

Only two specified the wage amount, both around 100 CUP per day or 2,000 CUP per month (based on a five-day work week), more than triple the mean state salary of 640 CUP in 2015. The other two CNA were unable to calculate because the remuneration is based on production or a combination of variables.

## 13. Problems with employees

None of the four that had employees reported problems with them.

## 14. Remittances

Three CNA did not receive remittances and two did; in the latter, one did not invest them in the business and the other said that the remittance helps them to be able to occasionally invest part of their earnings.

## 15. Government credits or bank loans

They all responded no. One member of the cafeteria that had been state owned commented: "we have not wanted to get into that." That negative response is the same as those from self-employed workers and usufruct farmers, probably due to the complexity and requirements for obtaining a small loan (see subsection "Obstacles" in the section titles "Antecedents" above).

## 16. Other sources of assistance

Three responded no and three said yes, both from family: a son and a brother.

## 17. Origin of inputs

The responses confirmed the serious difficulties in getting inputs. The four voluntary CNA said that they get supplies from diverse sources. The condiments one specified: "anywhere possible . . . after many months of discussion and work to convince them to break paradigms" [resistance of state entities to sell to the CNA]. The construction one responded: "in the most dissimilar places; it can be that today you'll find cement at the shopping [in CUC], but tomorrow it will be in the national currency market [CUP]." The renovation-construction CNA said that it asked its clients to buy "part of the materials, because it took a weight off our shoulders." The member at the cafeteria that used to be state-owned, explained: "many of the things we used to prepare or sell, we first had to find. . . . For example, we did not have enough bread and other things to finish out the day, so we . . . had to find them." Yet, in response to this particular question, she stated that the MINCIN was still selling them inputs, which seems to be a contradiction.

None of them made reference to El Trigal, the wholesale market that was open at the time of the interviews, which indicates how hard it was to get access to it; they also didn't mention the 20 percent discount that was supposed to be granted to CNA partners, despite the fact they explained the preferential treatment they got regarding taxes. No one mentioned the acquisition of inputs "illegally" or on the black market, as the self-employed and usufruct farmers did, still another hint that the CNA were more cautious than the other groups.

## 18. Competition

Three answered they didn't have competition, and two said they did: "there are private cafeterias around here, since the state ones are not nearby"; "there are a lot of people in this business (construction), from private individuals, brigadiers, the self-employed, the state, etc." None of them lowered their prices; the cafeteria that said it had private competition explained: "we have not changed the prices we had when belonged to the state, . . . some new products that are better are a bit more expensive, but we still have the lowest prices."

When asked if they thought their product or service was better than what the others in the business offered, the responses were somewhat vague: "that depends; there are those who offer a worse service, others that it's the same or more complete"; "we work very well, with no desire to stand out." The cafeteria said that its prices were lower than the rest but warned that its services "are not the best quality; we still use store-bought bread that the MINCIN assigns to us, but people buy it, just the same." The CNA on energy and condiments argued that their product/service was different.

## 19. Advertising

Most businesses advertise by word of mouth (recommendations that attract other clients), with posters on doors, business cards, the telephone book, and at fairs. None of them said they used the Internet or other electronic means.

## 20. Leasing from the state and its renewal

Only the state-origin cafeteria has to pay monthly rent to the state; the member interviewed verified this but did not say how much the rent was, probably because she did not know, as was the case with other responses. Regarding the lease renewal, she said: "we worry about this, because most things here are leased: the locale, refrigerators, the soda machine, and that makes one afraid to invest and later all this could end." The other four CNA are personally initiated; thus, they don't pay rent to the state.

## 21. Principal problems faced and changes desired

This is the group that responded the most briefly to these questions; in fact, most did not differentiate between problems and desired changes, another indication of the caution practiced by the interviewees.

### a. Problems faced

They all pointed to infringement of the law and the resistance that persists regarding the growth of CNA, and relations with the state or its experimental

TABLE 37. Comparison of important answers among the five CNA

| Answers | Cafeteria | Condiments | Construction | Energy | Const.-R |
|---|---|---|---|---|---|
| Origin (state, S, or private, P) | S | P | P | P | P |
| Degree of satisfaction | 8 | 4 | 9 | 2 | 7 |
| Number of members | 15 | 20 | 25 | 6 | 40 |
| Profits | X |  | X | X | X |
| Improvements | X | X | X |  | X |
| Number of employees | 0 | 10 | 20 | 0 | 25 |
| Remittances |  |  |  | X | X |
| Government credits |  |  |  |  |  |
| Other assistance (family) |  |  |  | X | X |
| Competition | X |  | X |  |  |
| Lowering of prices |  |  |  |  |  |
| Leasing from the state | X |  |  |  |  |
| Problems faced |  |  |  |  |  |
|   Bureaucracy, resistance | X | X | X | X | X |
|   Cost of improvements |  | X |  |  |  |
|   Experiment with CNA | X |  |  |  |  |
| Desired changes |  |  |  |  |  |
|   Relations with state enterprises |  | X | X |  |  |
|   Ability to import inputs |  |  |  |  | X |
|   End experimental stage | X |  |  |  |  |

nature that never ends, as well as obstacles to import inputs. Although the responses were not as explicit as those of the first two groups, they made direct or indirect reference to bureaucracy and legal nonfulfillment.

The condiments CNA—personally created—was the most straightforward: "The most serious problems are . . . the resistance that perseveres regarding the development of this new form of production, to such a point that it pushes us to the verge of bankruptcy all the time, due to the stubbornness against negotiating with us, even when it leads to economic advantages for both parties, a behavior contrary to what has been legislated by superior authorities. No one backs up cooperatives' costs because of those citizens' actions, which make things very difficult to work."

"Cooperatives are an experiment; they could end tomorrow because it didn't turn out well, or they're no longer convenient, and then what happens to you. In the end, the [cafeteria] cooperative was a good thing for us, but we were not the ones who created it."

"Despite the fact that the country's leadership today talks about the cooperative sector as if it was important, that is not the reality."

The CNA involved in energy complained: "People are not ready to understand that efficient use can be made of air-conditioning or electricity in buildings."

b. Changes or improvements desired

"For state enterprises to truly open up to having a relationship with the new ways of doing business, like ours" (energy).

"If this changes [resistance to CNA], the rest will be resolved" (condiments).

"It would be good if they finally said when the CNA experiment will be over and it finally stays, or said what was going to happen; it doesn't seem to me that they need to experiment so much" (cafeteria).

"For us to truly be able to achieve something without so many obstacles; for us to be able import a lot of the materials we need. Where does one find scaffolding? If I could import them, I'd have one here in three months; then I'd be able to accept some project" (renovation-construction).

Table 37 summarizes and compares the most important answers among the five CNA.

# 5

# BUYING & SELLING DWELLINGS

## ANTECEDENTS

The 1960 urban reform ordered the confiscation of most dwellings (property owners could keep one of them as their place of residence), prohibited their sale or leasing, practically banned private construction, and abolished mortgages. On the other hand, it granted the right to previous lessees to pay monthly rent to the state for 20 years, after which they became the dwelling's owners, for which reason 85 percent of the population owns their homes.[1] But the cited restrictions brought about adverse effects. The rate of construction of state dwellings was much lower than demographic growth. Many dwellings are in very bad condition because of a lack of maintenance (due to scarcity of construction materials, state restrictions on construction, and the inefficiency of the official agency in charge of repairs), as well as hurricanes, which in recent years damaged a million dwellings, 28 percent of the 3,882,424 existing stock (ONEI 2013b). Officially, the housing deficit is 600,000 units, but the real number is around a million (Mesa-Lago and Pérez-López 2013). The National Housing Institute reports that 1,170,000 homes (30 percent of the total) are in mediocre or bad condition (Benítez 2013). In Centro Habana, 49 percent of the dwellings are in bad condition and 9 percent are in a critical state. There are daily building collapses and 24,311 residents live in temporary shelters (Martín Herrera 2013).[2] In an attempt to alleviate those problems, permission was granted for the construction of private dwellings (called "by population's effort"), as was the swap of dwellings of a supposedly equal value; in practice, swaps created bureaucracy and corruption. The housing reform (Decree-Law 288, 2011) is an important step forward as it authorizes the buying and selling of dwellings, which heretofore had been prohibited for more than half a century, and guarantees rights regarding property, transfer, and inheritance.

## Size and trends

Data on housing transactions are in property registries and notary offices that pass them on to the Ministry of Justice, but those records are not public, and the ministry does not offer periodic reports. The little existing information can be obtained through newspaper articles, which endure frequent contradictions and gaps, so the information is deficient. The housing law was enacted on November 22, 2011, and very few dwellings were traded in December. In 2012, 45,000 dwellings were transferred, and in 2013 there were 200,000 inscriptions at the registry (probably accumulated since 2012); conversely, there were 88,000 transactions in 2013. By the end of 2016, data on 2014 and 2015 had not yet been released. Based on brokers' information, it has been estimated that the number of dwellings constructed fell to 70,000 in 2014, with a slight jump to 75,000 in 2015 (Morales 2016a). Systematic data on the breakdown of transactions between buying and selling and donations are not available either. From November 2011 to March 2012, 80 percent of the total transfers were donations (probably to legalize previous illegal sales), and 20 percent were purchases and sales. In 2013, of a total of 200,000 inscriptions in the property registry, 40 percent were purchases and sales and 60 percent donations, inheritances, and swaps. Although the comparison is not exact, the total transactions in 2013 are equal to 5.2 percent of the total existing dwelling stock, a raise over 1.2 percent in 2012 (table 38). The increase in transactions was due to the fall in housing prices, after very high prices peaked in 2012, as well as the raise in emigration because those who definitively leave the country sell their dwellings, thus expanding the supply.

According to a 2013 study based on 1,227 dwellings, the average sale price was 31,498 CUC (a fortune in Cuba), with a range from 21,464 CUC in Villa Clara to 59,191 in Playa Habana (Morales and Scarpaci 2013). Values of US $500,000 in Miramar and US $2 million for a penthouse in Havana were also reported (Arlidge 2013; AP, Apr. 30, 2013; Benítez 2013). Another 2014 sampling of 1,239 dwellings showed their values to have decreased in Matanzas, Havana, and Cienfuegos; the highest price was 31,863 CUC, in Cienfuegos, while in Havana it was 31,157 CUC. Although prices fell in the municipalities, within Havana, the price in Playa (the beaches) increased by 15 percent, and it was reported that a dozen dwellings had a price of one million CUC (about the same in dollars) or more. Conversely, the lowest prices were in provincial outskirts, in populations with lower purchasing power, and in

TABLE 38. Formal transfers of dwellings by type, 2012–14

| Years | Total transfers | Percentages | | Transfers/ total dwellings (%) |
|---|---|---|---|---|
| | | Purchases and sales | Donations | |
| 2012 | 45,000 | 20 | 80 | 1.2 |
| 2013 | 200,000[a] | 40 | 60[b] | 5.2 |

*Notes*: [a] Inscriptions in the property registry, apparently for a number of years; another figure is 88,000.
[b] Donations, inheritances, and swaps.
*Source*: Authors' own calculations, based on Morales 2014; Peters 2014.

marginal neighborhoods. In 2014, 50.8 percent of the dwellings for sale were in Havana, followed by 9.6 percent in Camagüey; the smallest proportion (1.3 percent) was in Isla de la Juventud (Morales 2014). After the start of normalization of relations between Cuba and the United States, prices experienced an upturn (Morales 2016a). On February 23, 2016, Revolico.com advertised the sale of a dwelling in Miramar for 900,000 CUC (the highest priced) and another in Marianao for 7,000 CUC (the lowest priced).

## Characteristics

There are no official data (e.g., age, sex, race, level of education, etc.) on homebuyers' and sellers' characteristics, nor on real estate brokers or realtors. The interviews offer valuable information about this.

## Advances

The 2011 reform authorized the purchase and sale of dwellings (at a price freely set by buyers and sellers) to Cuban citizens and those whose migratory status is that of a foreign resident, as well as to foreigners who are permanent residents. It also allowed for a second recreational home in the country or at the beach and guaranteed the right of inheritance, as well as the ability to transfer the dwelling to relatives of emigrants that leave Cuba permanently. If the emigrant abandons the dwelling, the state takes possession of it and, if there are claimant inheritors, the property is adjudicated by a hereditary order (Decree-Law 288, 2011). In addition, it was accepted that dwelling owners acting as self-employed workers could lease the dwelling or rooms to tourists, an activity that is greatly expanding. The reform legalized swaps; beginning in 2015, this activity is under the control of the Ministry of Justice, and both parties must execute the transaction before a notary public (Decree-Law 322, 2014). Equity accrued in the dwelling, which was frozen for more than 50 years, can now be sold in order to swap a residence, invest in a micro-business, move to a more modest dwelling with the purpose of saving money for retirement, or obtaining a sum to travel abroad permanently.

There has been an increase in the inscription and updating of buildings in the property registry. In 2011, there were only 200,000 registered (many of them needed updating), equivalent to 5 percent of the total dwellings stock (Peters 2014). In 2013, there were 873,314 properties inscribed in the property registry, of which 76 percent were private (663,719) and 24 percent were state-owned (based on *EFE*, May 11, 2013). Of the private dwellings inscribed, only part of them represented purchases or sales and the rest were updates or inscriptions in possible anticipation of a sale (table 38).

Taking into consideration the construction of various condominium buildings, combined with luxury golf courses, which are managed by the state for sale or lease to foreigners, a special admission permission was granted in 2014 for foreigners and their families to purchase or lease said dwellings and become temporary residents for one year with the possibility of extending the term for one more year; they could even remain abroad for a year without losing their residence status. This permission cost 200 CUC; extensions cost 140 CUC; permission is withdrawn if the foreigners conduct activities other than those authorized in Cuba (MININT 2014). Sellers must pay a tax of 4 percent of the dwelling's sale price; if said price is below the legally assessed value, the assessed value is used as the base for determining the tax.

In 2013, collateral guarantees (at a value set by the market) were reintroduced, backed by jewels, precious metals, agricultural equipment, livestock, and harvests. Mortgages on second recreational homes and vacant lots were also reauthorized, although not for primary dwellings (BCC 2013).

The government has freed up the sale of cement, concrete blocks, gravel, and other construction materials, which should facilitate the private construction of dwellings. In addition, it authorized activity in construction and renovation by self-employed workers and CNA, which was previously prohibited; two of the CNA interviewed do this kind of work and one of them is among the most successful (see chapter 4, the section titled "Results and Analysis of Interviews"). Murillo (2013) reported that the 2013 state plan for the sale of construction materials for dwellings was valued at 2.3 billion CUP (US $92 million).

Until the end of 2013, real estate brokers were not allowed, although they worked illegally. Since 2014, "agents for swaps and purchases/sales of dwellings" are authorized; they can charge a commission based on the value of the property in question (about 4 percent). Buyers prefer pre-1959 dwellings ("capitalist") because they are of better quality than many of those built by construction micro-brigades under the revolution (Vázquez, 2015; Revolico.com, Feb. 23, 2016).

In 2014, 378,000 state credits, a total of 2.231 million CUP, had been granted, an average of 8,546 CUP (US $342) per credit, 63 percent of which was used for the construction and repair of dwellings ("En la reunión" 2014). Furthermore, nonrefundable subsidies are conceded for the purchase of construction materials[3] to needy property owners whose homes were destroyed by hurricanes, and also to lessees living in multifamily dwellings or tenement blocs (*solares*) and state buildings. Between January 2012 and March 2013, 566 million CUP in subsidies were granted to 33,431 low-income beneficiaries for the repair of their dwellings damaged by hurricanes, an average of 16,930 CUP (US $677) per household, almost twice the average of micro-credits. The maximum subsidy for the construction of a dwelling measuring 25 square meters—a "basic unit"—is 85,000 CUP (US $3,400), a substantial sum in Cuba, and 5,000 or 10,000 CUP (US $208 or US $417) for repairs, according to the amount of work necessary (Consejo de Ministros 2013; *Granma*, May 6, 2013). In the provinces of Pinar del Río, Havana, Matanzas, Santiago de Cuba, and Granma, 89,179 subsidies were awarded in 2012–15, for a total of 988 million CUP ("Subsidios" 2016). This is equivalent to an average of 11,000 CUP (US $433), 66 percent of the national average in 2012–13 (US $677), which suggests a decline in average subsidies, but which is also a notable increase in the number of beneficiaries. In 2016, 59 percent of the subsidies was allocated to dwelling construction or repair, 27 percent to major conservation projects, and 14 percent to minor conservations; one-fourth of total subsidies was delivered to those who suffered home damage due to hurricanes (*Diario de Cuba*, July 4, 2016).

In 2014, the Council of Ministers made two concessions: they granted the right to private property to 20,000 victims of hurricanes who had begun to reconstruct their homes without permission to do so (they are eligible for subsidies) and approved the transfer of state dwellings under construction to be completed by "people's own efforts," giving priority to victims of hurricanes, those in shelters, and to special social cases. Conversely, it prohibited the sale or donation of dwellings that had been assigned by the state or constructed with subsidies during the first 15 years after acquisition. In the event of an infraction, the property's market value or the amount of the subsidy must obligatorily be returned to the state ("En la reunión" 2014).

Since 2015, procedures for dwelling transitions have been voided to all construction actions geared to preserve dwellings, as well as those that don't introduce structural changes. In addition, a new married couple may receive in donation from their parents—owners of the dwelling—to build a new structure upon the house roof, after a previous structural-resistance test is certified by the local architect (Decree-Law 322, 2014).

When purchase and selling began in 2011, advertising was limited to posters on homes and personal exchanges at public locations, where many buyers and sellers come together. By 2013, progress was noticed: the Internet site EspacioCuba ran 2,500 ads and had from 30 to 40 clients daily (AP, 30, 2013); Revolico.com became one of the principal avenues for advertising sales offers and purchase requests; by mid-2013, 100,000 dwellings had been advertised (Morales and Scarpaci 2013). Cuban television began to transmit sales ads (Arlidge 2013; *Granma*, July 11, 2013). In 2014, the Havana Brokers' House, with ONAT license, established its headquarters and began to publish a weekly bulletin, *El Papelito.com*, with two pages listing properties for purchase or sale, as well as rentals for foreigners and Cubans; its initial distribution was free but later it charged a fee; in addition, it offers legal and public notary assistance for purchases and sales charging a 4 percent commission on the price (Coyula 2014).

In 2011, unused state buildings, which are very costly to maintain and protect, were approved to be converted into private dwellings; in 2012, said conversion was authorized for 130 structures belonging to the Ministry of Health, as well as to MICONS and other state entities' structures (*Granma*, Feb. 19, 2014).

Two sentences from the Supreme Court in 2013 implicitly acknowledged a previously illegal purchase and sales transaction and authorized its payment in U.S. dollars, which suggests that the government wants to legalize previous transactions and strengthen market security (Circular 265, Apr. 2013; *Cubaencuentro*, Sept. 10, 2013; Peters 2014).

Regarding purchase and sales transactions, the director of Civil Notaries and Registries, Ola Lidia Pérez, said: "Sometimes there is talk of an excessive bureaucracy, but until informatics allows electronic communication between public notaries and registrars, we cannot function without some paper documents" (Fonticoba 2015). Some simplification of the process began in 2015, when construction functions previously carried out by municipal authorities were transferred to the Institute of Physical Planning (IPF): the review of applications to check if they meet all construction requirements; the evaluation of construction plans by an architect; and the final decision and authorization of a certificate of habitability. In addition, several of the agencies involved are coordinating their functions (Decree-Law 322, 2014).

## Obstacles

The state budget assigned to housing is the second lowest in public spending, and it declined from 2.9 percent to 1.3 percent of GDP in 2008–13; later, housing was merged with communal and personal services, which declined by 70 percent of the budget in 2008–15 (ONEI 2013a, 2014, 2015). The production of construction materials fell dramatically in 2011–14; cement roof tiles by 63 percent, clay bricks by 28 percent, terrace tiles by 25 percent, prefabricated concrete by 16 percent, lime by 9 percent, mosaic tiles by 6 percent, and cement by 3 percent. Output only increased 19 percent in ground rock, 15 percent in prefabricated cement blocks, and 10 percent in ceramic tiles (ONEI 2015). Architects cannot be self-employed in their profession, which is an obstacle for home construction and repair.

In 2013, the sale of construction materials was quite below the planned target because of insufficient equipment, poor quality of products, high prices, and the slow stock mobilization (Benítez 2013). The comptroller general, Gladys Bejarano, described in 2014 the deficiencies in the sales program due to a lack of construction materials, which led to people who had received subsidies being unable to buy such materials since the deadline to do so expired (*Granma*, March 3, 2014). In 2013, 56 percent of the subsidy beneficiaries had not been able to buy materials because of a deficit in their supply (*Juventud Rebelde*, March 12, 2014). In 2015, Bejarano carried out 366 audits, which detected obstacles and defaults in the distribution of subsidies; in Centro Habana, only 5 percent of all beneficiaries had received the construction materials (*Granma*, Jan. 28, 2015). In 2016, a National Assembly of People's Power (ANPP) commission evaluated the subsidies and detected some serious control needs: when money given as a subsidy is used in an improper manner, subsidy beneficiaries must take care of the money and search for advice so the construction is not left uncompleted (*Diario de Cuba*, July 4, 2016)

A significant impediment for the purchase and sale of dwellings is higher supply than demand due to the population's poor purchasing power. In 2015, the mean annual state salary was 7,680 CUP (US $307) and a very inexpensive home cost US $4,000, tantamount to 13 entire years of salary (see the sub-subsection "8. Price of the buying and selling" below in the subsection "a. Buyers and Sellers" in "Results and Analysis of Interviews"). Cubans lack the basic knowledge for evaluating their properties and set a market price on them: there are no assessors and, given the poor state of most homes, buyers have to invest about 50 percent in repairs above the purchase price, which is generally unknown (Morales and Scarpaci 2013; Reuters, March 20, 2013).

The sale of a home requires a previous inscription or an update in the property registry. The seller has to be sure that his or her dwelling is properly described in the property's deed; if it is not, a municipal architect must carry out an inspection and make the necessary corrections to the deed. The seller presents the official property deed to the registrar, who reviews the documents; if everything is in order, the deed is registered in 15 days, extendable to 30 days if needed; the seller should carry out the sale within that period of time (Decree-Law 288, 2011). There are 222 registries in the country and they were not up-to-date because very few people bother to inscribe their homes or update their conditions. In addition, a tendency to create multiple registries began without any regulations for their creation, organization, or management; hence, "the information at many of them is duplicated or is dispersed and fragmented, which conspires against the truthfulness of its content" (*Granma*, Dec. 19, 2014).[4] Both parties have to appear before the notary public, at the dwelling's location. The seller has to present the property deed at the property registry as well as a certification of the dwelling inscription. The buyer must open a bank account and get a certification that he or she has the money to pay for the property transfer, pay with a certified bank check, and swear that he or she has no other dwelling, and that the money for the purchase was obtained legally (Fonticoba 2015; on complex procedures, see sub-subsection "20a. Principal problems faced" and "20b. Changes desired" below).

Legal transactions and rules for the construction of homes are also complex and lengthy. Resident Cubans cannot be owners of more than two dwellings (very few have a second recreational dwelling; see sub-subsection "6. Ownership of a second, recreational dwelling" in subsection "a. Buyers and sellers" below); Cubans who reside abroad and visit Cuba where they have family cannot be owners but often use fronts for buying dwellings, which is a crime[5] (Palli 2013, 2014; Vázquez 2015). The application for construction requires eight visits to four state entities, which take about 132 days (*Granma*, July 8, 2013). *Juventud Rebelde* (Apr. 5, 2014) invited its readers to ask questions of the Ministry of Justice; one of them protested about the long time he had to be in line to submit the application and suggested that more hours be made available; the expert answered that the service had been expanded to twice a week, from 8 AM to 7 PM, while awaiting a more flexible schedule. If the state grants a parcel of land, the beneficiaries must start construction on it within a year, extendable to one more; if construction does not take place during that term, the grant is canceled. When there is a request to construct an additional dwelling on top of a building roof, the requester must present the property deed to the municipal IPF office with the required stamps, and the resistance report made by the local architect (Decree-Law 322, 2014).

There are no mortgages for financing the construction of dwellings, except on second, recreational residences and vacant lots. Nor are mortgage banks releasing bonds that could substantially increase credit for housing. Purchases are made in cash, which greatly limits the market; only buyers who receive foreign remittances, very prosperous self-employed workers, and those who have sold a dwelling have the ability to make a purchase.

The 4 percent tax on the sale price is often breached due to underdeclaration of value. In order to skirt the payment of taxes, the sale price is set as the "legal" value consigned in the property deed, a fraction of its true value (Peters 2014; see sub-subsection "14. Taxes" in subsection "a. Buyers and Sellers" below).[6] In addition, many new sales are masked as donations to legalize previous illegal transactions, functionaries are bribed, and foreigners acquire properties and place them under the name of a Cuban family member or friend (strawman). In 2014, in an attempt to try to control underdeclaration, the housing law was modified, creating a new "referential value" determined by variables such as number of bedrooms, type of construction, urban amenities, and the existence of garages, patios, and gardens ("En la reunión" 2014).[7] The notary public who prepares the deed has to give ONAT data and information, including the 4 percent tax payment, in order for ONAT to control said payment. The director of Civil Notaries and Registries has said that the notary public becomes a fiscal collaborator because he or she must testify on payment of the tax (Fonticoba 2015).

An analysis of subsidies for the purchase of construction materials carried out by the magazine *Bohemia* early in 2016 through 50 interviews with public functionaries in five provinces detected the following problems: (a) in 2012, the comptroller discovered improperly granted subsidies to people who did not meet the requirements (dwellings in good physical condition that didn't need help), while properties in critical condition were denied the subsidy; in 2013, it discovered errors in the registries regarding the distribution of subsidies and shortages of construction materials; in 2014, it found cases of corruption in the granting of subsidies and sale of construction materials, favoritism, and the disbursement of subsidies to the same person for two years in a row. (b) There were many people with a right to subsidies to improve their homes who were first denied and later granted one after much red tape; others received less than the amount for a basic unit; in a couple of cases, the subsidy was denied because the person had an "adequate" salary, without taking into account the person's family burden or the cost of reconstruction; the functionaries responsible alleged that they were complying "with guidance received from superiors," but it was clear that they were ignorant of the rule in place. (c) There were more than 38,700 records of applications for subsidies awaiting approval, despite the fact that Santiago de Cuba had 138 million CUP for said subsidies, which would expire by the end of the year; of the total number of beneficiaries, only 44 percent had managed to finish their construction. (d) Delays in ending construction were essentially due to the scarcity of construction materials or the delay in their distribution (the result of the output decline already analyzed), combined with the poor condition of bulldozers, loaders, and trucks, which made the transportation of these materials difficult; in some cases, when the materials arrived at the store, they already had owners (speculators). (e) Subsidies have a five-working-day deadline after they are invoiced, but the slowness of bank procedures sometimes prevents the actual use of such subsidies; in Matanzas, banks processed only five or ten cases daily ("Subsidios" 2016; see also Murillo 2013; Reuters, March 20, 2013; *Granma*, Oct. 4, 2013).

The conversion of state buildings into dwellings always requires approval of the Ministry of the Economy and Planning, evaluation by specialists in the IPF office, and the inscription of the building in the property registry. There is resistance from many managers who "do not seem to care much if the buildings are generating expenses for which reason the procedure doesn't flow with the necessary ease, keeping valuable real estate capital unused" (*Granma*, Feb. 19, 2014).

## Impact

There are no official statistics on the value of newly constructed or repaired private dwellings, which makes it impossible to estimate its percentage of the GDP. The increase in self-employment and CNA housing construction has not been quantified, thus we cannot calculate either the nonstate sector (NSS) contribution to new private jobs. Likewise, there is no data on the value of buying and selling (which is also underestimated due to underdeclaration), although notaries have this information and pass it on to the Ministry of Justice. As in many other regards, there is no statistical follow-up on the reforms, which makes it very difficult to evaluate its effects.

We do know, however, the total number of homes built and a breakdown of those constructed by the state and by the population's own efforts in 2006–15 (table 39). The year 2006 set a historic record for the revolution on the number of homes built (111,373), which has not been matched since. That year the population built almost 70 percent of the new dwellings (another record), while the state built only 26 percent. Between 2006 and 2011 (the year in which the housing reform was enacted), the percentage of homes built by the population relative to total construction declined from 69.9 percent to 27.5 percent, whereas those erected by the state increased from 26.7 percent to 70.6 percent. Probably as a result of the reform, there was a reversal in the previous trend; thus, the distribution of dwelling construction in 2015 was 54.7 percent by the population and 45.3 percent by the state, an indicator that the reforms were achieving a modest increase in the population's private initiative. Yet, total dwellings built in 2015 were still a fifth of the 2011 peak (fig. 20).

The ANPP commission assessed the state plan of dwelling construction and made the following conclusions: the number of finished buildings is well below the population needs; the plan is unfulfilled by 12 percent and, in some provinces such as Isla de la Juventud, by 92 percent. The quality of construc-

TABLE 39. Dwelling construction, total, population-built and state-built, 2006–14

| Indicators | 2006 | 2007 | 2008 | 2009 | 2010 | 2011 | 2012 | 2013 | 2014[b] | 2015 |
|---|---|---|---|---|---|---|---|---|---|---|
| Dwellings built | | | | | | | | | | |
| Thousand units | 111.4 | 52.6 | 44.8 | 35.1 | 33.9 | 32.5 | 32.1 | 25.6 | 25.0 | 23.0 |
| Units x 1,000 inhabitants | 9.9 | 4.6 | 4.0 | 3.1 | 3.0 | 2.8 | 2.8 | 2.3 | 2.2 | 2.0 |
| Dwellings built (thousands) by[a] | | | | | | | | | | |
| Population | 77.8 | 27.4 | 23.6 | 14.2 | 11.4 | 8.9 | 9.3 | 12.2 | 12.7 | 12.6 |
| State | 29.7 | 22.4 | 18.7 | 19.4 | 21.7 | 23.0 | 22.4 | 12.9 | 12.2 | 10.4 |
| % of dwellings over total by[a] | | | | | | | | | | |
| Population | 69.9 | 52.0 | 52.8 | 40.4 | 33.7 | 27.5 | 28.9 | 50.2 | 48.7 | 54.7 |
| State | 26.7 | 42.6 | 41.8 | 55.4 | 64.0 | 70.6 | 69.6 | 47.7 | 50.7 | 45.3 |

Notes: [a] Dwellings built by cooperatives make the difference to reach the total of 100 percent.
[b] Among the four provinces that suffered severe cuts in construction in 2013–14 were Las Tunas and Granma, the ones with the lowest socio-economic indicators in Cuba.

Source: Authors' own elaboration based on ONEI 2010, 2013a, 2015, 2016f.

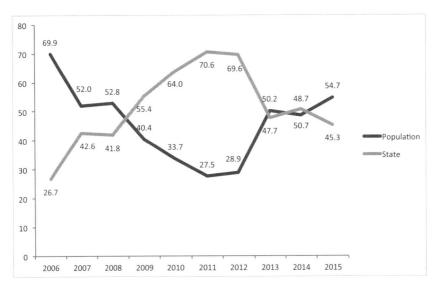

FIGURE 20. Housing constructed by the state and population, 2006–14

tion is deficient: "after a few months, the dwellings built already have cracks in walls and floor; it is absurd that the money devoted to build new dwellings has to be used to repair those of recent construction; somebody is doing a bad job" (*Diario de Cuba*, July 4, 2016).

## RESULTS AND ANALYSIS OF INTERVIEWS

Twenty-five interviews were conducted in September 2015. The same questionnaire (with 20 questions) was prepared for both buyers and sellers, but the pilot revealed that the questions did not always apply to both groups and they had to be separated.[8] As a result, ten interviews were conducted with buyers and another ten with sellers (in no case did a seller sell to a buyer or vice versa; all the interviews were independent). In addition, we felt it necessary to seek information from five real-estate brokers or agents (with 14 questions), as they have general knowledge on buying and selling that the other two groups lack. We also wanted to check the brokers' answers with those of the buyers and sellers. The 25 interviews were done in nine municipalities of Havana province.

Based on the 25 interviews, the interviewees' ages ranged from 24 to 62; 68 percent were under 44 years of age; 64 percent were men and 36 percent women; 77 percent of the interviewees identified their skin color as "white," 20 percent as "mestizo" (mulatto), and 8 percent as "black." Sixty-four percent of the interviewees had a university education, 16 percent had either technical school certification or precollege, and only 4 percent (one) had completed ninth grade. To summarize, approximately two-thirds of the

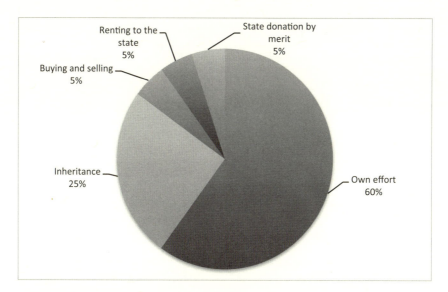

FIGURE 21. How did you acquire your dwelling?

interviewees were under 44, males, white, and had some university education. The professions and occupations were all virtually different. The five brokers were self-employed. What follows are the tabulated results of the responses and their analysis; they are divided into 20 buyers and sellers (with the same questionnaire) and five brokers (with a different questionnaire).

## a. Buyers and Sellers

The section numbers correspond to the questionnaire's 20 questions; where there is an additional question, it is discussed under the same number (see appendix 1).

### 1. Dwelling ownership

All the interviewees confirmed that they do or did own their dwellings. We inquired into the method of acquisition: 60 percent (12) got their dwelling through their own effort; 25 percent (five) inherited it; one bought it, one paid the state rent for 20 years, and another received it as a state donation for sports merit (fig. 21). We've said that 85 percent of the population owns its dwellings. It is interesting to note that 60 percent of those interviewed built their own dwellings, 25 percent inherited them, and only 10 percent acquired them via rent or a state donation.

### 2. Ownership of a second dwelling or empty lot

All interviewees said they did not own a second dwelling or empty lot, even though this is permitted by law (see 6 below).

TABLE 40. Location of dwelling bought or sold

| Dwelling location? | Number of interviewees | Percentage |
|---|---|---|
| Centro Habana | 6 | 30 |
| Cerro | 3 | 15 |
| Diez de Octubre | 3 | 15 |
| Vedado | 3 | 15 |
| Playa | 2 | 10 |
| Other | 3 | 15 |
| Total | 20 | 100 |

3. Buying or selling dwellings since the authorization

As it was expected, all the interviewees had bought or sold their dwellings since the 2011 law; half bought them, the other half sold them.

4. Dwelling donation

Ninety-five percent of the interviewees responded negatively to this question, while only one said his father had donated to him the land on which he built his house. Until the end of 2013, donations were much higher than buying or selling; because the interviews were conducted in 2015, it is likely that those who had acquired a dwelling in an illegal manner hurried to legalize their situations via donation, and now this group is smaller in number. Unfortunately, we do not have a breakdown of donation and buying and selling transactions for 2014 and 2015.

The question "With whom do you currently live?" was asked only to sellers (to find out what they did after the sale). We assumed that the buyers lived in dwellings they purchased. All the sellers live with family members; 60 percent (six) said it was with a spouse, 20 percent (two) said it was with their parents, and 20 percent said it was with their grandparents or in-laws. We asked another question to find out if the family member with whom they lived owned the dwelling, and all of them responded affirmatively.

5. Location of dwelling purchased or sold

Thirty percent of the purchased or sold dwellings were located in Centro Habana, 15 percent in Cerro, 15 percent in Diez de Octubre, 15 percent in Vedado, 10 percent in Playa, and 15 percent in other municipalities (table 40). This question will be related to question 8, prices of selling and buying.

We asked the buyers if the neighborhood to which they moved had improved; we did not ask the sellers because they did not remain in the neighborhood. Sixty percent said it had not and 40 percent said it had. This

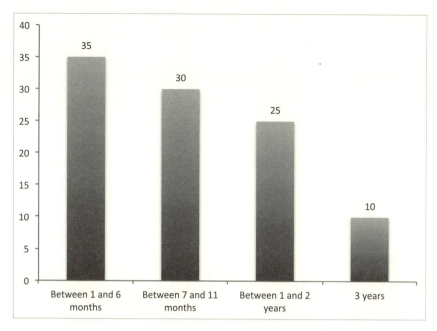

FIGURE 22. How long did it take you to buy or sell the dwelling?

can be explained not because the neighborhood itself had improved or not (it had not been long since the purchase), but because the buyer moved to a neighborhood better (or worse) than his or her previous one. For example, a buyer moved from a residential neighborhood (Casino Deportivo) to Centro Habana (a large part of which is in ruins), while another moved from Playa (Beach) to Cerro, which is also undergoing a decline in neighborhood quality. One interviewee moved within his same neighborhood, so it did not improve.

### 6. Ownership of a second, recreational dwelling

The housing reform allows owning a second home for recreational purposes, in the country or at the beach. None of the interviewees said they had such a dwelling, which confirms that few Cubans have them due to their limited resources and because having a primary dwelling is the highest priority.

### 7. Time it took to buy or sell a dwelling

It took 35 percent (seven) of the interviewees between three and six months to buy or sell their dwelling; 30 percent (six) said it took them between six and eleven months; 25 percent (five) between one and two years; and 10 percent (two), three years (fig. 22). On average, it took the sellers longer to sell than for buyers to buy: 11.6 months and 10.7 months, respectively; this is usually the case, but in Cuba the seller has to go through more transactions and requirements than the buyer, for example, validating the dwelling description on the title with an architect, registering the title, and so on (see sub-subsection "4. Dwelling donation" in subsection "a. Buyers and sellers" above).

8. Price of the buying and selling

Table 41 shows the prices at which the interviewees bought or sold their dwelling. Combining the first two categories, 90 percent ranged between 5,000 and 20,000 CUC, and only 10 percent (two) at between 21,000 and 30,000 CUC (dollar equivalents are similar). The average price of a dwelling sold was 15,450 CUC, and of one bought, 12,700 CUC.

The size, condition, and quality of the dwelling are important factors in setting the price, but another is its location: 75 percent of the dwellings are in less prestigious municipalities or neighborhoods (Cerro, Centro Habana, and Diez de Octubre) or are far from the capital (Güines, Madruga), and only 10 percent were in Playa (beaches), a high-prestige neighborhood. The Vedado neighborhood ranks between Playa and the rest, but its dwellings tend to be quite expensive.

Table 42 reveals that the prices in municipalities far from the capital (Catalina de Güines, Madruga, and to a lesser degree, Marianao) remain concentrated (67 percent) in the first column (5,000 to 10,000 CUC), with Marianao at the top; in Centro Habana, the price is divided in half between the first two columns (5,000 to 10,000 and 11,000 to 20,000 CUC); in Cerro, it is concentrated (67 percent) in the second column; in Diez de Octubre it is entirely in the second column, with a maximum of 15,500 CUC; this is also the case in Vedado, but one property there was sold at the top of the line (19,000 CUC); last, Playa is all in the third column (21,000 to 30,000 CUC). One must keep in mind that 30,000 CUC is almost 100 times the mean salary in the state sector.

9. Advertising

The responses are nonexclusive because various interviewees mentioned more than one way of advertising. Fifty percent found out or advertised by word-of-mouth; 27 percent used the Internet (Revolico.com); 15 percent placed posters in the seller's home façade, and one did so through a broker and another via radio and television (table 43). Basic methods of publicity (word-of-mouth and posters) amount to 65 percent, while the Internet and radio-TV only 31 percent. Sellers used word-of-mouth (44 percent), posters (25 percent), and the Internet (25 percent); buyers relied more on word-of-mouth (60 percent), followed by the Internet (30 percent).

TABLE 41. Value of sale or purchase

| Price in CUC | Number of interviewees | Percentage |
| --- | --- | --- |
| 5,000–10,000 | 6 | 30 |
| 11,000–20,000 | 12 | 60 |
| 21,000–30,000 | 2 | 10 |
| Total | 20 | 100 |

TABLE 42. Percentage distribution of municipalities by price of dwellings

| Municipalities | 5,000–10,000 | 11,000–20,000 | 21,000–30,000 | Total |
| --- | --- | --- | --- | --- |
| Others [a] | 67 | 33 | 0 | 100 |
| Centro Habana | 50 | 50 | 0 | 100 |
| Cerro | 33 | 67 | 0 | 100 |
| Diez de Octubre | 0 | 100 | 0 | 100 |
| Vedado | 0 | 100 | 0 | 100 |
| Playa | 0 | 0 | 100 | 100 |

Notes: Prices are ordered from lowest to highest in CUC.
[a] Catalina de Güines, Madruga, and Marianao

TABLE 43. Advertising methods

| How did you find out that the dwelling was for sale, or how did you advertise it? | Number of mentions | Percentage |
| --- | --- | --- |
| Word-of-mouth | 13 | 50 |
| Internet (Revolico.com) | 7 | 27 |
| Signs | 4 | 15 |
| Broker | 1 | 4 |
| Radio and TV | 1 | 4 |
| Total | 26[a] | 100 |

Note: [a] 26 mentions because the categories are nonexclusive.

TABLE 44. Sources for the purchase of dwellings

| How did you finance the purchase of your dwelling? | Number of interviewees | Percentage |
| --- | --- | --- |
| Own resources | 3 | 30 |
| Family or friends | 1 | 10 |
| Both | 6 | 60 |
| Total | 10 | 100 |

## 10. Financing for the purchase of a dwelling

We asked the buyers what their sources were for buying their dwellings: own resources, help from family or friends or both: 60 percent gave both, 30 percent their own resources, and 10 percent (one) family and friends (table 44). Of the seven buyers who received some type of help from family or friends, four said it came from within Cuba, two from abroad, and one from both.

## 11. Use of a broker

Of the 20 interviewees, only two, a buyer and a seller, used a broker; the seller paid 4 percent of the dwelling's price and the buyer gave the broker 400 CUC, about 4 percent of the price paid.

## 12. Inscription of dwelling at the property registry

All the interviewees answered affirmatively because it's not possible to buy or sell a dwelling without said inscription. Next, we asked the sellers—who are responsible for inscribing the dwelling in the registry—how long this procedure took them: 70 percent answered from one to six months, and 30 percent said from seven to twelve months (table 45). This confirms the complexity of this inscription and that it takes a long time.

Some of the comments made by interviewees were: "It took us almost a year to get the property registered; when it was not the architect making a mistake, it was the lawyer; something always happened and we had to go all the way back." "It took me more than six months, because it is a procedure for which one must go so many times; you have to take documents and several actions that sometimes don't work and that is why it takes so long." One interviewee for whom the inscription had only taken a month reasoned he had given the registrar an "incentive" to speed up the process. Another explained: "this inscription was not required before and only a very small proportion did it." These responses confirm the described obstacles (see subsection "Obstacles" in "Antecedents" above). We asked the sellers how much the registration had cost: 60 percent said between 60 and 200 CUP, 30 percent said 250 CUP, and 10 percent (one) said 600 CUP (table 45).

The registrar's fee is not based on the price of the sale; for example, a house costing 19,000 CUC paid 600 CUP, one priced 30,000 CUC paid 250 CUP, and another two worth 8,000 and 18,000 paid 250 CUP. The fee depends on the work and time it takes to clear up the property's deed, particularly if there is no previous inscription or its updating is very complex; the seller may also lack knowledge and be charged more, and there are differences among municipalities.

TABLE 45. Time and cost of inscription at the registry

| Time (months) | Number of interviewees | Percentage |
|---|---|---|
| 1–6 | 7 | 70 |
| 7–12 | 3 | 30 |
| Total | 10 | 100 |
| **Cost (CUP)** | **Number** | **Percentage** |
| 60–200 | 6 | 60 |
| 250 | 3 | 30 |
| 600 | 1 | 10 |
| Total | 10 | 100 |

TABLE 46. Cost of notary services

| Payment to notary | Number of interviewees | Percentage |
|---|---|---|
| 25–49 CUC | 12 | 60 |
| 50–100 CUC | 6 | 30 |
| 50–100 CUP | 2 | 10 |
| Total | 20 | 100 |
| **Payments "on the sly"** | **Number** | **Percentage** |
| Did not indicate | 12 | 60 |
| Did indicate | 8 | 40 |
| Total | 20 | 100 |

## 13. Notary

Ninety percent of the interviewees thought it was easy to find a notary public to conduct the transaction and only 10 percent said it was hard. Notaries are paid in CUP, like the property registrar; yet 90 percent of all notary fees were in CUC and, in two cases, they were both in CUP and CUC; only 10 percent paid only in CUP.

Table 46 shows notary fees and those who paid bribes ("on the sly"). Sixty percent of the interviewees paid from 25 to 49 CUC; 30 percent, from 50 to 100 CUC; and 10 percent from 50 to 100 CUP. Forty percent mentioned having paid "on the sly": "officially, I was charged 30 CUP . . . , but I had to pay him 30 CUC to make the process easier and to complete in the least time possible"; "I paid him 50 CUC 'on the sly'"; "I was able to find someone to help me so that everything would go faster; it cost me 40 CUC"; "I paid the customary, plus a good gift to make the transactions easier"; "if you don't

TABLE 47. Acceptance of tax based on assessed value

| Is the 4 percent tax appropriate? | Number of interviewees | Percentage |
|---|---|---|
| Yes | 15 | 75 |
| No | 5 | 25 |
| Total | 20 | 100 |
| **If it's based on assessed value** | **Number** | **Percentage** |
| Mentioned it | 9 | 45 |
| Did not mention it | 11 | 55 |
| Total | 20 | 100 |

pay a few CUC, you'll be delayed; "it cost me 35 CUC because I was recommended"; "50 CUP and 10 CUC as a gift." Of the two that only paid in CUP, one elaborated: "It was not easy because many people are doing these transactions and one must stand in line and wait a pretty long time."

As in the case of registrars, there is no direct relationship between the amount of payment to the notary and the price of the buying and selling; for example, 30,000 CUC was a high price and paid the notary 50 CUC, while a much lower price of 12,000 CUC paid 100 CUC. Unlike the case of the registrars, in which the payment is fixed by the complexity of the inscription, this factor is less important with a notary since he or she receives the confirmed deed. The notary fee seems to be set at random and indicates a lack of clients' knowledge, although it also may be due to existing differences among municipalities.

## 14. Taxes

Seventy-five percent of the interviewees said that the 4 percent tax the seller pays is adequate, and only 25 percent voiced objections: "they want to take advantage of everything," "surviving is really tough." The high level of acceptance of this tax is because it is calculated based on the assessed value, which is a fraction of the true value, hence reducing the tax amount (see subsection "Obstacles" in "Antecedents" above; table 47).

Fifty-five percent of the interviewees did not mention underdeclaration, but 45 percent clarified that their "yes" to the tax was conditioned: "it may seem as though the tax is appropriate, but in reality, the house is never sold at its assessed price; it always sells for much more"; "if we take into account the price for which a dwelling was assessed by the Housing Institute, it is not much, but if we had to pay this tax based on the dwelling's real value, it's a lot of money."

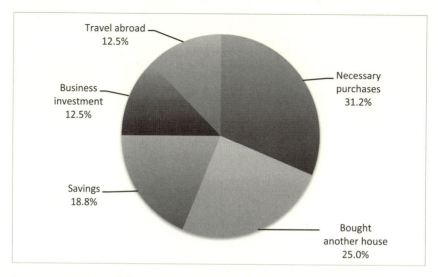

FIGURE 23. On what did you use the dwelling sale value?

### 15. Use of the dwelling's sale

We asked the sellers how they used the value of the sale. Thirty-one (five) bought needed goods (consumption), 25 percent (four) purchased and improved another dwelling, 18.8 percent (three) saved it, 12.5 percent (two) invested it in a business, and 12.5 percent (two) traveled abroad (fig. 23).

### 16. Right to inherit a dwelling

In order to check the interviewees' awareness of the law, we asked if they knew their families had the right to inherit their property and all answered affirmatively.

### 17. Bank loans for constructing or repairing dwellings

None of the interviewees had applied for micro-credit, which was the same among the other three groups, but 8 percent of the interviewees demanded better access to bank credit for financing their dwellings.

### 18. Subsidies for the purchase of construction materials

All the interviewees answered that they did not receive them, probably because their dwellings didn't require repair or they were not in need.

### 19. Access to and prices for construction materials

We asked all the interviewees if it was easy to find construction materials and if their prices were high or appropriate (table 48). For the first question, 66 percent answered that access to such materials was difficult, 35 percent said

TABLE 48. Access to and price of construction materials

| Access to construction materials | Number of interviewees | Percentage |
|---|---|---|
| Difficult or very difficult | 12 | 60 |
| Easy | 7 | 35 |
| Ambiguous | 1 | 5 |
| Total | 20 | 100 |
| **Prices** | **Number** | **Percentage** |
| High or very high | 17 | 85 |
| Doesn't say | 2 | 10 |
| Appropriate | 1 | 5 |
| Total | 20 | 100 |

TABLE 49. Principal problems faced

| Principal problems | Number of mentions | Percentage |
|---|---|---|
| Bureaucracy and paperwork | 10 | 33 |
| Lack of resources/low salaries | 8 | 27 |
| Access to and high prices of materials | 5 | 16 |
| Brokers and notaries | 3 | 10 |
| High cost of housing | 2 | 7 |
| Had no problem | 2 | 7 |
| Total | 30[a] | 100 |

*Note*: [a] 30 mentions because the questions were nonexclusive.

it was easy, and one was ambiguous. Some comments: "there are things one needs and cannot be found anywhere, things that should be in all hardware stores, but they're not; you can't find them in the private [self-employed] shops, and you have to go to the black market, with all the risks that implies"; "something is always unavailable, it gets delayed, everything is difficult." With respect to prices, 85 percent said they were high or too high, 5 percent said they were appropriate, and 10 percent did not say: "they are very high at the [TDR] stores, you have to look for them on the black market"; "prices are exaggeratedly high . . . compared to Cubans' incomes."

20. Principal problems faced and changes desired

As in the case of the two first groups, these were the longest responses.

### a. Principal problems faced

Ninety percent of the interviewees said they faced problems, and only 10 percent said they did not. The principal problems mentioned (categories are

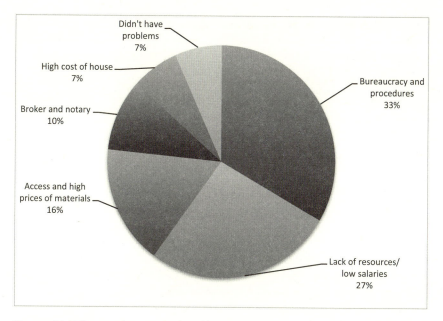

FIGURE 24. What are the principal problems you face?

nonexclusive) were: 33 percent, bureaucracy and paperwork; 27 percent, a lack of resources and low salaries; 16 percent, the shortage and high prices of construction materials; 10 percent, brokers and notaries; 7 percent, the high cost of housing; and 7 percent had no problems (table 49 and fig. 24). Among the sellers, the principal problem (47 percent) was the bureaucracy and paperwork, while among the buyers (50 percent) it was the lack of resources and low salaries.

Some answers identified the key problems: "the huge bureaucracy in this country to do anything"; "the bureaucratic process in which one must get mixed up"; "the paperwork is always complicated"; "the procedures that one must go through . . . , is pretty complex"; "transactions continue to be cumbersome."

"Saving for what an apartment costs for someone who lives with their salary is practically impossible at this time in Cuba, you have to have an extra income or delay many years to save up that amount"; "finding someone who has the money to buy the house is always difficult"; "you don't always find what you need . . . , sometimes you find something and have to wait for the other necessary inputs to become available, without which you can't start the repair to your dwelling, [it can take] two or three months or more"; "home maintenance becomes a titanic task."

"Agents and brokers are somewhat frivolous and not professional"; "there are many brokers who have differing criteria and sometimes that makes it quite difficult, and many take advantage of this"; "you have to give the notary

TABLE 50. What would you like to see change or improve?

| Desire for change or improvement | Number of mentions | Percentage |
|---|---|---|
| Less bureaucracy and paper work | 8 | 32 |
| Higher salaries | 5 | 20 |
| More supplies and lower prices for materials | 3 | 12 |
| Better access to the Internet and information | 3 | 12 |
| Greater access to credit | 2 | 8 |
| Others | 4 | 16 |
| Total | 25[a] | 100 |

Note: [a] 25 mentions because the categories are nonexclusive.

an incentive"; "the exaggerated sum you must pay for the dwelling." One of the interviewees who answered that he had no problems pointed out that "subsidies to low-income people have improved."

## b. Changes desired

Thirty-two percent would like a decrease in the bureaucracy and simplification of the procedures; 20 percent, higher salaries; 12 percent, greater supply of construction materials and lower prices; 12 percent, better access to the Internet and information; 8 percent, more access to credit; and 16 percent other things like inexpensive housing construction (table 50 and fig. 25).

Some desires were: "That the state eliminate all the obstacles it has put in place, so that people can do whatever they want with their property, and that those responsible for the transactions do their work as they should, without one having to bribe them to get fast results"; "I would like that those who govern start thinking about how to make citizens' lives simpler, and less on how to preserve ideas that have been demonstrated to bring nothing more than destitution"; "that transactions not be so tedious, nor so complicated; something as simple as selling a house becomes nonsensical"; "freedom for personal initiatives that increase personal liquidity."

"The adaptation of [real estate] market prices to current salaries"; "for people to have better salaries . . . that allow them to have their own housing"; "for people to have access to resources that allow them to buy or build a home."

"That sale of construction materials was more stable, that they have quality, because sometimes they are not of good quality"; "that construction materials improve, especially regarding prices, that they go down."

"There are places where people have no access, like *Revolico*, not everyone has access . . . to see what house is for sale"; "there should be an official place for getting information."

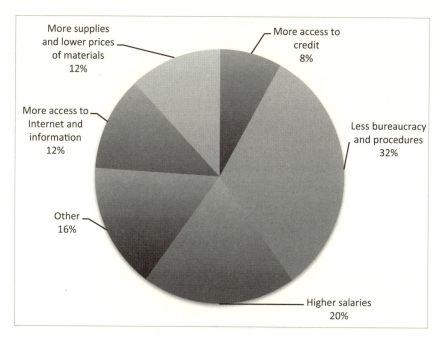

FIGURE 25. What would you like to see change or improve?

"That people have . . . the possibility of getting access to credit, which would allow them to have their own home"; "that people could pay [for the house] with bank credit."

## c. Brokers

As already discussed, we decided to obtain information from five real estate brokers or agents because they had certain knowledge about the buying and selling market that buyers and sellers usually lack; also, we wanted to corroborate sellers' responses with those of the brokers. Given the tiny sample, however, we did not tabulate tables with frequencies and percentages, but we do offer the information, which is valuable. The section numbers correspond to the 14 questions on the questionnaire (see appendix 1).

### 1. Length of time and work zone as a broker

The length of time working as a broker fluctuates between several months and five years; all but one worked in Havana.

### 2. Mechanism for being contacted by clients

The mechanisms brokers use to publicize their contact information: advertising on the Internet (mainly on Revolico.com), connecting through friends and word-of-mouth, establishing an office, handing out business cards, and visiting sites where people concentrate in search of buying and selling and exchanges. Although all brokers resort to a mix of these modalities, the most common is advertising on the Internet (all but one): "At this time, websites play a super important role in buying and selling all around the world"; "access to the Internet is not easy but I think it is crucial for being able to grow as a broker."

### 3. Advertising

Only one of the interviewees said he didn't advertise, although he has business cards. Four had websites for advertising, like *Revolico* and the Weekly Package; one is planning a promotional video that will be inserted into the package. Three use business cards. Two place a poster at the entrance to their office, with a phone number: "We have designed an entire advertising structure, firstly with a very attractive commercial poster . . . so that everyone, even those who are not potential clients, sees it." None advertised in the telephone book, radio, or television.

### 4. Supply and demand and impact on prices

We asked the interviewees how the relationship between supply and demand on the buying and selling market had behaved over time, how that affected prices, and causes for the fluctuations. They all agree that there has been a considerable increase in available housing; hence, supply is greater than demand—when a house is on the market for too long and doesn't sell, the owner lowers the price. All of this explains why prices have gone down (a broker predicts they will decrease further). One thinks that despite the decline in prices, they are still too high. This topic was virtually ignored by buyers and sellers, possibly because they lack a global perspective of the real-estate market's evolution, even though 6.7 percent identified the high cost of housing among the problems they faced.

### 5. Location of buying and selling

We asked what proportion of buying and selling is done among Havana residents and those in other provinces. For two of the brokers interviewed, all or nearly all their clients want to buy and sell in Havana. The other three brokers said that from 10 percent to 20 percent of the transactions are done in provinces close to Havana (particularly in Artemisa and Mayabeque).

### 6. Completed transactions

Of the clients contacted by the brokers, those who completed the transaction vary from one-fourth to one-half. "There are lots of people who when they see the house don't like it, but half of them end up finding one they like."

TABLE 51. Prices of purchases/sales according to brokers

| Price divisions | Amounts in CUC |
|---|---|
| Low | 4,000–5,000, 5,000, 8,000–10,000, 10,000, 7,000–12,000 |
| Intermediate | 20,000–30,000, 20,000–35,000, 30,000–50,000 |
| High | 60,000, 90,000, 100,000, 500,000, and a million |

## 7. Objectives in selling a dwelling

Answers to this question were not exclusive. All the brokers mentioned that an objective for the seller is to buy another dwelling (in two cases, a bigger or better situated one); three said that the goal was to leave the country; two answered that they wanted to have a money reserve, and one stated that it was to cover his needs. Sellers themselves referred to the same objectives, although with a different emphasis: satisfying needs was the primary aim (31 percent), buying another dwelling was the second (25 percent), and saving was the third (19 percent); conversely, no one said that the sale was to finance their permanent departure from the country (probably due to caution), although 12.5 percent mentioned taking a temporary trip, and 12.5 percent answered that is was to invest in a business, which was not mentioned by the brokers.

## 8. Price of buying and selling

According to the brokers, overall housing market prices vary a great deal: between 4,000 and one million CUC ("No one makes a sale in CUP anymore"). The range for low prices oscillates between 4,000 and 12,000 CUC; intermediate prices fluctuate from 20,000 to 50,000 CUC; and high prices vary from 60,000 to 1 million (table 51). The overall range contrasts with the actual price for buyers and sellers with the five brokers, of which 90 percent fluctuate between 5,000 and 30,000 CUC. The line for intermediate prices was between 11,000 and 20,000 CUC, and only one was 30,000 CUC, which indicates that the buyers and sellers had an intermediate-to-low buying capacity when compared to the overall market described by the brokers: "The minimum price is 4,000 CUC for something really small and in a-not-so-good place"; "for most people, the lowest prices are a fortune"; "dwellings in Miramar can cost nearly 1,000,000 CUC."

## 9. Transactions

We asked the interviewees if they thought the procedures for buying and selling are simple or complex. They all agreed that paperwork is easier now (two with the caveats "ideally" and "if things work as they should"), but they also concurred that in practice, "the bureaucratic infrastructure can make the process very difficult"; "they make procedures quite cumbersome and force you to offer a bribe, to put it subtly, if you don't want to be mixed up for months in paperwork"; "the most complicated thing . . . is to inscribe the dwelling at the property registry, since they tend to take a long time and make the transaction complicated"; "if you do not pay someone 'on the sly,' you could spend months and months stuck with red tape without closing the deal." The brokers' opinions were very similar as those of buyers and sellers.

10. Taxes

Three of the brokers disapproved of the 4 percent tax because it was too high: "I believe it is exorbitant"; "the state wants to take a slice out of you and that cannot be, things have to be balanced." One explained that the tax particularly affects sellers of properties, with prices ranging from low to intermediate; another said that even in the case of dear properties, the percentage could go so high as to equal the cost of a small property. Only one broker—the one who had been working for a few months and thus was less experienced—said that the tax seemed fine to him. Another broker cautioned: "if we apply the tax to the real price of selling a house, it's too much." These answers do not coincide exactly with those of the buyers and sellers, of which 75 percent were in agreement with the tax, but based on the assessed value and not the real one.

11. Licenses

How much did brokers pay in taxes? Like other self-employed persons, they pay a fixed monthly quota of 500 CUP for their license and, when income surpasses the minimum exempted annually, they have to prepare an affidavit and pay a tax on income after subtracting up to 10 percent for expenses; the annual totals in CUP were 3,745, 4,000 and 5,000. One broker did not make the annual payment because he had been in the business for a short time; and another didn't because he works as a part-time broker and is a state employee.

12. Compensation of income relative to costs

We asked if the earnings were higher than the cost of the license, annual tax, and expenses; they all responded affirmatively, confirming that the broker profession is lucrative, despite the already mentioned problems and others expounded upon in the next question. Nobody specified net earnings.

13. Principal problems faced in buying and selling and desires for change or improvements

The principal universal problem in buying and selling identified by all brokers is the high price of housing when compared to the population's low income, which is the reason they want prices to come down because increasing salaries is much tougher: "the potential market for buyers is small, not because their demand for housing is low, but because incomes can't afford it"; "I don't believe that salaries will increase . . . for which reason I think the most logical thing would be to reduce sale prices"; "it is more likely for prices to come down than for people to be able to find the money to pay 15,000 CUC for a dwelling."

The second problem noted by two of the brokers was: "the bureaucracy that is one of the most complex things, and the one that is most forcefully beating us"; "the bureaucratic apparatus can make [the procedures] very difficult." Only one broker asked to "increase the supply of construction materials at more accessible prices."

Brokers' opinions coincide with those of buyers and sellers, although a third of the latter pinpointed the bureaucracy as the foremost problem, only mentioned by two brokers. Another 27 percent of buyers and sellers said that low salaries were an obstacle to buying housing due to high prices. This difference in the priority of problems might be because the bureaucracy beats down buyers and sellers more than brokers. The lack of and high price of construction materials was the third problem listed by buyers and sellers (18 percent), while there was only one mention of it by brokers because it obviously affects them much less.

## 14. Most serious problems faced as a broker and desires for change and improvement

With this question, we wanted to separate the brokers' views on buying and selling problems from the problems of the brokers themselves. The latter's responses note that low salaries and high prices drastically limit the brokers' earnings because the number of potential clients diminishes: "There are millions of well-trained professionals in this country that need a house but cannot afford it because . . . their salaries are insufficient to live; not even saving for ten years would achieve that goal." One broker pinpointed the strong competition and bad practices (bribes) that instill fear in people about contracting a broker, and this reduces the amount of business the brokers get.

The desires expressed by brokers match what they said about their problems: "I believe that lower prices would favor us all because the volume of sales would be greater." They also want the bureaucracy to not be an obstacle in their work: "I'd like to see changes in the offices responsible for the procedures, that the work is done fast, with quality, not due to the mere act of receiving a small gift so that everything gets down more quickly." Lastly, about the professionalism of the brokers: "I'd like that frivolous people don't get into our line of work, discrediting those of us who see this as a professional job."

The low use of brokers is confirmed by the 10 percent of buyers and sellers who contracted them vis-à-vis the 90 percent who didn't contract them, and worked as "brokers on their own behalf." The lack of professionalism of brokers was mentioned by 10 percent of the buyers and sellers, and by two of the brokers. Four of the brokers use the Internet and this is not mentioned among the direct obstacles they face but is a problem confronted by 12 percent of the buyers and sellers, therefore making it quite difficult to connect with brokers. Something similar occurs with the little access to credit: it does not directly affect brokers but does so indirectly because if more credit were available, people would be able to buy more dwellings.

# 6

# COMPARISONS, CONCLUSIONS, & SUGGESTIONS

This chapter undertakes four tasks: (1) to contrast four characteristics of the interviewees (age, sex, skin color, and education), identified in all the interviews; (2) to compare the 80 interviewees' answers to the 18 questions common in the questionnaires, sometimes in all four groups, and others in only some of them (the number of interviewees varies and will be specified);[1] (3) to investigate the potential relationship among the four characteristics and the 18 common answers; (4) to extract the study's conclusions, and (5) to recapitulate the voices of the emerging nonstate sector (NSS), pointing out their problems and displaying their desires for change to improve and advance the sector.

We reiterate what was explained at the beginning of the book: this is not a survey based on a scientific sample (due to its impossibility) but is based on intensive interviews, hence what we analyze herein does not represent the universe of the four groups but does provide very useful information that helps fill the notably existing void (tabulations are from Vera Rojas and Pérez-Liñán 2016).

## INTERVIEWEES' CHARACTERISTICS

Table 52 summarizes the four characteristics (age, sex, skin color, and education), showing in each category the total number of interviewees and percentage distributions.

TABLE 52. Interviewees' Characteristics

| Characteristics | Number of interviewees | Percentage |
|---|---|---|
| **Age** | | |
| 22–30 | 17 | 21.25 |
| 31–40 | 29 | 36.25 |
| 41–50 | 12 | 15.00 |
| 51–60 | 13 | 16.25 |
| 61–75 | 9 | 11.25 |
| Total | 80 | 100.00 |
| **Sex** | | |
| Male | 59 | 73.75 |
| Female | 21 | 26.25 |
| Total | 80 | 100.00 |
| **Skin color** | | |
| White | 64 | 80.00 |
| Mulatto | 9 | 11.25 |
| Black | 7 | 8.75 |
| Total | 80 | 100.00 |
| **Education** | | |
| Primary/secondary | 13 | 16.25 |
| Mid-level technical | 15 | 18.75 |
| Pre-college | 19 | 23.75 |
| University | 33 | 41.25 |
| Total | 80 | 100.00 |

## Age

The age of those interviewed oscillates between 22 and 75 years, with the larger concentrations being from 31 to 40 years (36 percent) and from 22 to 30 (21 percent); together they equal 57 percent of the interviewees, while the groups from 41 to 75 equal 43 percent. The average age is 41 years; in the four groups, the lowest age is 34 among the self-employed, followed by 40 among buyers and sellers; the higher average age is 51, among usufruct farmers. This suggests that the largest group, the self-employed, attracts more young people and encourages employment. It is surprising that the tough labor of usufruct farmers has the highest average age, with 28 percent of them between 61 and 75. Home sellers are older than buyers (44 and 36 years, respectively); buyers are the youngest subgroup. It was not possible to compare the age cohort in the sample with that of the labor force because there is no disaggregation in the latter (ONEI 2015).

## Sex

Seventy-four percent of the interviewees were male and only 26 percent female, 11 percentage points less than the 37 percent of female participation in the employed labor force (ONEI 2016a); hence, women were underrepresented in the sample. All the usufruct farmers were male; of the members of nonagricultural production and service cooperatives (CNA), 80 percent were male and 20 percent female (similar to the 21.8 percent of national female participation in this group); and of the self-employed, 56 percent were male and 44 percent female (much higher than the 29.2 percent of female participation among all self-employed); among buyers and sellers, 45 percent were males and 55 percent females (the only group in which the majority were women), and all brokers were male. We lack national figures on the participation of women in the labor force in the other two groups (see table 2). The hard work of usufruct farmers may explain that all of them were male, but hard work doesn't factor in with self-employed workers and CNA members. Thus, the NSS does not seem to have promoted female employment.

## Skin color

Eighty percent of the interviewees were white, 11 percent mulatto, and 9 percent black; the corresponding numbers in the 2012 population census are 64.1 percent, 26.6 percent, and 9.3 percent, respectively (ONEI 2016b); the first group is overrepresented in the interviews, the second underrepresented, and the third is virtually the same. We cannot compare the racial composition of the labor force because the ONEI does not publish this data. Among the four groups, usufruct farmers and brokers were all white; among buyers and sellers, 75 percent were white and 25 percent Afro-Cuban; among the self-employed 72 percent and 28 percent, respectively, and among the CNA, 60 percent and 40 percent. Only this last figure rises above the 36 percent of Afro-Cubans in the national population, but the proportion of the CNA members in the total NSS is only 0.5 percent; thus, its weight is negligible compared to weights of 41 percent of the self-employed and 27 percent of usufruct farmers, among whom the vast majority is white. Mulattoes have a lower participation in the sample than in the general population, whereas blacks' participation is about the same.

## Education

The distribution of the interviewees according to their level of education confirms the notable advances achieved in education in Cuba, with percentage of interviewees increasing as one goes up the education scale: 16 percent only have an elementary-secondary education, 19 percent a mid-technical educa-

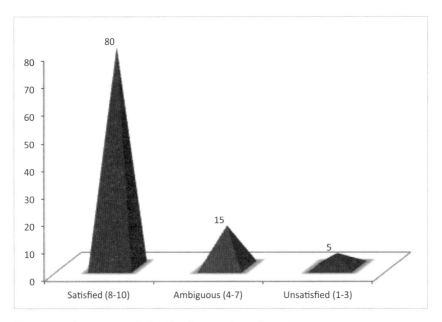

Figure 26. Are you satisfied with what you do and earn?

tion, 24 percent precollege, and 41 percent a university education. These levels are better than the national averages of the labor force, where 27 percent have only a primary-secondary education and 22 percent have a higher or university education (ONEI 2015). Among the four groups, the least educated is usufruct farmers, in which 48 percent have an elementary-secondary-level education; to the contrary, the best educated group is that of the buyers and sellers, with 60 percent having a university level (CNA members also have 60 percent but based on a tiny sample), and the self-employed with 48 percent. The sample suggests that those in the NSS have more education than the national average, except usufruct farmers, whose level is lower; this in turn indicates that a well-educated sector is working in the NSS, attracted by the promise of higher income.

To summarize, the average interviewee is 41, male, white-skinned, and has a mid-technical or university education. Women, Afro-Cubans, and those with only primary-secondary education are underrepresented in the sample.

## COMPARISON OF THE SAME QUESTIONS IN THE FOUR GROUPS

Eighteen identical questions were selected for the four groups; 15 of them are based on 55 to 88 observations, which we consider sufficient enough for an analysis; but three are based on 30 observations, and we will mention them because they are interesting, but less weighty than the previous ones. Only two questions have 80 observations (asked to all interviewees), deal-

TABLE 53. Previous occupation

| Previous occupation | Number of interviewees | Percentage |
|---|---|---|
| State employee | 21 | 70 |
| Student | 3 | 10 |
| Unemployed | 2 | 7 |
| Other | 4 | 13 |
| Total | 30 | 100 |

ing with the principal problems they face and what they would like to see change or improve. Ten questions have 55 interviewees, two questions have 75 interviewees, and one question has 65 interviewees. Appendix 2 shows the number of interviewees who answered identical questions in the groups, and those involved in each.

## 1. Degree of satisfaction

We asked 55 interviewees (self-employed workers, usufruct farmers, and CNA members) to rank themselves on a scale between 1 (less satisfied) and 10 (most satisfied): 80 percent (44 interviewees) were satisfied (scale 8 to 10), 15 percent (eight) were ambiguous (scale 4 to 7), and only 5 percent (three) were dissatisfied (scale 1 to 3) (fig. 26). Satisfaction runs very high despite bureaucratic obstacles. In group interviews, the highest level of satisfaction, 72 percent (scale 8 to 10), was among the self-employed that also had the lowest level (8 percent) of dissatisfaction (scale 1 to 3); they were followed by usufruct farmers with 64 percent and 12 percent, respectively; there were only five CNA members and hence their percentages are not comparable, but were 60 percent and 40 percent respectively.

## 2. Previous occupation

Of 30 interviews (self-employed and CNA members), 70 percent were state employees before, 10 percent were students, 7 percent unemployed, and 13 percent other (table 53). Among the self-employed, 76 percent had been state employees, while all CNA members were.

## 3. Annual taxes

Taxes must be paid annually when income (after authorized deductions) exceeds a specific amount (in addition, there are monthly license/taxes we were not able to tabulate). We asked this question about taxes to 55 interviewees (self-employed workers, usufruct farmers, and CNA members), of which 42 percent (23) didn't know or did not respond, which distorts the

TABLE 54. Contracted employees

| Employees hired | Number of interviewees | Percentage |
| --- | --- | --- |
| None | 24 | 43 |
| 1–5 | 20 | 36 |
| 6–10 | 7 | 13 |
| 11–15 | 1 | 2 |
| 16–20 | 1 | 2 |
| Doesn't know; no answer | 2 | 4 |
| Total | 55 | 100 |

results. Of the remaining 58 percent (32): 20 percent paid between 300 and 1,000 CUP, 18 percent between 1,001 and 5,000 CUP, and 15 percent between 5,001 and 20,000 CUP; only 5 percent (three) did not pay. The higher payment bracket is equal to between 75 percent and three times the mean annual salary in the state sector.

## 4. Employees

Among 55 interviewees (self-employed workers, usufruct farmers, and CNA), 53 percent (29) hired salaried employees, 43 percent (24) did not hire any, and 4 percent (2) did not know or did not respond. There is evidence that some did not declare their employees.[2] Among the 53 percent that had employees, 36 percent contracted from one to five, 13 percent from six to ten, 2 percent from eleven to fifteen, and 2 percent from sixteen to twenty. Thus, a large majority (79 percent) either did not contract any or had fewer than five employees (table 54). The self-employed contract more employees (68 percent) than do usufruct farmers (44 percent).

## 5. Salaries

Fifty-five interviewees (self-employed workers, usufruct farmers, and CNA members) answered the question about the frequency of salary payment to employees: 31 percent paid a daily wage, 13 percent paid monthly, 5 percent weekly, and 11 percent other. We could not tabulate salary amounts due to their enormous variety.

## 6. Problems with employees

Of 55 interviewees (the self-employed, usufruct farmers, and CNA members) who contract employees, 35 percent have no problems and 27 percent do; the self-employed are the ones who face the most problems.

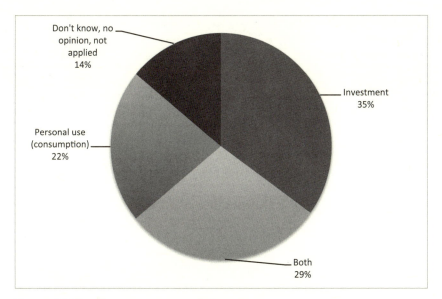

FIGURE 27. How do you use your profits?

## 7 & 8. Profits and their use

Among 55 interviewees (the self-employed, usufruct farmers, and CNA members), 93 percent made profits and 7 percent did not; this explains the high level of satisfaction in the NSS, despite bureaucratic obstacles. We asked 65 interviewees (the previous 55 plus 10 dwelling sellers) how they use their profits (or the value of the sale, which was excluded in the earlier question): 35 percent (23) invested their profits, 29 percent (19) mixed investment and personal use (consumption), and 22 percent (14) only devoted them for personal use; 14 percent (9) did not know, did not respond, or did not make a profit (fig. 27).

Self-employed workers and usufruct farmers represent almost two-thirds of the total number of interviewees who were asked about their use of profits. The self-employed invested 60 percent of their profits, and usufruct farmers only 12 percent. The latter devoted 44 percent of profits for consumption, probably because their income is lower than that of the self-employed and the cost of their inputs is proportionally higher.

## 9, 10, & 11. External remittances, government loans/credit, or other assistance

Of 55 interviewees (self-employed workers, usufruct farmers, and CNA members), 76 percent did not receive remittances and only 24 percent did (table 55).[3]

Usufruct farmers received proportionately more remittances (32 percent) than the self-employed (12 percent). Of the five CNA members, three recei-

COMPARISONS, CONCLUSIONS, & SUGGESTIONS 123

TABLE 55. Foreign remittances, state loans, and other assistance

| Receives remittances | Number of interviewees | Percentage |
|---|---|---|
| No | 42 | 76 |
| Yes | 13 | 24 |
| Total | 55 | 100 |
| **State credit** | | |
| No | 75 | 100 |
| Yes | 0 | 0 |
| Total | 75 | 100 |
| **Other assistance** | | |
| Yes | 44 | 68 |
| No | 21 | 32 |
| Total | 65 | 100 |

ved remittances, a 40 percent higher percentage than the other two groups, but based on much fewer observations. As we have noted, all these proportions are far below the national average of 65 percent of the population that receives remittances. It may be that interviewees underdeclared remittances due to apprehension or don't need them due to their more comfortable situation, especially among the self-employed.

Seventy-five interviewees (all but the brokers) were asked if they received small state loans, and all answered negatively, blaming bureaucratic obstacles and excessive procedures in exchange for receiving a very small sum.

Sixty-five interviewees (all but sellers and brokers because the question did not apply) were asked if they received some other form of assistance (from family members, internal and external, or from friends), 68 percent (44) did receive it, and 32 percent (21) did not. Remittances, loans and other assistance are compared in figure 28.

## 12. Competition

This question was asked only to 30 interviewees (self-employed workers and CNA members), as it was not suitable for sufruct farmers and buyers and sellers: 77 percent (23) said they faced competition and only 23 percent (7) said they did not.

## 13. Price reduction

We asked 55 interviewees (all but buyers and sellers) if they reduced their prices: 84 percent (46) said they did not, and only 16 percent (9, all self-employed) said they did through negotiation. All the usufruct farmers

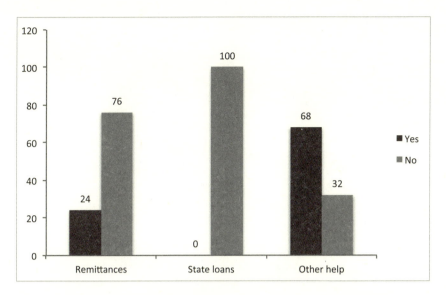

FIGURE 28. Do you receive foreign remittances, state loans, or other assistance?

answered they did not, due to the very high cost of inputs and very low prices paid by *acopio*; the self-employed alleged that their produce/service is superior or different or that they have no competition.

## 14. Product or service

The question about whether the interviewees believed that their products or services were better than what others offered was answered by only 30 interviewees (self-employed workers and CNA members), but supplements the previous question, so we kept it. Fifty percent answered positively, while 17 percent said that their product or service was different, and 20 percent expressed it was the same; 13 percent did not know or did not answer.

## 15. Acquisition of inputs

We asked to 55 interviewees (self-employed workers, usufruct farmers, and CNA members) where they obtained their inputs; the categories were non-exclusive, and there were 80 mentions (fig. 29).[4] Twenty-five percent (20), all self-employed, bought inputs at TRD, paying high prices due to their 240 percent or more markup; another 35 percent (20), all usufruct farmers, got inputs from cooperatives (CCS); 16 percent (13) on the black market or "on the sly" (self-employed workers and usufruct farmers) because of high prices at the TRD stores; 9 percent (7) from another producer (all usufruct farmers) or from the self-employed (all self-employed); 4 percent (3) either did not buy any (usufruct farmers) or did so through family (self-employed); 4 percent (3) at the agricultural market (also at high prices); 4 percent (3),

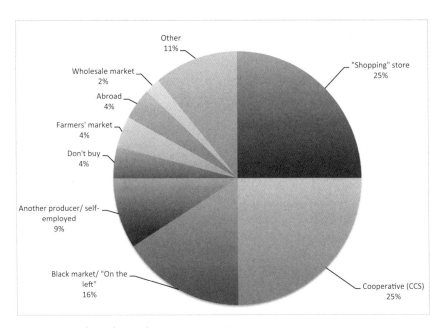

FIGURE 29. Where do you buy your inputs?

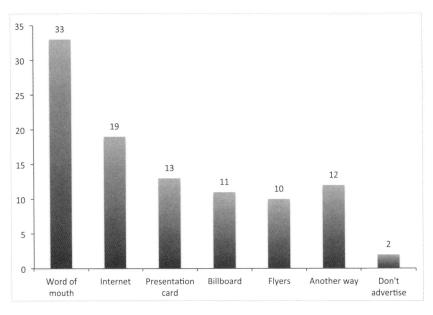

FIGURE 30. How do you advertise?

all self-employed, abroad probably through "mules" (carriers) or by requesting them from relatives; 2 percent (2) at the wholesale market (all self-employed), thus indicating its exiguous nature; and 10 percent (8) other ways, most of them at multiple locations (CNA members).

## 16. Advertising

This question was asked to 55 interviewees (all but usufruct farmers because they don't advertise); there were 100 mentions, as categories were nonexclusive. Thirty-three percent (33 mentions) advertised by word-of-mouth; 19 percent via the Internet (all but CNA members); 13 percent with business cards (except buyers and sellers); 11 percent with posters (all the interviewees); 10 percent with flyers (all self-employed); 10 percent other ways, like fairs, telephone book, radio and TV; and only 2 percent did not advertise (fig. 30). Rudimentary forms of advertising like word-of-mouth (predominant), business cards, flyers, and posters are the overwhelming majority (67 percent), while the Internet and other ways are a minority of 31 percent, although growing. Revolico.com and the Weekly Package are the most used mediums.

## 17. Principal problems faced

This question and the following one were asked of the 80 interviewees. They were not given alternative responses to choose; instead, the questions were completely open. All interviewees answered in considerable detail; thus, what follows here and in the next section are the literal voices from the NSS on their principal problems and desires.

There were 116 mentions because the categories are nonexclusive. Almost all, 97.4 percent (77 mentions), said they had problems and only three (2.6 percent) said they did not. Among the former, 31.9 percent signaled out as problems the limited access to inputs and their high prices (all but the CNA members); 26.7 percent complained about the bureaucracy, obstacles, and too much state interference (all groups); 7.8 percent mentioned high prices, including housing and low income or salaries (especially in buying and selling); 4.3 percent pointed out limited access to the Internet or technology and its high cost (self-employed); and 26.7 percent indicated other problems that were specific to each group: poorly trained personnel, transportation cost, negative human behavioral aspects (self-employed); inadequate marketing, low *acopio* prices, lack of water (usufruct farmers); high cost of improvements to buildings or equipment (CNA); bad management or high notary and broker fees (buyers and sellers), and insufficient professionalism and inappropriate competence (brokers) (table 56 and fig. 31).

## 18. Changes or Improvements Desired

As in the previous question, this one was asked of the 80 interviewees. Their desires for change or improvement corresponded to the problems identified and added two more. There were 104 mentions because the categories are

TABLE 56. Principal problems faced

| Problems | Number of mentions | Percentage |
| --- | --- | --- |
| Poor access to and expensive inputs, wholesale market | 37 | 31.9 |
| Bureaucracy, obstacles, and state interference | 31 | 26.7 |
| High prices and low income/salaries | 9 | 7.8 |
| Poor access and expensive Internet | 5 | 4.3 |
| Others | 31 | 26.7 |
| No problems | 3 | 2.6 |
| Total | 116[a] | 100.0 |

Note: [a] 166 mentions because the categories are nonexclusive.

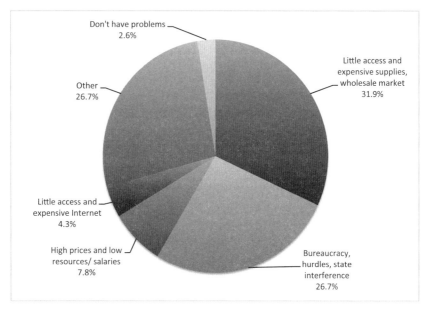

FIGURE 31. What are the principal challenges you face?

nonexclusive (table 57 and fig. 32). Equal to the first problem, the first desire was for greater access to inputs (including construction materials) and lower prices: 24 percent (from all four groups). The second desire matching the second problem was for more freedom, fewer obstacles and regulations and less state interference and resistance against the NSS: 24 percent (from all groups). The third desire (self-employed and usufruct farmers) was intertwined with the first: 10.6 percent wanted the state to offer incentives, guarantees, and recognition of their worth, as well as to reduce taxes. If the first and third desires are combined, the sum is almost 35 percent (36 mentions), thus becoming the principal plea.

TABLE 57. What would you like to see change or improve?

| Changes or improvements desired | Number of mentions | Percentage |
|---|---|---|
| Greater access to inputs and lower prices, wholesale market | 25 | 24.0 |
| More freedom, fewer obstacles, regulations, state interference, and resistance | 25 | 24.0 |
| More state incentives, guarantees, recognition, fewer taxes | 11 | 10.6 |
| Higher incomes/salaries | 9 | 8.7 |
| Better access to the Internet and lower prices | 6 | 5.8 |
| Greater access to credit | 3 | 2.9 |
| More professionalism in brokers and notaries, no bribes | 4 | 3.8 |
| Others | 21 | 20.2 |
| Total | 104[a] | 100.0 |

Note: [a] 104 mentions because the categories are nonexclusive.

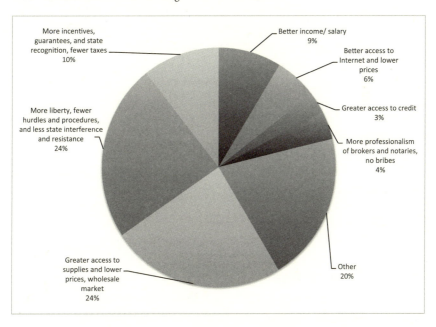

FIGURE 32. What would you like to see improve or change?

The fourth desire matches the third problem: 8.7 percent (buyers, sellers, and brokers) sought better salaries to afford the high cost of housing. The fifth desire matches the fourth problem: 5.8 percent (self-employed and buyers and sellers) wanted access to the Internet and lower prices. Two additional wishes were: 2.9 percent (self-employed and buyers and sellers) aspired for greater access to credit and fewer requisites, and 3.8 percent (buyers, sellers, and brokers) coveted more professionalism in notaries and brokers, and the end of bribes.

Lastly, 20.2 percent pinpointed other yearnings specific to each group. The self-employed want to join together and create an organization to watch out for their interests and improve the area in which they work. Usufruct farmers wished for the *acopio* to cease buying and distributing everything, and for the state to pay higher prices for their products. CNA members wished to have a better relationship with state enterprises, to end the CNA experimental nature, and to be able to import needed inputs. Buyers and sellers wanted less costly housing built; and brokers wished that salaries were adequate to housing prices, so that more dwellings could be sold.

## ASSOCIATIONS BETWEEN CHARACTERISTICS AND RESPONSES

In our analysis of the four characteristics (age, sex, skin color, and education) and the common answers, we found 20 statistically significant associations.[5] Yet, associations dealing with skin color were significant in only one case and it was not relevant. In addition, various important and interesting associations did not end up being significant regarding degree of satisfaction (e.g., age, education, and sex), due to the small size of our sample. In this section, we eliminated less important relations and left 11 with some value. To simplify the reading, we decided not to reproduce the tables with all the results of our analyses, but they are in our files. All the associations exclude answers in which the interviewee said he or she didn't know or didn't respond, and the question was not applicable. Of the 11 associations selected, two are based on the 80 interviews, one on 75, one on 65, five on 55, one on 32, and one on 29 interviews.

### 1. Age and occupation, previous unemployment

Of 29 interviewees, 69 percent were previously employed by the state, with the greatest frequency being (91 percent) of the age cohorts from 31 to 40 years, followed by the 22 to 30 cohorts (70 percent), and the least frequency in the 41 to 50 age cohorts (25 percent). About 7 percent of the sample was previously unemployed (much greater than the national average of 2.7 percent of the labor force), with the highest rate among the 41-to-50-year-old cohorts.

### 2. Age and remittances

Based on 55 interviews, 76 percent did not receive remittances and 24 percent did. The receipt of remittances seemed to depend on the age of the interviewee: the older the interviewees, the more remittances they received, and the younger received fewer remittances. The older interviewees (from 51 to 60 years old and 61 or over) received remittances more frequently (62 percent and 44 percent) than the young ones between 22 and 30 years old (9 percent); 91 percent of the youngest interviewees did not receive remittances. It is likely that the older received more remittances because their children or grandchildren abroad sent them.

## 3. Age and assistance

Of 65 interviewees, 66 percent received assistance and 34 percent did not. Opposite to remittances, the youngest interviewees received more assistance from family members and friends—especially domestic—than the older ones: those in the 22-to-30-year-old and the 31-to-40-year-old brackets got more assistance (100 percent and 64 percent, respectively) than those 61 or older (44 percent).[6]

## 4. Age and the purchase of inputs at TRD

Of the 55 interviewees, 64 percent did not buy in the TRD stores ("shopping") and 36 percent did. Age seems to be a factor in these purchases: the lower the age, the less was bought at TRD, and vice versa: the 22-to-30-year-old cohort purchased 64 percent of their inputs at such stores; the 31 to 40 year-old acquired 44 percent, the 41 to 50 year-old obtained 33 percent, and the 51-to-60-year-old cohorts did not buy at all.

## 5. Sex and the purchase of inputs at TRD

Among the 55 interviewees, 36 percent purchased inputs for their activities in TRD stores and 64 percent did not. Sex seemed to be a factor; thus, 75 percent of women bought at the "shopping" stores, while only 26 percent of the men did so. Men had more access than women to other sources to obtain inputs: the black market, cooperatives, another producer, and the self-employed.

## 6. Age and use of profits

The use of profits seems to depend on the age of the interviewee: the younger, the more they totally or partially invest them, and vice versa. The 22-to-30-year-old cohort devoted 58 percent to investment; the 31 to 40 year-old assigned 50 percent, but the 61 and older group only invested 22 percent and used 44 percent for consumption. If total and mixed uses are combined, the younger ones devoted 100 percent to total or partial investment, while the older ones assigned 77 percent to total or partial consumption.

## 7. Education and use of profits

The distribution of profits also seemed to depend on the level of education achieved: the more educated, the more investment, and vice versa. Based on 55 interviews, 41 percent invested all their profits, while 34 percent divided them between investment and consumption, and only 25 percent devoted them entirely to consumption. The interviewees with more education tended to use their profits for investment (68 percent with a university degree) than interviewees with less education (18 percent only with primary-secondary education); this last cohort used their profits for consumption (36 percent) or a combination of this with investment (46 percent). Some interviewees who used all their profits for consumption said that it was because their profits were very low and did not leave enough to invest.

## 8. Education and annual taxes

Based on 30 interviewees, those with the most education paid more taxes than those with less education: 67 percent of the interviewees with a university education paid between 5,000 and 20,000 CUP, while 41 percent of the interviewees with primary-secondary schooling paid between 300 and 1,000 CUP. In addition, 25 percent didn't pay taxes. When this relationship is combined with the previous one, it can be inferred that those with more education have higher profits and invest more in their business; hence, they should have a higher income and pay more taxes.

## 9. Education and desires for change

Among the 80 interviewees, 31 percent believed that the bureaucracy, obstacles, and so on were a principal problem that needed to change; the more education, the more mentions, and vice versa: 42 percent among university graduates, 47 percent among those with mid-technical education, but only 8 percent among those who only had primary/secondary education. One can infer that the most educated operate at a higher level of complexity and face more obstacles than the less educated ones who are involved in a simpler activity and have a lower income.

## 10. Age and desire for changes

Among the 80 interviewees, 14 percent mentioned "more state incentives, guarantees and recognition": the greater the age, the more mentions, and vice versa. By age cohorts: 22 to 30, 6 percent; 31 to 40, 10 percent, 51 to 60, 25 percent, and 61 or older, 40 percent. It is possible that the older interviewees felt more vulnerable, which is why they wanted more state guarantees, support, and recognition.

# CONCLUSIONS

## Antecedents

Raúl Castro's most important structural reform probably has been the opening and expansion of the NSS in Cuba, which in 2014 embraced one million people and grew from 16 percent to 29 percent of the labor force in 2009–15, although there was a decline in 2015 followed by a small rebound in the first quarter of 2016. A serious problem is the lack of information on the NSS; this study contributes to filling that void with 80 intensive interviews conducted on part of the island, between September 2014 and December 2015, with self-employed workers, usufruct farmers, members of new cooperatives (CNA), and private housing buyers, sellers, and brokers. We reiterate that this is not a scientific survey representative of the universe, but it offers valuable information that was not elsewhere available.

The study has detailed the advances made by the four groups in the NSS up until November 2016, among them:

- mostly private property of micro-businesses;
- proliferation of *paladares*, several of them gourmet;
- leasing of housing and rooms to tourists;
- private taxis and old, vintage taxis;
- transfer of state establishments to the self-employed and CNA;
- authorization to the self-employed and CNA to contract directly with state enterprises;
- expansion of land cultivated by the private sector (including usufruct), and state-recognized ownership of improvements;
- profit incentive for CNA to renovate locales and improve the quality of goods or services, with various successful cases;
- sale at market prices of product/services from self-employed, CNA, and buying and selling of dwellings;
- granting of some temporary tax exemptions;
- authorization of real estate brokers, a recent increase in constructed and repaired housing by the population, and subsidies to needy people who have been affected by hurricanes, for buying construction materials at freed prices.

The economic impact is very difficult to assess due to a lack of statistics, but we summarize what we found in 2014–15:

- the self-employed represent nearly 10 percent of employment but only 5 percent of GDP (due to their low qualifications), as well as 2 percent of budget income, 8 percent of final consumption, and 54 percent of the total sale of agricultural products;
- usufruct farmers represent 6 percent of the labor force and generate—along with private farmers and agricultural cooperatives—83 percent of the agricultural output, in comparison with the state's 17 percent;
- CNA members have the least impact, due to their small numbers (only 0.1 percent of the labor force), for which reason their sales are 4 percent of total sales, and their contribution to budget income is only 0.3 percent;
- the construction of private housing by the population is 54.7 percent compared to the state's 45.3 percent, but the former was 70 percent in 2006;
- there are no data for dwellings sold in 2014–15, the value of buying and selling, and the number of workers who construct private housing.

We conclude that the NSS has achieved advances but not sufficiently enough to have considerable effect on macro-economic indicators (except in job creation by the self-employed). The explanation for this are the serious obstacles that the NSS faces (analyzed in this book), among which the most remarkable are the following:

- strong restrictions, bureaucratic obstacles, and excessive taxes, especially the tax burden on the self-employed who hire most employees, which is counterproductive to the creation of private jobs and encourages under-declaration;
- severe shortage of inputs and their high prices (the only wholesale market was notoriously insufficient to satisfy the enormous demand and was closed in 2016);
- scarce access to and high cost of the Internet, which forces people to use rudimentary methods of advertising;
- restriction of self-employment to mostly underqualified jobs and its ban for university professionals;
- ten-year contracts imposed on usufruct farmers;
- excessive paperwork needed to get a small loan, to request the building of a home or an usufruct farmer's parcel, and to get CNA approval (the final decision is left to the Council of Ministers);

- irregularities in the granting of housing subsidies and the lack of a mortgage as a collateral guarantee for having a primary dwelling;
- high cost involved in the sale of housing and scarce income of buyers.[7]

The problems mentioned restrict the NSS growth, which is essential to providing private jobs to more than one million unnecessary state workers that remain to be dismissed. A logical conclusion is that the expansion of the NSS would improve the standard of living for all citizens, would create employment thus allowing the state to save money on the salaries of unnecessary employees, would increase GDP, and would generate overall welfare.

The interview answers confirm what is written above with their own narrative, concrete details about their experiences, an identification of their achievements and problems, as well as the interviewees' desires for change or improvement. These are the voices of change that are at the crux of this book.[8]

The average interviewee was 41 years of age, male, has white skin, and has a mid-technical or university education. Underrepresented in the sample are women, Afro-Cubans, and those with only primary or secondary school education.[9]

## Principal interview results

Herein we summarize the most relevant results of the interviews with the four groups and analyze some associations between group's characteristics and answers to common questions.

- 80 percent of all the interviewees are satisfied with what they do and earn, and only 5 percent are dissatisfied ("I am satisfied with what I do but not with what I earn"); the most satisfied (three higher levels) are the self-employed, then the usufruct farmers, and the CNA members appear to be the least satisfied.
- 53 percent of self-employed workers, usufruct farmers, and CNA members hire salaried employees, 36 percent of the interviewees have from one to five employees, the self-employed hire more than the usufruct farmers (66 percent versus 44 percent), and among those that have employees, only one-third has problems, principally the self-employed.
- Among those who have employees, 31 percent pay them a daily wage, 13 percent monthly, 5 percent weekly, and 11 percent some other way; we were not able to tabulate salary amounts due to the enormous variety of payment methods and sums.
- 93 percent of self-employed workers, usufruct farmers, and CNA members make profits and only 7 percent do not (this is similar among the

self-employed and usufruct farmers), which explains the high level of satisfaction despite the obstacles the NSS face.

- 66 percent invest all their profits or mix them with consumption; the self-employed invest more than the usufruct farmers (79 percent versus 56 percent), perhaps because the latter have lower incomes and pay more for their inputs.
- The better educated invest more of their profits than the less educated, possibly because they have higher incomes and can invest instead of consume their profits; in addition, the least educated are the usufruct farmers.
- The younger interviewees assign more of their profits to investment than the older ones.
- Among 29 percent of the self-employed, the investment is recovered in less than a year, and 53 percent in between two and four years.
- 77 percent of the self-employed and CNA members endure competition (this question did not apply to usufruct farmers and buyers and sellers); 84 percent do not reduce the price of their product/service due to the high cost of inputs or the very low *acopio* price; the self-employed allege that their product/service is better or different.
- No usufruct farmer has constructed a house or stable on his parcel, although it is permitted, because he or she has housing nearby, the cost of building is high or it takes time, or there is need of the land for crops; 56 percent of the usufruct farmers sell their production to the *acopio*, and 40 percent of them sell between 51 percent and 100 percent of their crops.
- Only 24 percent of self-employed workers, usufruct farmers, and CNA members receive external remittances (76 percent do not receive them). It is possible they have a higher income than the average population or have reservations about declaring remittances; usufruct farmers receive more remittances (32 percent) than the self-employed (12 percent); older interviewees receive more remittances than younger ones.
- 68 percent receive assistance from family members and friends (mostly in Cuba), the self-employed get more assistance (84 percent) than usufruct farmers (52 percent); in addition, it seems that the last group has fewer resources; the younger ones receive more help from family members and friends than the older ones.
- No interviewee receives small loans or state credit because of the excessive requirements and very complex bureaucratic procedures to receive a small sum.

- 58 percent of self-employed workers, usufruct farmers, and CNA members pay annual taxes: 20 percent pay between 300 and 1,000 CUP; 18 percent from 1,001 to 5,000 CUP; and 15 percent from 5,000 to 20,000 CUP (the latter sum is three times the mean annual state wage); the remaining 42 percent don't know or do not answer if they pay taxes or not; it was impossible to tabulate the monthly payment of taxes due to their diversity.
- The better educated pay more annual taxes than the less educated; it is possible that the former have a higher income and hence pay more taxes.
- 25 percent of the self-employed, usufruct farmers, and CNA members buy inputs at TRD at very high prices; 25 percent do so at CCS (all usufruct farmers), 16 percent do so on the black market or "on the sly," 4 percent at the agricultural market, and only 2 percent (all self-employed) at the only wholesale market, a clear indication of its insufficiency.
- The younger the age the less they buy at TRD and vice versa; women buy at those stores more than men; the latter use more diverse sources.
- 67 percent of the interviewees (excluding usufruct farmers) advertise using basic methods (word-of-mouth, business cards, flyers) and only 19 percent use the Internet due to its difficult access and high cost.
- 92 percent of the self-employed plan to expand geographically or by contracting more employees or leasing more rooms to tourists.

## VOICES OF CHANGE: PROBLEMS AND DESIRES

The last two questions in all questionnaires were asked to the 80 interviewees (there were more than 100 mentions). We did not give them previous alternative responses to select one or two, but instead left the question completely open. Thus, what follows are their actual words, pinpointing the principal problems they face and their desires for improvement or change.

## 1. Problems

- 97 percent say they have problems and only 3 percent don't.
- Among those who have problems, 32 percent identify limited access to and high prices of inputs.
- 27 percent denote the bureaucracy, obstacles, and too much state interference.
- 8 percent complain of the high prices of goods (including housing) and low income or salaries—a severe obstacle for buying them.

- 4 percent mention limited access to and the high cost of Internet.
- 26 percent spell out other problems specific to each group, such as insufficiently qualified personnel, inadequate commercialization, low prices of *acopio*, high cost of improvements to building and equipment, low professionalism, murky management and bribes, transportation costs, and negative behavioral aspects.

## 2. Desires for improvement or change

The five primary desires connect with the four primary problems identified:

- 24 percent want greater access to inputs and lower prices.
- 24 percent crave more freedom, fewer obstacles, regulations, and state interference; those with more education identify this as the main problem that requires a change.
- 11 percent ask the state to offer guarantees, incentives, and recognition, and to reduce taxes (the combination of this category and the prior one add up to 35 percent); older interviewees mention this change more than the young.
- 8 percent seek better salaries due to the high price of inputs and housing.
- 6 percent covet more access to the Internet with lower prices.
- 3 percent wish for more professionalism among notaries and brokers, and for the bribes to end.
- 20 percent mention other desires that will be explained in the next section.

## 3. Specific suggestions

In this section, we extract concrete suggestions from the interviewees so that the NSS will advance and achieve better results on behalf of the economy and the Cuban people.

- Eliminate excessive bureaucracy, simplify and make complex procedures easier: "that the state eliminates all the obstacles it has put in place, so that people can do with their goods what they want, and that those responsible for the procedures do their jobs as they should, without one having to pay a bribe to get fast results"; "that the processes not be so cumbersome, not so complicated . . . but easier and quicker."
- Expand self-employment activities, especially qualified ones, and be flexible in the definition of these occupations to allow others not specifically determined (the government should make a list of the disallowed activ-

ities and allow freedom for the rest): "More freedom in private business to be able to do other things"; "much clearer regulations regarding what one can do in the private sector, that they be more permissive."

- Allow university professionals to be self-employed, to avoid their exodus from state employment due to low salaries: "I was a doctor and decided to leave primarily because I did not earn enough to cover my needs"; "that a broader range of possibilities be opened up for professionals . . . that would be useful for the development of entrepreneurs and small and medium businesses." This measure would take advantage of highly underutilized human capital, raise the income of professionals, and further develop the NSS.

- Reduce excessive taxes on the NSS: "Taxes are too high . . . they are abusive; they are giving foreigners up to eight years of tax exemption on profits for millions in investment and, of course, recover them, whereas profits of the self-employed who are trying to survive are often taxed at a rate of 59 percent." The multiplicity of taxes and their heavy burden impede the development of the NSS; if this sector would grow more with the incentive of an integrated and smaller tax burden, its contribution to fiscal income would increase.

- Eliminate or modify the labor force tax on the self-employed that charges an increasing rate according to the number of salaried employees hired, punishes the self-employed who create more jobs, encourages underdeclaration of the number of employees hired, and creates obstacles for the goal of eliminating unnecessary state workers: "Officially, I have no employees." This could be resolved with a flat tax rate, regardless of the number of employees.

- Allow the CNA to hire permanent employees and outside the cooperatives in order to increase their production or services: they wish "to contract employees for a longer period [of a year], and not only from cooperatives."

- Execute the often-ignored legal norm that the NSS can contract with state enterprises: "there are many bureaucratic obstacles when it comes to negotiate with them, because they refuse, they want to do business with essentially state enterprises and not private ones"; "that state enterprises open up to a relationship with new forms of production"; "it is still hard for us to insert ourselves as a legal entity and we cannot sell to industry, buy from a factory, or sell to a state market." This measure would generate mutually beneficial interrelations for state enterprises, the NSS, and the economy.

- Create wholesale markets all over the country and reduce their prices, as well as those at TRD stores, which would eliminate the black market and promote production: "prices are too expensive at the 'shopping' store"; "I buy secretly on the black market [which] sometimes has better prices than the stores"; "we need a wholesale market [to] not have such high prices"; "the state excessively inflates prices at its stores . . . they should gamble on making more in quantity and not on the price of the product."

- Extend the contract period for usufruct farming from 10 to 50 years or make it indefinite, like in China and Vietnam, in order to provide stability and incentives to invest in the land and increase output: "the period for usufruct is short"; "they should give more time to the contract"; "if one has the land in production, they should give guarantees that they are not going to take it away."

- Increase the leasing term to CNA of state origin; end state resistance and the CNA experimental stage to give them more security and stimulate investment and production or services: "we're worried about the term, since the majority of our things are leased from the state . . . and that makes us afraid of [investing] and later all this could end"; "resistance to this new form of production persists, [which] causes us to constantly risk bankruptcy, due to the stubbornness of some who won't negotiate with us, even when it entails economic advantages for both and ignores what has been legislated"; "the CNA still is an experiment that could be over tomorrow"; "announce once and for all when this experiment will be over."

- End *acopio* and increase state prices for agricultural products, which together with access to cheaper inputs would achieve the much-desired price reduction for consumers: "I don't want the *acopio* to keep everything one produces"; "prices would be reduced if everybody sells freely and cheaper."

- Make procedures to apply for micro-bank-loans more flexible: "I started the procedure and dropped it when I didn't move forward"; "I tried and by the third week I regretted it because there is so much bureaucracy." It is internationally proven that micro-credits have a high rate of return and promote the development of micro-businesses and the country.

- Eliminate the requirement that NSS have to prove where they get their inputs, which is a serious barrier to their expansion and stability: "to be able to buy without worrying about later having to justify where I got things."

- Support the creativity and dynamism of self-employed workers and CNA members, who want to expand not only within Cuba, but also abroad: "I'd like to have a virtual office on the Internet to be able to sell my services abroad"; "I see a container leaving for the Caribbean, why shouldn't we be able to sell in the Bahamas or the Cayman Islands?"; and "may they acknowledge our right to export and import products." This would expand Cuban exports and help reduce imports and the trade commercial goods deficit.[10]

- Increase access to the Internet, lower its cost, and facilitate other forms of advertising: "there is very little access to the Internet"; "I'd like it if all my clients had email, that they could consult my Facebook page"; "I haven't placed any ads in . . . the phone book, not so much due the cost, but rather because sometimes one must be prudent."

- Allow self-employed workers to group themselves to carry out their own functions: "We are affiliated with unions, it would be better for self-employed workers . . . to come together, create our own organization within our territory, be responsible for issuing licenses . . . generate consensus with the local government . . . and recommend what the territory wants. If there were a framework for us to be able to systematically meet . . . , I am sure that we would be able to contribute more, and better."

The following four phrases summarize the aspirations of the emerging NSS:

"Allow free rein to the fertile imagination we Cubans are exhibiting, which should be done unhindered and unrestricted; the government should facilitate that flow, not obstruct it, and control only what must be controlled" (self-employed).

"The current way of thinking must be changed, not only among us, but by our leaders—they have to give us more freedom to grow and keep cooperating" (CNA member).

"If the state wants us to produce more and better, it should help us to do so . . . and give Cuban small farmers a greater chance to cultivate the land" (usufruct farmer).

"I would like that those who govern us think more on how to make citizens' lives simpler and less on how to preserve ideas that have been demonstrated bring nothing more than destitution" (dwelling seller).

# NOTES

## 1. The Emerging, Nonstate Sector in Cuba and Its Importance

1. Where no specific source is provided, the information comes from Mesa-Lago 2012 and 2014 and Mesa-Lago and Pérez-López 2013.

2. The term "private" is not used often in Cuba, and it was not mentioned in the official media until 2014; "nonstate," "small farmers," "self-employed workers," "dwellings built by the population," etc., are used in its place. The party guidelines in 2016 used the word "private" for the first time (PCC 2016b).

3. A 2012 law attempted to give greater autonomy to the UBPC, but the results are not clear.

4. "We recognize the objective existence of market relations," but "socialist planning is the principal way for the direction of the economy," and "socialist [state] ownership of the fundamental means of production is the foremost form in the national economy" (PCC 2016b: 1)

5. For an analysis of the Congress, see Mesa-Lago 2016.

6. Several resolutions have been enacted on leasing state property to the self-employed and CNA, as well as on wholesale markets, but there is not a comprehensive law on the NSS (see chapters 3 and 5).

7. Another table in the Yearbook (9.3) includes "land tenants by legal persons," separating state enterprises and farms, UBPC, CPA, CCS, and "others," but it doesn't offer the number of people in each category.

8. Unemployment increased from 2.5 percent in 2010 to 3.5 percent in 2012 (according to the state's plan to reduce its personnel), but it decreased to 2.7 percent in 2014 and 2.4 percent in 2015 (ONEI 2015, 2016a). Thus, in 2016, it was impossible to dismiss 36 percent of the labor force and to have 40 percent of the labor force employed in the nonstate sector because the latter did not expand sufficiently. The

143

Seventh Congress of the party announced that there wouldn't be more dismissals in the state sector.

9. In one case, at least, the survey results could not be published for five years; conducted among senior citizens in 2008, the survey's results were not available by the end of 2016.

10. There was an important study done on 9 of the 201 approved self-employed occupations, in all of Cuba, carried out via U.S.-based phone calls or email, which gathered their fixed capital expenses, cost of necessary inputs, and strategies to purchase them (CSG 2015).

11. There were five interviews conducted with those who swapped dwellings in Havana in 2013, and another seven in 2015 (Morales and Scarpaci 2013, Morales 2016a).

12. Roberto Veiga and Lenier González Mederos conducted the interviews and checked the entire document. Responses were processed and tabulated by Sofía Vera Rojas, who also cross-referenced questions common to all groups with several variables and elaborated upon drafts of figures. Carmelo Mesa-Lago wrote the entire book; he is only responsible for "Antecedents" sections. Aníbal Pérez-Liñán supervised the answers, made suggestions, and read the entire document.

## 2. Self-Employed Workers

1. In March 2016, the percentage of women and youngsters had risen to 31 percent (*EFE*, 4-29-2016).

2. *El País* (March 28, 2014) reported that the government had offered administration and market economy courses to 68,000 "entrepreneurs" but did not quote a source.

3. Authorization for affixing a poster requires one to fill out an application with stamps, present the housing deed—if not available, approval by the owner—an activity plan, and the blessings of the Office of the Historian (*Café Fuerte,* Apr. 15, 2015).

4. Revolico.com was removed in May 2015 but many clients protested and it was restored (*Diario de Cuba,* May 21, 2015).

5. In order to drive the normalization process, at the end of 2014 U.S. President Barack Obama authorized imports from the NSS as well as exports of multiple goods to them, but the Cuban government still had not permitted them by November 2016.

6. A journalist asked if the new rules wouldn't "stimulate the creation of an underground commerce network" (black market), but there was no response (*Juventud Rebelde,* Oct. 2, 2013).

7. This paragraph is based on Pons 2015.

8. Initially, it was 15 percent and should have been reduced 5 percent per year to 5 percent in 2016.

9. The following are deductible: paid taxes, rent, and social security, plus a standard percentage, which fluctuates between 10 percent and 50 percent; it is not possible to deduct other costs (including investment), even if they are documented.

10. In addition, there is a tax on advertising and the rent paid for using state buildings.

11. In July 2016, the government announced that it would apply capped prices to private taxis (*14ymedio*, July 15, 2016).

12. As a more rational solution, several Cuban social scientists proposed creating competitive cooperatives entrusted with the distribution (González 2016; Pérez Villanueva 2016; Veiga, 2016).

13. In January 2016, the foreign press reported that the government had opened shopping stalls and capped prices in Artemisa, Havana, and Ciego de Ávila, and that carts selling agricultural produce in the streets of Havana had disappeared (*EFE,* Jan. 20, 2016; Reuters, Jan. 25, 2016). In May, policemen confiscated products and imposed fines on middlemen who tried to access selling posts in Mayabeque (*Cubanet,* May 31, 2016)

14. Of the total, 12 percent are medical doctors, 12 percent economists, 8 percent attorneys, and 8 percent computer scientists.

15. Neither pork nor toilet paper can be bought in free agricultural markets, as they are only sold at the TRD and the black market, respectively.

## 3. Usufruct Farmers

1. In Cuba, the only owners of agricultural lands are peasants to whom the state granted small parcels at the start of the revolution and whose number fell from 200,000 to 99,500. For an analysis of property rights in Cuban structural reforms, see Mesa-Lago 2013 and Palli 2013. The best analysis of usufruct is Nova and González-Corzo 2015.

2. However, there was a decline in noncultivated lands in the state sector and UBPC/CPA but a 20.4 percentage point increase in the CCS/private sector, which is difficult to explain.

3. In 2007, idle lands were distributed to: 51 percent state, 44 percent UBPC/CPA, and only 5 percent CCS/private. Distribution was not published after this time period.

4. Cuban agronomist Armando Nova confirmed in an email (Nov. 8, 2014) the error in the 2012 statistics.

5. Unlike the case of individuals, Decree-Law 273 (2010) confers surface rights to luxury golf courses of foreign investors for a term of up to 99 years.

6. A 2013 law allows ties between cooperatives and CCS.

7. The ANPP reported in 2015 that 73 percent of state enterprises that had losses in 2014 were agricultural; one delegate commented on the serious problems in agriculture: its bad organization, lower capital investment in its businesses, insufficient training of personnel, and poor use of research (*Havana Times,* July 14, 2015).

8. Based on an annual payment of 5 percent of sales, we estimate that the volume of these payments was 400,000 CUP in 2015, 52 times the mean average salary of a state employee.

9. The production of citrus fruits was a significant source of exports; it declined from 981,000 tons in 1989 to 96,810 in 2014 (Mesa-Lago 2012, updated with ONEI 2015).

## 4. Members of Nonagricultural and Service Cooperatives

1. The two most recent and important studies on CNA are Piñeiro 2015 and Ritter and Henken 2015.

2. In view of this last figure, it is doubtful that there were 2,150 barber and hair-

dressing cooperatives, as reported in *Bohemia,* no. 68 (2013). Also, if in that year 5,490 CNA members were leasing 2,141 state buildings (*Granma,* July 1, 2013, July 6, 2013), there should have been 7,640 CNA partners vis-à-vis the official figure of 2,300 in 2013. Table 46 reports that number for 2013.

3. In 2013, a state wholesale enterprise in Isla de Juventud opened for the sale of food, intermediate and consumption goods, and for leasing refrigeration and transportation equipment (*EFE,* March 8, 2103), but no more information was published.

4. This is equal to US $400 and US $2,000, respectively.

5. The Cuban journal *Temas* reported public criticisms of CNA concerning the slow approval of proposals, the existence of hundreds of shelved records, and the authority of functionaries at any level to veto them (Chappi 2014).

6. Earlier, Raúl Castro had said, "it is an experimental process and, although it is progressing, its fundamental purpose is to detect possible faults and correct them.... We cannot rush ourselves in the constant approval of these cooperatives. We will go at the appropriate pace" (*Granma,* March 3, 2014).

7. Usufruct was approved in 2008, self-employment has been encouraged since 2010, and CNA officially began in 2013, although they have been experimental since 2011. The party guidelines promise "to advance in the experiment of the CNA" (PCC 2016b: 2).

## 5. Buying and Selling Dwellings

1. Not everyone acquired the dwelling by renting from the state; others constructed or inherited it (see sub-subsection "1. Dwelling ownership" in subsection "a. Buyers and sellers").

2. Intense rains in Havana in December 2013 caused 135 collapses (*Agencia Xinhua,* Dec. 2, 2013).

3. Rules determine the goods that one can acquire at state hard-currency shops (TRD) with subsidies (Consejo de Ministros 2013).

4. In 1960, the national cadaster began but was later abandoned: "there is no legal regulation that forces people to inform the national registry about construction modifications they make, thus neither the urban or rural registry are sufficiently updated" (*Granma,* March 3, 2014).

5. In December 2015, 20 homes were confiscated because their owners were not really Cubans but Italian, Russian, Chinese, or Spanish fronts.

6. Suppose that the dwelling value on the deed is 20,000 CUC but it has been really purchased for 40,000 CUC; the 4 percent tax on this would be 800 CUC in the first case, but 1,600 CUC on the second.

7. The new referential value controls an old problem: the value of a dwelling acquired after paying 20 years of rent to the state was fixed at 10 percent of the dweller's salary, creating serious distortions in the dwelling's value.

8. For example, the question "Who is the owner of the dwelling?" was asked only of sellers, while the question "Did you buy in a better neighborhood?" was asked only of buyers.

## 6. Comparisons, Conclusions, and Suggestions

1. We eliminated three common questions because they had less than 30 interviewees, and we left the questions that had between 30 and 80 interviewees.

2. The national average for employees contracted by one self-employed worker is 0.3 percent.

3. Only 15 percent of Cuba Emprende (2016) trainees got remittances; a survey showed that 32 percent of the self-employed used remittances to start their businesses (Padilla, 2014). The 24 percent in our sample is between those two figures.

4. Dummies were generated to carry out the association analysis with interviewees' characteristics.

5. A satisfaction level of $p = < 0.05$ in the Fisher exact test or in the Pearson chi-square test.

6. Notwithstanding this, 75 percent of the interviewees from 51 to 60 years old also said they received assistance.

7. Fidel Castro's death, which occurred after this book was finished, opened an interrogation on whether the reforms and the nonstate sector would stagnate or accelerate.

8. Due to the small size of our sample, it was not possible to find significant relationships of characteristics (age, sex, skin color, and education) with satisfaction/dissatisfaction and profits; we chose the nine most relevant relationships to discuss herein.

9. Recall that the sample of CNA members was tiny and hence its results are not solid.

10. Among the measures taken by Obama is the approval for NSS to export and import, but by the end of 2016 the Cuban government had not yet authorized this.

# APPENDIX 1

## QUESTIONNAIRE FOR THE INTERVIEWS

### SELF-EMPLOYED

1. Are you satisfied with your occupation and what you earn? (order from 1 lowest, to 10 highest)
2. Were you previously unemployed, worked informally, employed by state, or retired?
3. What is your occupation? (food-beverage vendor, *paladar* restaurant, truck driver, repairman [of what], dwelling lessor)

    If it is a *paladar*: how many chairs?; if it is a dwelling lessor: how many rooms?

    Do you operate out of your home or do you rent a locale (arcade, inside)?
4. How much did you pay for the license? (CUP or CUC)
5. How much do you pay in taxes (monthly or annual?)

    If you can, separate them: profits, sales, labor force, social security (are you enrolled?), others
6. Do you contract employees?

    If yes: How many? (family members, from elsewhere, contract an accountant)

7. By what method do you pay your employees?

    (Discretionary) What salary do you pay your employees and with what frequency? (day, month)

8. Do you have problems with the labor force?

    Yes_____ Why? _____ No_____

9. Do you have profits or utilities after taxes? (month, year)

    If yes: How and for what do you use it?

10. How long would or did you take to recover your investment in your business?

11. Do you receive remittances from abroad?

    If yes: Do you invest (part of) it in your business?

12. Have you received a small loan or credit from the government?

    If yes: How much? When do you have to pay it back? How much interest do you pay?

13. Have you received other help in establishing your business? (family members, friends or both (inside and outside the country)

14. Do you have competition?

    If yes: Do you lower the price of the product/service to attract more clients?

15. Do you believe your product/service is better than what others in your business offer?

    (How?)

16. Where do you obtain inputs for the business? (wholesale market, agricultural market, TRD or shopping store, other)

17. How do you advertise your business? (word-of-mouth, poster, blog, others)

18. Do you plan to expand your business/activity?

    If yes: How much and how?

19. What are the most serious problems you face? What would you like to see change or improve?

## USUFRUCT FARMERS

1. Are you satisfied with your occupation and what you earn? (order from 1 lowest, to 10 highest)

2. Did you have previous experience in agriculture?

    If yes: Have you been trained by the state or someone else?

3. What is the size of your parcel? (for example, 0.13 hectares [0.32 acres] or 0.67 hectares [1.65 acres])

4. Did you remove the *marabú* from the land? (how did you do it, by hand, with equipment)

   If no: Why?

5. Do you have a house or barn on the parcel, or are you building it?

   If no: Why?

6. What do you grow? (main crop, others)

7. Have you planted or are you planting fruit trees, other trees? (if not said before)

8. How much do you pay in taxes? (monthly or annually)

   What are the taxes you pay? (separate them: profits, sales, labor force, others)

9. Do you contract employees?

   If yes: how many? (family members, from elsewhere)

10. By what method to you pay your employees?

    (Discretionary) What salary do you pay your employees? (day, month)

11. Do you have problems with the labor force?

    Yes_____ Why?_____ No_____

12. Do you have profits or utilities after taxes? (month, year)

    If yes: How do you use it for?

13. Are you tied to a cooperative or state farm?

    If yes: Kind of cooperative? (UBPC, CPA, CSS). Benefits derived from this tie?

    Would you rather be independent?

14. Do you receive remittances from abroad?

    If yes: Do you invest (part of) it in the farm?

15. Have you received a small loan or government credit?

    If yes: How much? When do you have to pay it back? How much interest do you pay?

    If no: Why not?

16. Have you received any other help for your usufruct farm? (family members, friends, inside and outside Cuba)

17. What portion of your production do you sell to the *acopio*?

    (A) Would you prefer to market your production directly or through the state?

    Yes_____ No_____Why?

(B) Do you think prices of the products you produce could be reduced at the stand?

Yes_____ No_____ Why?

18. How do you obtain tools, seeds, fertilizer? (wholesale or agricultural market, shopping store, other)

19. Do you worry that your 10-year contract will not be renewed when it expires or even before?

20. Do you know that when you die, family members who worked with you can inherit the contract and investment made by you?

21. What are the most serious problems you face? What would you like to see change or improve?

## MEMBERS OF NONAGRICULTURAL PRODUCTION COOPERATIVES (CNA)

1. Are you satisfied with your occupation and what you earn? (order from 1 lowest, to 10 highest)

2. What did you do before? (worked for the government, doing the same thing you're doing now)

3. What does the cooperative do? (barbers, manicurists, shoe or electrical appliance repair, etc.)

4. How many members does the cooperative have? (has the number grown since it was set up?)

5. What are the advantages and disadvantages of working at a cooperative compared to your prior work with the state? (we are our own bosses and make the decisions, earn more, improve the locale, give better service to clients)

6. Are there limitations on your business? If it is a barber shop or nail salon, are there a limited number of seats?

7. What is the monthly rent you pay the state (CUP or CUC), and how much do you pay in tariffs for public utilities and phone, as well as in taxes? (separated, if possible)

   If it concerns a cooperative that rents rooms to tourists, what is the monthly quota (CUP or CUC) paid to the state?

8. Do you have utilities or profits after taxes? (month, year)

   If yes: How and what do you use them for?

9. How are the net profits divided up (after paying taxes) among members (equal parts, according to the capital or work they contribute)?

10. Have improvements been made to the business, like painting and fixing up the locale, buying new equipment?

11. Do you contract employees?

    If yes: How many? (family members, nonfamily members)

12. By what method do you pay your employees? Daily, weekly, monthly salary, according to their efforts (a percentage of what they produce or make)?

    (Discretionary) What salary do you pay your employees? (day, week, month)

13. Do you have problems with the labor force?

    Yes_____ Why?_____ No_____

14. Do you receive remittances from abroad?

    If yes: Do you invest part of it in the cooperative?

15. Have you received a small loan or credit from the government or a bank?

    If yes: How much? When do you have to pay it back? How much interest do you pay?

16. Have you received some other sort of assistance for the business? (family members, friends, inside or outside Cuba)

17. How do you obtain the inputs you need? (wholesale or agricultural market, shopping store, other, "on the sly")

18. Do you have competition?

    If yes: Do you reduce the price of the product/service to attract more customers?

    Do you believe your product/service is better than what others in your business offer? How?

19. How do you advertise your business? (word-of-mouth, posters, blog, others)

20. Does the cooperative have a time limit on its lease with the state?

    If yes: For how long? Do you worry that they will not renew your lease when the contract expires or even sooner?

21. What are the most serious problems faced by the cooperative? What would you like to see change or improve?

## BUYING AND SELLING OF DWELLINGS (BUYERS AND SELLERS)

1. Were you or are you the owner of your dwelling?

    If yes: Did you acquire it paying the state rent for 20 years, via an exchange, or own effort?

2. Do you own a dwelling or vacant lot?
3. Have you sold or bought a dwelling (house or apartment) since buying and selling was authorized?
4. Have you donated or received a donation of a dwelling or plot of land? (from a family member, from someone else)

    For sellers:

    With whom do you currently live?

    Do you own the dwelling?

5. Where was the dwelling you sold or where is the one you bought?

    In case of the latter, is the neighborhood in which you bought a better one?

6. Do you have a second dwelling for recreation or rest? (at the beach or in the country)
7. How long did it take you to buy/sell your dwelling? (from the time you listed it for sale until it sold)
8. What was the value of the purchase/sale or donation? (in CUP, CUC, foreign currency)
9. How did you find out the dwelling was for sale or what did you do to advertise yours? (word-of-mouth, poster, at an open market, blog)
10. Did you buy the dwelling with your own resources or receive assistance from a family member or friend abroad?
11. Did you use a broker to handle the purchase/sale?

    If yes: How much did you pay for his or her services (CUP or CUC)? Was it a percentage of the value?

12. Was your dwelling or the one you bought on the property registry?

    If no: How difficult was it to inscribe or update the dwelling in the registry?

    How much did you pay to the property registrar? (total or percentage of value)

13. Was it easy to find a notary to conduct the transaction? How much did he or she charge you?
14. Do you believe that the 4 percent tax on the dwelling's sale price is adequate?
15. What have you done with the value of the sale of your dwelling? (buy another one of equal or lesser value, invest part of it in a business, buy needed things, travel abroad)
16. Do you know that family members have the right to inherit your dwelling, even if you emigrate abroad (after a procedure with the government is done)?

17. Have you received a government loan to repair your dwelling before selling it or after purchasing it?

    If yes: What is the value of the loan, when do you have to pay it back, and what is the interest rate?

18. Have you received a state subsidy to buy construction materials in order to build a dwelling?

    If yes: What was the value of the subsidy? Was it easy or difficult to obtain?

    What was the procedure you followed?

19. Is it easy now to find construction materials and do you believe prices are high or adequate?

20. What are the most serious problems you faced during the buying and selling or construction of your dwelling? What would you like to see change or improve?

## BUYING AND SELLING OF DWELLINGS (BROKERS)

1. How long have you been working as a real estate broker and in which of the city's zones?
2. What methods do you use for being contacted by buyers and sellers?
3. If you advertise, how do you do it, and if you don't, do you plan to, and how?
4. How has the relation between supply and demand evolved in buying and selling? How has this influenced prices? What are the causes of these fluctuations?
5. Approximately what proportion of buying and selling is done among Havana residents, and how much with a resident in other provinces? (name the provinces)
6. What proportion of the people that you contact carry out the purchase/sale?
7. What are the primary objectives for selling a dwelling?
8. In your opinion, what is the minimum, medium, and high price in buying and selling?
9. In what currency?
10. Do you believe the actual transactions for buying and selling are simple or complex?
11. Do you believe the 4 percent tax on buying and selling is adequate or not?
12. How much do you pay for your license annually?
13. Does the income you receive compensate for the license, taxes, and other expenses?

14. What are the most serious problems buyers and sellers or dwelling builders face?
15. What they would like to see change or improve?
16. What are the most serious problems you face as a broker in buying and selling? What would you like to see change or improve?

# APPENDIX 2

## LIST OF COMMON QUESTIONS TO ALL GROUPS

1. Satisfaction: self-employed (25), usufruct (25), member CNA (5) = 55
2. Previous occupation: self-employed (25), CNA (5) = 30
3. Annual tax: self-employed (25), usufruct (25), CNA (5) = 55
4. Employees: self-employed (25), usufruct (25), CNA (5) = 55
5. Payment of employees: self-employed (25), usufruct (25), CNA (5) = 55
6. Problems with employees: self-employed (25), usufruct (25), CNA (5) = 55
7. Profits: self-employed (25), usufruct (25), CNA (5) = 55
8. Use of profits: self-employed (25), usufruct (25), dwelling sellers (10), CNA (5) = 65
9. Remittances: self-employed (25), usufruct (25), CNA (5) = 55
10. State credit/loan: self-employed (25), usufruct (25), buying and selling (20), CNA (5) = 75
11. Other assistance: self-employed (25), usufruct (25), buying and selling (20), CNA (5) = 75
12. Competition: self-employed (25), CNA (5) = 30
13. Lowering of price: self-employed (25), usufruct (25), CNA (5) = 55
14. Better product/service: self-employed (25), CNA (5) = 30

15. Inputs: self-employed (25), usufruct (25), CNA (5) = 55
16. Advertising: self-employed (25), buying, selling, and brokers (25), CNA (5) = 55
17. Problems: self-employed (25), usufruct (25), buying, selling, and brokers (25), CNA (5) = 80
18. Change/improvement: self-employed (25), usufruct (25), buying, selling, and brokers (25), CNA (5) = 80

# BIBLIOGRAPHY

Amuchástegui, Domingo. 2016. "Amid private-sector struggles, state freezes coop startups. *Cuba Standard* (July).
Arlidge, John. 2013. "Cuba home of the oddest property market." *Financial Times*, June 21.
Armengol, Roberto. 2013. "Competitive solidarity and the political economy of *invento*." *Cuba in Transition* 23. Washington, DC: ASCE.
Banco Central de Cuba (BCC). 2013. Instrucción No. 1. Havana, February 7.
Banco Central de Cuba (BCC). 2014. Resolution No. 35. *Gaceta Oficial*, May 21.
Benítez, Daniel. 2013. "Cuba's housing situation." *Havana Times*, July 9.
Castro, Raúl. 2013. "Discurso en la Clausura del Segundo Período de la Asamblea Nacional del Poder Popular." *Granma*, December 23.
Castro, Raúl. 2016a. "Informe central al VII Congreso del PCC." *Granma*, April 17.
Castro, Raúl. 2016b. "Discurso en el período de sesiones de la Asamblea Nacional del Poder Popular." *Granma*, July 8.
Chappi Docurro, Tania. 2014. "Cooperar es progresar." *Catalejo el Blog de Temas*, October 1.
Chappi Docurro, Tania. 2016. "La propiedad y sus derechos." Summary of the debate in *Ultimo Jueves de Temas*, March.
"Cierran mercado mayorista." 2016. *Cuba Debate*, May 31.
Cobo, Narciso. 2016. "Cuentapropismo y pequeña empresa: una mirada desde el derecho." *Cuba Posible*, January 18.
Consejo de Ministros. 2013. Acuerdo No. 7.387. Regulation of housing subsidies. May 6.
Coyula, Regina. 2014. "Los papeles de El Papelito." *14ymedio*, June 26.
Cuba Emprende. 2016. http://proyectocubaemprende.org/ateliers_calendario/index_frontend.

"Cuba entrega más de 1,7 millones de tierras en usufructo desde 2008." 2015. Havana, EFE, May 16.

Cuba Standard. 2015. *Economic Trend Report 4th Quarter*. Miami.

Cuba Study Group (CSG). 2015. *Suministrando el Crecimiento: Retos y Oportunidades para Emprendedores Cubanos*. South Bend, IN: Team of Kellogg School of Management, July 28.

Decree-Law 288. 2011. Housing reform. November 22.

Decree-Law 315. 2014. Infractions of regulations for self-employment. *Gaceta Oficial*, January 15.

Decree-Law 318. 2013. Regulations of *acopio* and state leases to CNA. October 20.

Decree-Laws 259, 300, and 304. 2008, 2012. Regulations of usufruct. July 10 and October 22.

Decree-Laws 305 and 309. 2012. Nonagricultural cooperatives (CNA). November 15 and 28.

Decree-Law 322. 2014. Modifications to housing law. July 31.

Díaz, Ileana, and Dayma Echevarría. 2015. "Mujeres emprendedoras en Cuba: Análisis imprescindible." In Pérez Villanueva and Torres 2015, 145–58.

Díaz, Ileana, Héctor Pastori, and Camila Piñeiro. 2012. "El trabajo por cuenta propia en Cuba: Lecciones de la experiencia Uruguaya." *Boletín Cuatrimestral*. Havana: Centro de Estudios de la Economía Cubana.

Economic Commission for Latin America and the Caribbean (ECLAC). 2014. *Anuario Estadístico para América Latina y el Caribe*, Santiago de Chile.

"En la reunión del Consejo de Ministros . . . fueron aprobadas cinco medidas relacionadas con la vivienda." 2014. *Granma*, November 30.

"Expectativas por cuenta propia." 2014. *Granma*, January 31.

Feinberg, Richard. 2013. *Soft Landing in Cuba? Emerging Entrepreneurs and Middle Classes*, Washington DC: Brookings Institution.

Figueredo, Oscar, Eduardo Domínguez, and Ladyrene Pérez. 2016. "Modificación de precios: Llegó el tema a la Asamblea Nacional." *Cuba Debate*, July 5.

Fong, Igor G., and Heriberto Rosabel. 2015. "En Cuba, banca: Créditos sin demanda." *Bohemia*, April 14.

Fonticoba, Onaisys. 2014. "Agricultura: aciertos y dificultades." *Granma*, July 4.

Fonticoba, Onaisys. 2015. "Compraventa de viviendas ¿qué hacer?" *Granma*, June 23.

Foresight Cuba. 2016. "Precios tiendas TRD mayo 2016." May 29.

Frank, Marc. 2016. "Havana suspends new licenses for private restaurants, owners fret." *Reuters*, October 17.

Frank, Marc, and Rosa Valdés. 2014. "Cuba looks to cooperatives to slow the rise of capitalism." *Reuters*, April 13.

Gámez, Nora. 2016. "¿Qué puede comprar un trabajador cubano con su salario mensual?" *Nuevo Herald*, May 3.

González, Lenier. 2016. Comments to Mesa-Lago on changes of prices and distribution of agricultural products. Havana, February 26.

González, Víctor. 2014. "Un éxito empresarial, las carnicerías sin moscas." *14ymedio*, November 6.

González-Corzo, Mario, and Orlando Justo. 2014. "Cuba's emerging self-employed entrepreneurs: Recent developments and prospects for the future." *Journal of Development Entrepreneurship* 19, no. 3:1–26

Havana Consulting Group (THCG). 2014. *Sector privado Cubano: A pesar de las limitaciones compite con fuerza con el sector estatal*. Miami, December.

Henken, Ted. 2015. "The Cuban reset." November 18.

Law No. 113. 2012. Tax reform. *Gaceta Oficial*, November 21; also Resolutions Nos. 41–42 and No. 353 (2013).

Leiva, Miriam. 2015. "Resultados del XI Congreso de la ANAP." *Cubanet*, May 25.

León, Jessica, and David Pajón. 2015. "Política crediticia en Cuba: Evolución reciente y efectos sobre el sector no estatal." In Pérez Villanueva and Torres 2015, 103–13.

Malmierca, Rodrigo. 2014. Interview in "Cuba rumbo a Panamá, haciendo justicia y aportando al desarrollo." *Granma*, April 6.

Malmierca, Rodrigo. 2016. Cited in "Cuba reconoce que su economía no crecerá en 2016." EFE, November 1.

Martín González, Marianela. 2015. "Sin crecimiento en la producción agrícola no habrá riqueza en el país" [Report of Marino Murillo to XI Congress of ANAP]. *Juventud Rebelde*, May 16.

Martín Herrera, Marcelo. 2013. Documentary *Elena* exhibited at ICAIC, Havana, April.

"Más de 12.000 unidades de la gastronomía y los servicios técnicos y personales pasan a la gestión estatal." 2014. *Cubadebate*, October 1.

"Más que un asunto de números." 2013. *Catalejo Último Jueves*, March 10.

Mata, Zunilda. 2016a. "Los dueños de piscinas se rebelan contra la burocracia." *14ymedio*, August 23.

Mata, Zunilda. 2016b. "El camino cuesta arriba de una cooperativa gastronómica." *14ymedio*, September 16.

Mesa, Natacha T. 2015. "Cooperativas no agropecuarias: Razones para un nuevo cuerpo legal cooperativo en Cuba." In Pérez Villanueva and Torres 2015, 63–74.

Mesa-Lago, Carmelo. 2012. *Cuba en la era de Raúl Castro: Reformas económico-sociales y sus efectos*. Madrid: Editorial Colibrí.

Mesa-Lago, Carmelo. 2013. "Los cambios de propiedad en las reformas estructurales en Cuba." *Espacio Laical*, no. 223 (February).

Mesa-Lago, Carmelo. 2014. "Institutional changes in Cuba's economic and social reforms." In *Cuba Economic Change in Comparative Perspective*, edited by Richard Feinberg and Ted Piccone. Washington, DC: Brookings Institution and Universidad de Havana.

Mesa-Lago, Carmelo. 2016. "El lento avance de la reforma en Cuba." *Política Exterior*, no. 171 (May–June): 94–104.

Mesa-Lago, Carmelo, and Jorge Pérez-López. 2013. *Cuba under Raúl Castro: Assessing the reforms*. Boulder-Londres, Lynne Rienner.

Ministerio de Comercio Interior (MINCIN). 2013. Resolution No. 52, February 14.

Ministerio del Interior (MININT). 2014. Resolution No. 4, May.

Ministerio de Trabajao y Seguridad Social (MTSS). 2014, 2015. Reports and regulations on self-employment. Havana.

Ministerio de Turismo (MINTUR). 2015. Resolution No. 29, June.

Monreal, Pedro. 2016. "Si la empresa privada es la respuesta, entonces, ¿cuál es la pregunta?" *Cuba Posible*.

Morales, Emilio. 2014. "Crecen las ventas, bajan los precios, pero todavía el mercado inmobiliario está en un bajo perfil." Miami: Havana Consulting Group, July 3.

Morales, Emilio. 2015. "Real estate in Cuba, situación actual." Miami: Havana Consulting Group, March.
Morales, Emilio. 2016a. Estudio sobre real estate en el Mercado Cubano, Informe Anual 2015. Miami: Havana Consulting Group, February.
Morales, Emilio. 2016b. "Remittances market: One of the most attractive in Latin America." *THCG Business Report*, no. 3 (June): 2–5.
Morales, Emilio, and Joseph Scarpaci. 2013. "Mercado inmobiliario en Cuba: El boom de la especulación." Miami: Havana Consulting Group, May.
Murillo, Marino. 2013. "Informe a la Asamblea Nacional." *Granma*, July 5 and 8.
Murillo, Marino. 2014. "Reunión del Consejo de Ministros." May 11.
Murillo, Marino. 2015a. Informe a la Asamblea Nacional en "Ratifica Asamblea Nacional que economía cubana crece 4 percent en 2015." *Cuba Debate*, December 29.
Murillo, Marino. 2015b. "Persisten reservas de eficiencia en la economía cubana." *Granma*, December 20.
Murillo, Marino. 2016a. "Actualizar sin alejarse de la esencia de nuestro sistema social." *Granma*, April 7.
Murillo, Marino. 2016b. "Intervención en el VII Período Ordinario de la Asamblea Nacional." *Granma*, July 9.
Nova González, Armando. 2013. *El modelo agrícola y los lineamientos de la política económica y social en Cuba*. Havana: Editorial Ciencias Sociales.
Nova González, Armando, and Mario González Corzo. 2015. "Cuba's agricultural transformations." *Journal of Agricultural Studies* 3, no. 2:175–93.
"Nuevos cursos de capacitación para trabajadores en el sector no estatal." 2016. *Granma*, June 1.
Oficina Nacional de Estadísticas e Información (ONEI). 2010, 2011, 2012, 2013a, 2014, 2015. *Anuario Estadístico de Cuba 2009, 2010, 2011, 2012, 2013, 2014, 2015, 2016a*. Havana.
Oficina Nacional de Estadísticas e Información (ONEI). 2013b. *Informe final del Censo de Población y Viviendas*. Havana.
Oficina Nacional de Estadísticas e Información (ONEI). 2016b. *Organización institucional: Principales entidades, correspondiente al período Octubre–Diciembre 2015*. Havana, January.
Oficina Nacional de Estadísticas e Información (ONEI). 2016c. *El color de la piel según el Censo de Población y Viviendas*. Havana, February.
Oficina Nacional de Estadísticas e Información (ONEI). 2016d. *Venta de productos agropecuarios indicadores seleccionados, Enero–December 2015*. Havana.
Oficina Nacional de Estadísticas e Información (ONEI). 2016e. *Sector agropecuario. Indicadores seleccionados enero-diciembre 2015*. Havana, February.
Oficina Nacional de Estadísticas e Información (ONEI). 2016f. *Panorama Económico y Social en Cuba 2015*. Havana, April.
Oficina Nacional de Estadísticas e Información (ONEI). 2016g. *Sector agropecuario: Indicadores seleccionados enero-marzo de 2016*. Havana, May.
Oficina Nacional de Estadísticas e Información (ONEI). 2016h. *Venta de productos agropecuarios: Indicadores seleccionados enero-marzo 2016*. Havana, May.
Ojeda, István. 2016. "Precios; no bastan los buenos deseos." *Periódico26.cu*. Las Tunas, January 20.

Padilla Pérez, Maybell. 2015. "Self-employment in Cuba: Results of a survey." *Cuba in Transition*, no. 24. Miami: ASCE.

Palli, José M. 2013. "Superficie and usufruct rights in Cuba: Are they really insurable rights?," *Cuba in Transition*, no. 23. Miami: Association for the Study of the Cuban Economy.

Palli, José M. 2014. "The housing institute fades away." *CubaNews* (November).

Pañellas, Daybel, Jorge E. Torralbas Pañellas, Jorge E. Torralbas, and Claudia M. Caballero. 2015. "Timbiriches y otros negocios: Cuentapropismo e inequidades sociales en la capital cubana." In *Retos para la Equidad Social en el Proceso de Actualización del Modelo Económico Cubano*, edited by María C. Zabala, Dayma Echevarría, Marta R. Muñoz and Geydis E. Fundora, 215–42. Havana: Editorial Ciencias Sociales.

Partido Comunista de Cuba (PCC). 2016a. *Congreso PCC: Conceptualización del modelo económico y social Cubano de Desarrollo Socialista y Plan Nacional de Desarrollo Económico y Social hasta 2030: Propuesta de Visión de la Nación, Ejes y Sectores Estratégicos*. Havana, May 24.

Partido Comunista de Cuba (PCC). 2016b. *Actualización de los Lineamientos de la Política Económica y Social del Partido y la Revolución para el Período 2016–2021*. Havana, August.

Pedraza, Lina. 2015. "Proyecto de ley de presupuesto del estado para 2016." *Granma*, December 30.

Pérez, Lorenzo. 2015. "Los impuestos en Cuba ¿qué se debe cambiar?" *Palabra Nueva*, May.

Pérez Villanueva, Omar Everleny. 2016. "El cubano espera una economía reflejada en su bienestar." *Palabra Nueva*, March 8.

Pérez Villanueva, Omar Everleny, and Ricardo Torres Pérez, eds. 2015. *Miradas a la economía Cubana: Análisis del sector no estatal*. Havana: CEEC, Editorial Caminos.

Peters, Philip. 2014. *Cuba's new real estate market*. Washington, DC: Brookings Institution.

Piñeiro Harnecker, Camila. 2014. "Diagnóstico preliminar de las cooperativas no agropecuarias en La Habana, Cuba." *Cuba y la Economía*, Havana, May 30.

Piñeiro Harnecker, Camila. 2015. "Nuevas cooperativas cubanas: Logros y dificultades." in Pérez Villanueva and Torres 2015, 53–71.

Pons, Saira. 2015. "Tax law dilemmas for self-employed workers." CEEC, Universidad de Havana, May 20.

"Presentan Informe del Ministerio de Agricultura en Parlamento Cubano." 2014. *Cuba Debate*, July 2.

Puig, Yalma. 2014. "Taxis bajo un nuevo modelo de gestión." *Granma*, January 8.

"Raúl: Lo que hacemos debe ser sometido constantemente a la crítica constructiva..." 2015. Reports of Raúl Castro and Marino Murillo at the Meeting of the Council of Ministries 2015. *Granma*, May 31.

Ravsberg, Fernando. 2015. "Don't bite the hand that educates you: On Cuba's teachers." *BBC Mundo*, October 17.

Redacción. 2015. "Sin mucho cambio cifra de cooperativas no agropecuarias en 2015." *Cuba y la Economía*, August 4.

Resolutions No. 60, 61 and 62. 2016. MINCIN, Regulations on leasing state enterprises in commerce, gastronomy and services to self-employed, and relations between productive entities and wholesale distributors with CNA and self-employed. *Gaceta Oficial Extraordinaria*, April 13.

Resolutions No. 333 and 334. 2011. November 11. No. 516, December 23, non-agricultural and service cooperatives (CNA).

Resolutions No. 353, 41, and 42. 2013. Regulations on self-employment. *Gaceta Oficial*, September 23.

Resolution No. 427. 2012. Ministerio de Finanzas y Precios, regulación de CNA.

Ritter, Archibald R. M., and Ted Henken. 2015. *Entrepreneurial Cuba: The changing policy landscape*. Boulder: First Forum Press.

Rodríguez, Isaac. 2014. "El cuentapropismo salvaje." *Granma*, February 7.

"State firm quietly opens first wholesale store." 2016. *Cuba Standard*, July 10.

"Subsidios: Sin margen para el error." 2016. *Bohemia*, January 20.

"Turismo: Alianza provechosa." 2015. *Bohemia*, March 9.

Vázquez, Karelia. 2015. "Manual para comprar casa en Cuba." *El País*, October 13.

Veiga, Roberto. 2016. "La ineficiencia, el caos o un nuevo modo de gestión: Opiniones sobre la comercialización agropecuaria." *Cuba Posible*, February 26.

Vera Rojas, Sofía, and Aníbal Pérez-Liñán. 2016. Tabulations and analysis of answers in interviews made to self-employed workers, usufruct farmers, CNA members, and selling/buying dwellings, Pittsburgh.

Vidal, Pavel. 2016a. "Un peligroso repliegue de las reformas en la agricultura cubana. Una propuesta para que continúe el experimento." *Cuba Posible*, May 16.

Vidal, Pavel. 2016b. "La hora de la pequeña y mediana empresa privada." *On Cuba*, June 23.

Vuotto, Mirta. 2016. "Las cooperativas no agropecuarias y la transformación económica en Cuba: Políticas, procesos y estrategias." *REVESCO Revista de Estudios Cooperativos*.

Werner, Johannes. 2014. "Industrial co-op growing fast." *Cuba News* (November).

Whitefield, Mimi. 2015. "Cuba: A new-style Cuban cooperative." *Miami Herald*, September 2.

# ABOUT THE AUTHORS

**Lenier González Mederos**, interviewer and compiler of the interviews in Cuba; graduate of the University of Havana with a degree in social communication; Doctoral coursework in sociology at the University of Florence; former coeditor of *Espacio Laical*; currently co-director of *Cuba Posible* (Havana), one of the most important and influential journals in Cuba.

**Carmelo Mesa-Lago**, Distinguished Service Professor Emeritus of Economics and Latin American Studies, University of Pittsburgh; visiting professor or researcher in 8 countries, lecturer in 39; author of 96 books or monographs and 303 articles or chapters in books published in 7 languages in 34 countries, approximately half of them on Cuba; founder and editor of *Cuban Studies* for 18 years. His most recent books are *Cuba en la era de Raúl Castro: Reformas económico-sociales y sus efectos* (2012) and *Cuba under Raúl Castro: Assessing the Reforms* (with Jorge Pérez-López, 2013); International Labour Organization Decent Work Research Prize shared with Nelson Mandela.

**Aníbal Pérez-Liñán**, consultant for the processing and tabulation of the interviews; professor of political science, University of Pittsburgh; editor *Latin American Research Review*; distinguished researcher at the Kellogg Institute for International Studies, Notre Dame University; visiting professor in seven countries; author of two books and more than 60 articles or chapters in edited books on political institutions and democratization.

**Roberto Veiga González**, interviewer and compiler of the interviews in Cuba; graduate of the University of Havana with a degree in law; doctoral coursework in political science at the University of Florence; former coeditor of *Espacio Laical*; currently co-director of *Cuba Posible* (Havana), one of the most important and influential journals in Cuba.

**Sofía Vera Rojas**, processor and tabulator of the interviews; doctoral candidate in political science at the University of Pittsburgh, with a specialization in compared politics. Her research interests include political parties, electoral behavior, and democracy in Latin America.

# INDEX

Page numbers followed by "f" and "t" refer to figures and tables, respectively. Page numbers in *italics* refer to interview responses. Page numbers followed by "ch" and "n" refer to page references in the notes.

accounting classes, 76
*acopio* (procurement quota), 2, 22, 50, 51, 52, 140; and CNAs, 72, 136; and usufruct farmers, 50, 51, 52, *61–64*, *62*f15, *67–68*, *67*t35, 125, 127, 130, 136
advertising: and CNAs, *84*; comparison of interviewees responses, *126*f30, 127; *ofertas*, 17; principal interview result concerning, 137; tax on, 144ch2n10; use of by buyers and sellers, 91–92, *102*, *103*t43; use of by real estate brokers, *112*; use of by self-employed workers, 38, 39f8
Afro-Cubans, 24, 119; underrepresented in survey interviews, 120, 135
age of interviewees: age and assistance, 131, 147ch6n6; average age of interviewees, 135; comparison of interviewees characteristics, 118, *118*t52; principal interview result concerning, 136, 137; self-employed workers, *24*; significant associations found with other characteristics, 130–32
aging population, 6

agricultural lands, 45, 46, 48, 49, 145ch3n1. *See also* idle lands; usufruct farmers
agriculture products, 21, 22, 24, 36, 50, 51, 52, 53, 72, 73, 134; increasing prices as a specific suggestion, 140. *See also* UBPC (basic units of cooperative agricultural production)
agro-livestock production cooperatives (cooperativas de producción agropecuaria). *See* CPA (agro-livestock production cooperatives)
AlaMesa (start-up company), 17
ANAP (National Association of Small (Private) Farmers), 4, 77
ANEC (Asociación Nacional de Economistas y Contadores de Cuba ). *See* National Association of Economists and Accountants (ANEC)
annual salary, mean, 57, 93, 122, 137, 145ch3n8
ANPP (National Assembly of People's Power), 11, 16, 19–20, 21, 23, 46, 49, 93, 96, 145ch3n7
*Anuario Estadístico de Cuba* (Cuban Statistical Yearbook), 4
Artemisa (province), 22, 49, 53, 72, 77, 112, 145ch2n13

167

assistance, receipt of: age and assistance, 131, 147ch6n6; other sources of assistance, 33, *34*t12, *60*t31, 61; principal interview result concerning, 136

Banco Metropolitano (state owned bank), 50, 73, 75
Banco Popular de Ahorro (state-owned bank), 50, 75
banking and bank loans, 75; bank credit, 16–17, 20, 76, *107*; for construction or repairs to a dwelling, *107*; loans for self-employed businesses, 17, 20, *33–34*, *34*t12; loans for usufruct farmers, *60*tt30–31, *61*; loans to CNAs, 73, 75–76, *83*; make micro-loans more flexible as a specific suggestion, 140; mortgage banks, 94; private farmers receiving bulk of loans, 20; for self-employed businesses, *33*, *33*t11; slowness of bank procedures, 96; usufruct farmers' access to micro-credit and bank loans, 49–50, 51. *See also* financing
barbers and hairdressing cooperatives, 145ch4n2
basic units of cooperative agricultural production (unidades básicas de producción cooperativa). *See* UBPC (basic units of cooperative agricultural production)
Bejarano, Gladys, 52, 93
black markets, 18, 37–38, *37*f7, 51, 64, 78, 83, 108, 125, *126*f29, 131, 137, 140, 144ch2n6, 145ch2n15; elimination of as a specific suggestion, 140
*Bohemia* (magazine), 18, 21, 95, 145ch4n2
bureaucratic obstacles facing the NSS sector, *108*t49, *109*, 134, 138, 139. *See also* paperwork; regulations
buyers and sellers of private dwellings, 1, 87–116; access to and prices of construction materials, *107*, *108*t48, *109*; advances made by, 89; advertising used, 91–92, *102*, *103*t43; antecedents, 87–88; buying or selling since authorization, *101*; changes and improvements desired, *110–11*, *110*t50, *111*f25; characteristics of, 89, 98–99; conversion of unused state buildings into private dwellings, 92, 96; Council of Ministers rules on private dwellings, 91; distribution of housing by price of dwellings, *103*t42; dwelling ownership, *100*; economic impact of, 134; foreigners purchasing, 89, 90, 92, 95; formal transfers of dwellings by type (2012–2014), 89t38; high costs involved and scarce income of buyers, 135; inheriting a dwelling, 88, 89, 99, 99f21, *107*, 146ch5n1; investments, *107*f23; length of time to buy or sell a dwelling, *101–2*, *101*f22; location of dwelling bought or sold, *100*t40, *101–2*; need to separate buyers and sellers in survey interviews, 98, 146ch5n8; number of transactions (2011–2014), 8; ownership of a second property, 89, 90, 94, *100*, *101*, *113*; price of the buying and selling, *102*, *103*t41; price of the buying and selling according to real estate brokers, *113*, *113*t51; principal interview result concerning, 135–37; principal problems and obstacles facing, 92–96, *108–10*, *108*t49, *109*f24; receiving a dwelling as a donation, *101*; referential value of dwellings, 95, 146ch5nn6-7; resources used for purchase of dwellings, *103*t44, *104*; sales at market prices for products/services, 133; size and trends, 88–89, 89t38; sources for acquisition, 89, *99*, 99f21, 146ch5n1; surveying of, 10, 144ch1n11; taxes on dwellings' sales prices, 95, *106*t47, 146ch5n6; temporary shelters, 87, 91, 133, 146ch5n2; total, population-built, and state-built numbers for 2006–2014, 97t39; use of brokers, *104*; use of the dwelling's sale value, *107*, *107*f23; ways of acquiring a dwelling, 99f21. *See also* construction of houses or barns; housing; housing reforms; real estate brokers, surveying of
"by population's efforts." *See* "population's efforts" (construction of private dwellings)

Camagüey (province), 14, 77, 89
capping prices in state markets, 21–22, 36, 51, 145ch2n13. *See also acopio* [procurement quota]
Casa Potín (gastronomic CNA), 18
Castro, Fidel, death of, 147ch6n7
Castro, Raúl, 2, 19; and agrarian reform, 21, 45; and CNAs, 71, 77, 146ch4n6; on growth of economy in 2016, 22; and the NSS, 52, 133
Catalina de Güines, houses bought and sold in, *102*
Catholic Church and "Cuba Emprende" training program, 16

CCS (Credit and Services Cooperative), 3, 4, 6t2, 8f2, 51, *59–61*, *60*, *62*, *64*, *125*, *126*f29, 143ch1n7; and CNAs, 72, 137; CSS/private sector, 46, 47t18, 48, 49, 53, 145ch3nn2–3; and idle lands, 145ch3n3; law allowing ties between cooperatives and CCS (2013), 145ch3n6; and noncultivated lands, 145ch3n2; and usufruct farmers, 51, *59–61*, *60*t28, *62*, *64*, *64*f16

Central Bank, 75

Centro Habana. *See* Havana

Centro Padre Félix Varela training program, 16

Cerro, houses bought and sold in, *100*, *100*t40, *101*, *102*, *103*t42

changes and improvements desired: by buyers and sellers of private dwellings, *110–11*, *110*t50, *111*f25; by CNAs, *86*; comparison of interviewees responses, 127–30, *129*f32, *129*t57; principal interview result concerning, 137–41; by real estate brokers, *115–16*; by self-employed workers, *42–44*, *42*t16, *43*f11, *67*; significant associations found between education or age and desires for change, 132; by usufruct farmers, *66*f18, *67–68*

characteristics: of buyers and sellers of private dwellings, 89, *98–99*; of CNAs, 71–72; comparison of interviewees characteristics, 117–20, *118*t52; of self-employed workers, 13–14; of usufruct farmers, 48, *53*. *See also* age of interviewees; education levels of interviewees; sex of interviewees; skin color of interviewees; women

Ciego de Ávila, 145ch2n13

Cienfuegos, 39–40, 88

citrus fruit production, 68, 145ch3n9

Civil Notaries and Registries, 92, 95

CNA (nonagricultural production and service cooperatives), 8, 15, 69–86; advances made by, 72–74; advantages and disadvantages, *80*; and advertising, *84*; allowing CNAs to hire permanent employees as a specific suggestion, 139; antecedents, 69–70; authorization for self-employed and CNAs to contract with state enterprises, 133; barbers and hairdressing cooperatives, 145ch4n2; changes and improvements desired, *86*; characteristics of, 71–72; CNAs concentrated in commerce, 71; comparison of important answers among 5 CNA interviewed, *85*t37; and competition, *84*; confusion on definition, 76; and construction, 90; creation of, 74–75, 146ch4n7; desiring acceptance from state enterprises, 80, 86, 130; difficulty in getting interviews with, 78; economic impact of, 77, 134; employees of CNAs, 76, *82*, 139; experimental nature of, 77, 146ch4nn6–7; financing of, 69, *83*; four groups of CNAs approved, 70; improvements to the businesses, *82*; increase leasing term to CNA of state origin as a specific suggestion, 140; independence of, 70; input sources, 75, *83*; limitations, *81*; membership, 79; need for accounting training, 76; not having public acceptance, *80*, *85*; number of CNAs, 70t36, 71f19; obstacles facing, 74–77; partners in CNAs, 70, 145ch4n2; previous occupations, *79*; and pricing policies, 69, 76–77; principal interview result concerning, 135–37; principal problems facing, *84–86*; and profits, 75, *81–82*, 133; on public utilities and telephone costs, *81*; sales at market prices for products/services, 133; satisfaction with occupation and earnings, *78–79*; size and trends, 70–71, 71f19; slow approval of proposals, 146ch4n5; state-origin cafeteria as a CNA, *78*, *79*, *80*, *81*, *83*, *84*, *85*, *86*; support CNA who wish to expand as a specific suggestion, 140–41; on taxes, *81*; tourism activities being transferred to, 15–16; transferred from state enterprises, 10, 15, 69, 71, 73, 74, 75, 76, 78, 79

collateral guarantees, 17, 20, 90, 135

competition: and CNAs, *84*; comparison of interviewees responses, 124, *125*; principal interview result concerning, 136; and self-employed workers, *34–37*, *35*f6, *36*t14

concentration of wealth, 4, 19, 51

confiscation: of dwellings, 87, 146ch5n5; of tools/equipment, 20, 37

Conoce Cuba (start-up company), 17

construction of houses or barns, 90, 91, 95, *110*, *115*, 133; application process, 94; assessing state plan for, 96, 98; bank loans and subsidies for construction, *107*; and construction materials, 87, 92–93, *107–8*, *108*t48, *109*; economic impact of, 134;

construction of houses or barns (*cont.*): government facilitating, 90; graph of housing constructed by state and population 2006–2014, 98f20; no regulation to report construction modifications, 146ch5n4; numbers of constructions, 88–89; "by population's efforts" (construction of private dwellings), 87–88, 91; principal interview result concerning, 136; subsidies for, 91, 95–96; total, population-built, and state-built numbers for 2006–2014, 97t39. *See also* buyers and sellers of private dwellings

convertible Cuban peso (peso cubano convertible). *See* CUC (convertible Cuban peso)

cooperative subsector of NSS, 4, 5t1, 6t2, 8, 8f2; creating competitive cooperatives, 145ch2n12; law allowing ties between cooperatives and CCS (2013), 145ch3n6; as midpoint between private and state property, 3; usufruct farmers ties to cooperatives, 51, *59–61*, *60t28*, *62*, *64*, *64f*16, *64f*16. *See also* CCS (Credit and Services Cooperative); CNA (nonagricultural production and service cooperatives); CPA (agro-livestock production cooperatives); UBPC (basic units of cooperative agricultural production)

Council of Ministers, 2, 15, 70, 74, 77, 91, 134

CPA (agro-livestock production cooperatives), 3, 4, 6t2, 8f2, 53, 70, 72, 143ch1n7; and CNAs, 72; and cultivated, noncultivated and idle lands, 46, 48, 145ch3n2, 145ch3n3; and usufruct farmers, *51*, *59*, *61*

credit, 20, *60t30*, 94, *110*, *111*, *111*f25, 116, 129f32; bank credit, 16–17, 20, 76, *107*; government (state) credits/loans, *33*, *33*t11, *61*, *83*, *85*t37, 91, 123–24, 124t55, *125*f28, 136; greater access to, *110*t50, 128, 129, 129t57; micro-credit, 1, 9, 49–50, 51, 73, 75, 91, *107*, 140; principal interview result concerning, 136. *See also* banking and bank loans; CCS (Credit and Services Cooperative); financing

Credit and Services Cooperatives (Cooperativas de Crédito y Servicios). *See* CCS (Credit and Services Cooperative)

credit cards, not available to self-employed, 21

Crédito y Comercio (state-owned bank), 50

"Cuba Emprende" training program, 16, 32, 147ch6n3

Cubanacán, 15

Cuban Communist Party (Partido Comunista de Cuba). *See* PCC (Cuban Communist Party)

Cuban national peso (Peso cubano nacional). *See* CUP (Cuban national peso)

Cubatxi, 15

CUC (convertible Cuban peso), 15–16, 23, 27, 27t4, 37, 58, 69, 105; what constitutes a fortune, 88

CUP (Cuban national peso), 16, 27, 27t4, 56, 57t24, 69, 105, 113; 25 CUP = 1 CUC = US $1, xi

Decree-Law 259 (2008), 45
Decree-Law 273 (2010), 145ch3n5
Decree-Law 288 (2011), 88
Decree-Law 289 (2012), 16, 73
Decree-Law 300 (2012), 45, 50
Decree-Law 315 (2014), 20
Decree-Law 318 (2013), 50, 52, 72
Decree-Law 322 (2014), 89, 91
development plan (through 2030), 3, 11
Diez de Octubre, houses bought and sold in, *100*, *100*t40, *102*, *103*t42

earnings. *See* salaries; satisfaction with occupation and earnings
economic impact of four sectors of NSS, 133–34
economic model, 3
education levels of interviewees, 135, 145ch2n14; comparison of interviewees characteristics, *118*t52, 119–20; principal interview result concerning, 136, 137; self-employed workers, 24
electricity tariffs, 81
*El País* (newspaper), 144ch2n2
*El Papelito.com* (weekly housing sales), 92
El Trigal (wholesale market), 17–18, *38*, 50, 72, 75, *83*
employees, interviewees having: comparison of interviewees responses, 122, *122*t54; principal interview result concerning, 135; self-employed workers having employees of their own, *28–31*, *29*tt5–7, *30*t8, 147ch6n2; usufruct farmers having employees of their own, *57*t26, *58*, *58*t27
employment situation, 4; CNA's contribution to, 77; employed labor force by employment

situation (2005–2015), 5t1; estimated number of people in the nonstate sector, 2014, 6t2. *See also* labor force
equity in property, 89–90
EspacioCuba (internet site), 92
exports, 141, 144ch2n5, 147ch6n10

financing: accessing credit, *111*, *111*f25; and CNAs, 69, *83*; comparison of interviewees responses on remittances government loans/credit or other assistance, 123–24, *124*, *125*f28; micro-credits from state, 9, 49, 51, 55, 91, 107; principal interview result concerning, 136; resources used for purchase of dwellings, *103*t44, *104*. *See also* banking and bank loans; credit; investments
Fisher exact test, 147ch6n5
Five-Year Plan (2012–2016), 11
foreigners: leasing rooms to, 26; purchasing a dwelling, 89, 90, 92, 95; receiving tax incentives, 43, 139
foreign investment, 145ch3n5; excluding self-employed, 21
foreign remittances, 9, 94, 124t55, 125f28; and self-employed workers, *32*; and usufruct farmers, *61*. *See also* remittances

gastronomical state enterprises: and CNAs, 71, 75; transferred to self-employed category, 13, 15, 21. *See also paladares* (small private restaurants)
GDP (gross domestic product): agricultural output, 52; CNAs impact on, 77; and housing, 96; nonstate sector as percentage of in 2015, 9; percentage generated by self-employed, 23–24
*general plan* for taxes. *See* taxes
Gold Pig (*Cerdo de Oro*) (CNA), 73–74
golf courses, surface rights to, 145ch3n5
González Corzo, Mario, 145ch3n4
González Mederos, Lenier, 144ch1n12
government credits. *See* credit
*Granma* (newspaper), 15, 17, 21
Granma (province), 91, 97
gross domestic product. *See* GDP (gross domestic product)
Guidelines of the 2016 Congress, 4

Havana, 18, 22, 49, 75, 145ch2n13; Centro Habana, houses bought and sold in, *100*, *100*t40, *101*, *102*, *103*t42; CNAs concentrated in, 72; housing in, 88, 89, 91; intense rains causing buildings to collapse, 146ch5n2
Havana Brokers' House, 92
household consumption: average monthly costs, 22–23; contribution of self-employed to, 23
housing: allowance for foreigners to purchase or lease, 89, 90, 92, 95; confiscation of dwellings because owners not Cubans, 146ch5n5; formal transfers of dwellings by type (2012–2014), 89t38; housing deficit, 87; housing prices, 88–89; rules on ownership, 94. *See also* buyers and sellers of private dwellings; construction of houses or barns; property registry
housing reforms, 90, 91; Decree-Law 288 (2011), 87–88, 89; Decree-Law 322 (2014), 89, 91; trying to control underdeclaration of housing, 95; urban reforms of 1960, 87

idle lands, 45–46, 145ch3n3; evolution of agricultural land, cultivated, noncultivated and idle, 49f12; in 2007, 2013, and 2014, 48t19. *See also* noncultivated lands
imports, 37, 43, 75, 144ch2n5, 147ch6n10
income taxes. *See* taxes
independent, usufruct farmers on being, 60–61, 60t29
inheritance: of a dwelling, 88, 89, *99*, *99*f21, *107*, 146ch5n1; of usufruct, 49, 65, 65t34
inputs, sources of: for CNAs, 75, *83*; comparison of interviewees responses on acquisition of inputs, 125–26, *126*f29; eliminate requirement that NSS have to prove where they got them as a specific suggestion, 140; importing of, 18, 144ch2n5; for self-employed businesses, 37–38, *37*f7; shortages as an obstacle facing the NSS sector, 134; for usufruct farmers, 64, 64f16, 67
Institute of Physical Planning (Instituto de Planificación Física). *See* IPF (Institute of Physical Planning)
Internet, 17, 40, 75, 116; increase access and lower costs of as a specific suggestion, 141; as a problem faced by interviewees, *40*f10, *41*, *41*t15, *42*, *42*t16, *43*, *43*f11, *68*, *110*, *110*t50, *111*f25, *127*, *128*f31, *128*t56, *129*, *129*f32,

Internet: as a problem faced by interviewees (*cont.*), *129*t57, 138, 141; use of for advertising, *38, 39*f8, 84, 102, *102*, *103*t43, 111, 112, *126*f30, *127*, 134, 137

interviews and survey: antecedents of conclusions reached, 133–35; comparison of interviewees characteristics, 117–20, *118*t52; comparison of interviewees responses to questions addressed to all four groups, 120–30; dummies generated to carry association analysis, 147ch6n4; elimination of common questions with less than 30 interviewees, 147ch6n1; guidelines used for, 10; list of common questions to all groups, 157–58; need to separate buyers and sellers in survey interviews, 98, 146ch5n8; principle interview results, 135–41; questionnaires used for interviews of specific groups, 149–56; significant associations between characteristics and responses, 130–32, 135, 147ch6nn5–8; size of sample of CNA members and summary results, 78, *85*t37, 147ch6n9; state limitations on conducting, 9, 144ch1n9; study methodology, 9–11; summary of aspirations of emerging NSS, 141; summary of characteristics of average interviewee, 135; summary of major problems and desired changes, 137–41; summary of principle interview results, 135–37; those responsible for conducting survey interviews, 144ch1n12. *See also* buyers and sellers of private dwellings; CNA (nonagricultural production and service cooperatives); self-employed workers; usufruct farmers

investments, 1, 9, 50, 76, 145ch3n7; by buyers and sellers of private dwellings, *107*f23; by CNAs, 76; foreign investment, 21, 145ch3n5; principal interview result concerning, 123f27, 131, 134, 136, 140; by self-employed workers, 21, *30*t9, *31–32, 32*f5, *33*t10, 144ch2n9; by usufruct farmers, 48–49, 51–52, *55*, 59, 59f14, 65

IPF (Institute of Physical Planning), 92

Isla de la Juventud (province), 89, 146ch4n3

Isladentro (start-up company), 17

*Juventud Rebelde* (newspaper), 94

Karabalí cabaret, 74

labor force: employed labor force by employment situation (2005–2015), 5t1; estimated number of people in the nonstate sector in 2014, 6t2; predominant state economy (includes 71% of labor force), 1; reduction of number of state employees, 2, 6–7; size of peaking in 2009, 6; taxes on, 19. *See also* employment situation

landowners: distribution of nonstate sector by its components, 8f2; in NSS (nonstate sector), 6t2, 7, 8

legal persons (micro-, small-, and medium-private enterprises), 4, 45; "land tenants by legal persons," 143ch1n7. *See also* natural persons (individuals)

licenses: for CNA bank accounts, 75; for real estate brokers, 92, *114*; for self-employed workers, 8, 12, 19, 20, 21, *26–27, 38, 39*, 141

Long-Term Plan (through 2030), 11

Madruga, houses bought and sold in, *102*

*marabú* (spiny brush), eradication, *54–55, 55*t21; and tax exemption, 49, 51

Marianao (province), 74, *102*

market, role of, 3, 143ch1n4

market economy, courses in, 16, 144ch2n2

MasterCard, 21

Matanzas (province), 72, 88–89

Mayabeque (province), 22, 23, 49, 72

Mercantile Registry, 75

Mesa-Lago, Carmelo, 22, 144ch1n12

micro-businesses/micro-enterprises, 4, 14, 16, 17, 20, 21, 34, 59, 90, 133, 140

micro-credits and micro-loans, 1, 9, 16, 49–50, 51, 55, 72, 73, 75, 91, 107; make more flexible as a specific suggestion, 140

Ministry of Construction (Ministerio de Construcción) (MINCON), 92

Ministry of Domestic Trade (Ministerio de Comercio Interior) (MINCIN), 15–16, 73, 83, 84

Ministry of Finances and Prices, 73

Ministry of Health, 92

Ministry of Justice, 88, 89, 94, 96

Ministry of Labor and Social Security (Ministerio de Trabajo y Seguridad Social), 12, 13–14, 16, 24, 25

Ministry of Tourism (Ministerio de Turismo) (MINTUR), 15–16, 75

Miramar neighborhood of Havana, 18, 88, 89, 113
mortgages, 87, 90, 94, 135
MTSS (Ministry of Labor and Social Security), 12, 13–14, 16, 24, 25
Murillo, Marino, 15, 22, 45–46, 50, 52, 70, 74, 90

National Assembly of People's Power (Asamblea Nacional del Poder Popular). *See* ANPP (National Assembly of People's Power)
National Association of Economists and Accountants (ANEC), 16, 76
National Association of Small [Private] Farmers (Asociación Nacional de Agricultores Pequeños). *See* ANAP (National Association of Small (Private) Farmers)
National Auditing Office, 76
National Office of Statistics and Information (Oficina Nacional de Estadísticas e Información). *See* ONEI (National Office of Statistics and Information)
National Office of Tax Administration (Oficina Nacional de Administración Tributaria). *See* ONAT (National Office of Tax Administration)
natural persons (individuals), 4, 45–48. *See also* legal persons
new cooperatives, members of, 1, 133
new occupation for self-employed, approval of, 12, 13, 18
nonagricultural production and service cooperatives (cooperativas de producción no agrícola y de servicios). *See* CNA (nonagricultural production and service cooperatives)
noncultivated lands, 46, 47t18, 48, 48t19, 49, 49f12, 145ch3n2. *See also* idle lands
nonstate sector. *See* NSS (nonstate sector)
notary publics, 74, 75, 88, 94, *109–110*, 109f24, *127*; cost of notary service for buying and selling a dwelling, 92, *105–106*, 105t46; need for (Decree-Law 322 [2014]), 89; and payments of taxes on dwellings' sales prices, 94, 95; simplifying communication between notaries and registrars, 92
Nova González, Armando, 45, 50, 145ch3nn1–4
NSS (nonstate sector), 1–11; advances made by "private" subsector in the NSS, 133; allowing NSS to contract with state enterprises as a specific suggestion, 139; distribution of nonstate sector by its components, 8f2; economic impact of, 133–34; employed labor force by employment situation (2005–2015), 5t1; estimated number of people in the nonstate sector, 2014, 6t2; evolution of state and nonstate sector (2005–2014), 7f1; expansion of, 2, 133, 135; growth of employment in, 6–7; impact of Fidel Castro's death on reforms, 147ch6n7; improvements for workers in, 15; law of enterprise to regulate, 3, 143ch1n6; need for government to facilitate rather than obstruct, 141; Obama approval of NSS to export and import, 144ch2n5, 147ch6n10; obstacles facing, 134–35; opening and expansion of in 2014, 133; as percentage of GDP in 2015, 9; principal interview result concerning, 135–37; quantification of, 4–9; Raúl calling for limits to be imposed, 52; receiving credit and loans, 16–17; regulation of by the state, 4; summary of aspirations of emerging NSS, 141; summary of major problems and desired changes, 137–41. *See also* cooperative subsector of NSS; "private" subsector of NSS

Obama, Barack, 144ch2n5, 147ch6n10
*ofertas* (ads), 17. *See also* advertising
Office of the Historian, 144ch2n3
ONAT (National Office of Tax Administration), 12, 16; and CNAs, 73, 74–75; licensing real estate brokers, 92; and notary publics, 95; and self-employed workers, 20, 26, *43*
ONEI (National Office of Statistics and Information), 119; monitors CNAs, 70; Statistical Yearbooks, 11, 45; "Survey of Self-Employed Workers," 9; on usufruct farmers, 45, 46
ownership, 3–4, 45, 46, 69, 99, 101, 133

*paladares* (small private restaurants), 9, 14, 15, 21, 22, 133. *See also* gastronomical state enterprises
paperwork, 17, 113–14; excessive (as an obstacle for the NSS sector), 61, 75, *108*t49, *109*, 134. *See also* bureaucratic obstacles facing the NSS sector
*Paquete Semanal*, 17, 38
partners in CNAs, 70, 145ch4n2

payment methods, 135; for CNA employees, *82*; used by self-employed workers to pay own employees, *28–30*, *29*tt5–7

PCC (Cuban Communist Party), 51; conducting regular opinion polls, 9; Seventh Congress of (2016), 3–4, 11, 14, 52, 71; Sixth Congress of (2011), 71

Pearson chi-square test, 147ch6n5

Pedraza, Lina, 23

Peoples Savings Bank, 17

Pérez, Ola Lidia, 92

Pérez-Liñán, Anibal, 144ch1n12

Pérez Villanueva, Omar Everleny, 22, 71, 75, 76

personal income taxes. *See* taxes

personal services: CNAs in, 71–72; state budget merging housing with communal and personal services, 92

Pinar del Río (province), 50, 91

Piñeiro Harnecker, Camila, 71

Playa, houses bought and sold in, *100*, *100*t40, *102*, *103*t42

Playa Habana, 88

"population's efforts" (construction of private dwellings), 3, 87–88, 91, 96; total, population-built, and state-built numbers for 2006–2014, 97t39. *See also* construction of houses or barns

previous occupations: of CNAs, *79*; comparison of interviewees responses, *121*, *121*f26; of self-employed workers, *25–26*; significant associations found between age and previous occupations, 130

pricing policies: and CNAs, 69, 76–77; comparison of interviewees responses on price reductions, 124–25; for self-employed businesses, *34*t13, *35*; for usufruct farmers, *63*, *63*t33, *67–68*

principal problems facing interviewees: buyers and sellers of private dwellings, 92–96, *108–10*, *108*t49, *109*f24; CNA (nonagricultural production and service cooperatives), 84–86; comparison of interviewees responses, 127–30, *128*f31, *128*t56; principal interview result concerning, 137–41; real estate brokers, *114–15*; self-employed workers, *40–42*, *40*f10, *41*t15; usufruct farmers, 65, *65–67*, *66*f17

private dwellings. *See* buyers and sellers of private dwellings

private entrepreneurialship (*emprendimiento*), two types of, 4

private farmers, 72; and CSS, 3; receiving loans, 20

private market stalls, 22, 145ch2n13

private property and micro-businesses, 133; cooperative subsector as midpoint between private and state property, 3

"private" subsector of NSS: advances made by "private" subsector in the NSS, 133; advances of, 133; clarification on meaning of, 143ch1n2; role of private ownership of production, 3–4. *See also* salaried employees; self-employed workers; "small farmers"; usufruct farmers

private taxis transferred to nonstate sector, 15

"privatization or alienation," 4

problems with employees: CNA members not reporting any, *82*; comparison of interviewees responses, 122; self-employed workers having, *30–31*, *30*t8; usufruct farmers not reporting any, *58*

product and service comparisons between self-employed and competitors, *36–37*

production distribution of usufruct farmers, *63t32*

profits: and CNAs, 75, *81–82*, 133; comparison of interviewees responses, 123, *123*f27; principal interview result concerning, 135–36; profit tax, 73, 146ch4n4; for self-employed businesses, *30*t9, *31*, *32*f5; significant associations found between age and use of profits, 131; significant associations found between age or education and use of profits, 131–32; for usufruct farmers, *59*, *59*f14

property, taxes on sale of. *See* taxes

property registry/registries, 74, 75, 88, 90, 93–94, 96, *114*; no regulation forcing people to inform, 146ch5n4; time and cost of inscription in, *104*, *105*t45

publicity: authorization for posters, 144ch2n3; for self-employed businesses, 17. *See also* advertising

purchasing power of people, 88, 93

race of interviewees. *See* skin color of interviewees.

real estate brokers, *109*; authorization for buying construction materials, 133; authorization of in 2013, 90; changes and improvements desired, *115–16*; compensation of income relative to costs, *114*; completed transactions, *112*; contacts by clients, *111–12*; on licensing, *114*; location of buying and selling, *112*; on objectives of sellers, *113*; price of the buying and selling according to real estate brokers, *113*, *113*t51; principal problems facing, *114–15*; on property sales tax, *114*; on supply and demand and impact on pricing, *112*; surveying of, *111–16*; on transaction process, *113–14*; use of, *104*

referential value of dwellings, 95, 146ch5nn6–7

regulations: affecting self-employed workers, 17, 20; applying to self-employed, 18–19; for getting loans, 20; government actions (2013–2016) hurting self-employed, 21; self-employed workers needing less bureaucracy and restrictions, *41*, *42*t16, *43*f11. *See also* bureaucratic obstacles facing the NSS sector

remittances, 123; and CNAs, *83*, *85*t37, 123–24; comparison of interviewees responses, 123–24, *124*t55, *125*f28; and Cuba Emprende trainees, 147ch6n3; foreign remittances, 9, 32, *61*, 94, 124t55, 125f28; principal interview result concerning, 136; significant associations found between age and remittances, 130–31; use of by self-employed workers, 32, 33, 123, 147ch6n3; and usufruct farmers, *61*, 123. *See also* foreign remittances

Revolico.com, 17, 38, 89, 92, 102, *110*, 111, 112, 127, 144ch2n3

Rodríguez, Gustavo, 77

salaried employees, 3, 4, 12, 14, 16, 20, 122, 135, 139

salaries: annual mean salary, 57, 93, 122, 137, 145ch3n8; comparison of interviewees responses, 122, 128f31, 128t56, 129t57; cuts to, 22; impact of on buying and selling of dwellings, *110*, *110*t50, *111*f25, 115, 129, 130, 137, 138; increases in, 2, 74; low salaries, 21, *108*t49, *109*, *109*f24; potential expansion of NSS impacting, 135

sales at market prices for products/services, 133

sales tax. *See* taxes

Santa Clara District Center of Training Felicia Pérez (Catholic nonprofit organization), 16

Santiago de Cuba (province): housing in, 91, 95

satisfaction with occupation and earnings, 130–32; of CNAs, *78–79*; comparison of interviewees responses, *120*f26, 121; principal interview result concerning, 135; of self-employed workers, *24–25*; usufruct farmers, 53, *54*f13

self-employed workers, 1, 2, 12–44, 36, *38*; advances made by, 14–17; allowing self-employed to group themselves and organize as a specific suggestion, 141; allowing university professionals to be self-employed as a specific suggestion, 139; architects not allowed to be, 93; authorization for self-employed and CNAs to contract with state enterprises, 133; changes and improvements desired, *42–44*, *42*t16, *43*f11, *67*; changes in ways of counting, 13; characteristics of, 13–14; and competition, *34–37*, *35*f6, *36*t14; and construction, 90; definition and antecedents, 12; description of current employment, *26*, *26*t3; distribution of nonstate sector by its components, 8f2; economic impact of, 23–24, 134; encouraged since 2010, 146ch4n7; evolution of numbers of, 2009–2015, 13f3; expansion of, 9, 14, 24, 137; expansion of as a specific suggestion, 138–39; government actions (2013–2016) hurting, 21; having employees of their own, *28–31*, *29*tt5–7, *30*t8, 147ch6n2; impact of state moving from self-employment to cooperative model, 77; investments, 21, *31–32*, *32*f5, *33*t10, 144ch2n9; legalizing of self-employment, 14; locations of, 14; national average for employees contracted by a self-employed worker, 147ch6n2; numbers of, 71; obstacles facing, 17–23; occupations allowed to work in, 18–19; percentage also having a state job, 14; percentage of women, 8; previous occupations, *25–26*; pricing policies, *34*t13; principal interview result concerning, 135–37; principal labor activities of, 14; principal problems facing, *40–42*, *40*f10, *41*t15; procurement and payment of license, *26–27*; profits, *30*t9, *31*, *32*f5; real estate brokers as, 114; restriction of to mostly underqualified jobs and banning university professionals, 134; sales at market prices for products/services, 133; satisfaction with occupation and earnings, *24–25*, *25*f4;

self-employed workers (*cont.*): "savage self-employment," 21–22; size and trends, 12–13, 13f3; small business expansion, 39–40, 40f9; sources of inputs for, 37–38, 37f7; support self-employed who wish to expand as a specific suggestion, 140–41; taxes paid by, 27–28, 27t4; tourism activities being transferred to, 16; training for, 16; transferring state establishments to, 15, 73, 133; use of advertising, 38, 39f8

sellers. *See* buyers and sellers of private dwellings

sex of interviewees, 1, 14, 48, 72, 89, 117, 135, 147ch6n8; comparison of interviewees characteristics, *118*t52, 119, 130; significant associations found with between sex and purchase of inputs at TRD, 131

"shoppings." *See* TRD (state hard-currency shops ["shoppings," as Cubans call them])

shortages affecting self-employed workers, 17

*simplified plan* for taxes. *See* taxes

size and trends of sectors: in CNA sector, 70–71, 71f19; housing sector, 88–89, 89t38; in self-employed sector, 12–13, 13f3; in usufruct farming sector, 45–46, 47t17, 48

skin color of interviewees, 1, 10, 24, 48, 72, 89, 135; comparison of interviewees characteristics, *118*t52, 119

small business expansion and self-employed workers, 39–40, 40f9

"small farmers," 2, 20, 141, 143ch1n2. *See also* usufruct farmers

social security contributions: by CNAs, 73, 77; by self-employed, 12, 14, 19, 27, 28, 144ch2n9

State Council, 2

state credits/loans. *See* credit

state enterprises, 3, 72, 76, 143ch1n7, 145ch3n7; and acceptance of CNAs, 80, 86, 130; allowing NSS to contract with state enterprises as a specific suggestion, 139; CNAs transferred from, 10, 69, 71, 74, 75, 76, 78, 79; inactive state enterprises, 15; and the self-employed, 21, 35; self-employed workers and CNAs authorized to contract directly with, 133. *See also* CNA (nonagricultural production and service cooperatives); gastronomical state enterprises; TRD (state hard-currency shops ["shoppings," as Cubans call them])

state hard-currency shops. *See* TRD (state hard-currency shops ["shoppings," as Cubans call them])

state markets, 21–22, 23–24, 36, 51, 81, 139

state-origin cafeteria as a CNA, 78, 79, 80, *81*, 83, 84, 85, 86

state property: cooperative subsector as midpoint between private and state property, 3; leasing of, 143ch1n6, 145ch4n2; tax on rent paid for using, 144ch2n10

state sector: budget assigned to housing, 92; capping prices for private taxis, 144ch2n11; capping prices in markets, 21–22, 36, 51, 145ch2n13 (*see also acopio* [procurement quota]; control of usufruct farming, 45; conversion of unused state buildings into private dwellings, 92, 96; employed labor force by employment situation (2005–2015), 5t1; evolution of state and nonstate sector, 2005–2014, 7f1; facilitating construction, 90; and idle lands, 145ch3n3; increase leasing term to CNA of state origin as a specific suggestion, 140; leasing products to CNAs and CCSs, 72; limitations on conducting surveys, 9, 144ch1n9; mean monthly salary in, 23; and noncultivated lands, 145ch3n2; offering market economy courses, 144ch2n2; plan to transfer state establishments to self-employed and CNAs, 73, 133; preference for cooperatives, 8, 73, 77; as previous occupation of many self-employed, 25–26; reduction of number of state employees, 2, 6–7, 143ch1n8; and role of the market, 3, 143ch1n4; separating state enterprises and farms, 143ch1n7; state budget merging housing with communal and personal services, 92; theft (desviación) of state resources, 18; transfer of state establishments into self-employed and CNA sectors, 10, 15, 69, 71, 73, 74, 75, 76, 78, 79; urban reforms of 1960, 87

"structural" reforms, 2, 8, 11, 133

study methodology, 9–11; guidelines used for interviews, 10; list of common questions to all groups, 157–58; questionnaires used for interviews of specific groups, 149–56. *See also* interviews and survey

subsidies, *110*; for dwellings damaged by hurricanes, 91, 133; irregularities in granting housing subsidies, 135; for purchase of construction materials, 91, 93, 95–96, *107*; rules determining goods that can be acquired at TRDs with subsidies, 146ch5n3; state-subsidized products, 75

Supreme Court legalizing real estate transactions, 92

surface rights to golf courses, 145ch3n5

"Survey of Self-Employed Workers," 9

surveys. *See* interviews and survey

taxes: categories of, 19; and CNAs, 73, *81*; comparison of interviewees responses, 121–22; *general plan* for taxes, 19, 27; granting of some temporary tax exemptions, 133; income taxes, 16, 19, 39, 49, 73; on labor force, 19, 144ch2n8; no mention of by CNAs, *81*; as an obstacle for the NSS sector, 134; personal income taxes, 93, 144ch2n9; principal interview result concerning, 137; profit tax, 73, 146ch4n4; on property sales prices, 90, 94–95, *106*, *106*t47, *114*, 146ch5n6; reducing excessive taxes as a specific suggestion, 139; reduction of for *marabú* eradication, 49, 51; sales tax, 49; on self-employment, 16, 17, 19–20, 23, 27–28, 27t4; significant associations found between education and annual taxes, 132; *simplified plan* for taxes, 19, 27; and usufruct farmers, 49, 57t24-25

taxis, 9, 15, 18, 144ch2n11; private taxis and old, vintage taxis as an advancement, 133

technical services: CNAs in, 13, 15, 71–72, 73, 78; self-employed workers in, 78

telephone costs, 15, 81

*Temas* (journal), 146ch4n5

temporary shelters: hurricane damage causing, 91, 133; intense rains causing buildings to collapse, 87, 146ch5n2

textile manufacturer in Marianao, 74, 75

theft: by employees, 15, *30*, 30t8, 70, *74*, *80*; of state resources (*desviación*), 18

tourism, 15, 18, 22, 72; courses on, 16; driving tourists, 21, 26, 27, 39; leasing of housing and rooms to tourists, 21, 26t3, 89, 133, 137; state tourist establishments, 13, 15–16, 41, 50

training programs, 16, 32, 147ch6n3

TRD (state hard-currency shops ["shoppings," as Cubans call them]), 18, 21, 22, *37–38*; cuts in TRD prices in 2016, 22–23; only source of some items, 37, 145ch2n15; principal interview result concerning, 137; reduction of prices as a specific suggestion, 140; rules determining goods that can be acquired, 146ch5n3; significant associations found between characteristics and purchase of inputs at TRD, 131; and usufruct farmers, *64*

trends in sectors. *See* size and trends of sectors

UBPC (basic units of cooperative agricultural production), 3, 46, 48, 51, 70, 143ch1n7; and CNAs, 72; and idle lands, 145ch3n3; law giving reater autonomy (2012), 143ch1n3; and noncultivated lands, 145ch3n2; and usufruct farmers, 59

unemployment, 6, 143ch1n8

university professionals not allowed to be self-employed, 134, 139

urban reform of 1960, 87

usufruct farmers, 1, 2, 45–68; and *acopio* (procurement quota), 50, 51, 52, *61–64*, *62*f15, *67–68*, *67*t35, 125, 127, 130, 136; advances made by, 48–50; and agricultural, cultivated, and noncultivated farms, 8f2, 47t18, 49f12; approval of in 2008, 146ch4n7; changes and improvements desired, *66*f18, *67–68*; characteristics of interviewees, 48, *53*; on choosing to be independent, 60t29, *61*; and clearing of *marabú*, 49, 51, *54–55*, 55t21; construction of houses or barns, *55*, 56t22; and contract renewals, *64–65*; definition and antecedents, 45; and distribution of usufruct land, 51–52; economic impact of, 134; expansion of land cultivated by (including usufruct), 133; extension of contract period from 10 to 50 years as a specific suggestion, 140; foreign investment, *61*; fruit tree planting, 56; government credits and bank loans, *61*; having employees of their own, *57*t26, *58*, 58t27; impact of usufruct farming in agriculture, 52–53; inheritance of usufruct, *65*; investments, 48–49, 51–52, *55*, 59, *59*f14, *65*; numbers of, 47t17; obstacles facing, 50–52; other sources of assistance, *61*; and ownership of agricultural lands, 45, 145ch3n1;

INDEX 177

usufruct farmers (*cont.*): previous agricultural experience, *54*; principal interview result concerning, 135–37; principal problems facing, 65, *65–67*, 66f17; production distribution, 63*t*32, *63*; profits, *59*, 59f14; satisfaction with occupation and earnings, *53*; size and trends, 45–48, 47t17; sizes of parcels of land, *54*, 55t20; surveying of, 10; and taxes, 56–57, 57tt24–25; ten-year contracts as an obstacle, 134; ties to cooperatives, 51, *59–61*, 60*t*28, *62*, *64*, 64f16; types of crops or livestock, 55–56, 56t23

value of dwellings. *See* referential value of dwellings
Vedado, housing in, *100*, *100*t40, *102*, *103*t42
Veiga, Roberto, 144ch1n12
Vera Rojas, Sofia, 144ch1n12

Vidal, Pavel, 22
Villa Clara (province), housing in, 88–89

Weekly Package (*Paquete Semanal*), 17, 38
wholesale markets, 17–18, *38*, 50–51, 72, 75, 146ch4n3; and CNAs, 72; creation of as a specific suggestion, 140; experimental wholesale market, 18, 72; self-employed workers need for, *41*. *See also* El Trigal (wholesale market)
women: as buyers and sellers of dwellings, 98, 119; comparison of interviewees characteristics, *118*t52; in NSS labor force, 6t2, 7–8, 24; as percentage of self-employed, 8, 14, 24, 144ch2n1; and TRDs, 131, 137; underrepresented in survey interviews, 119, 120, 135

Zona+ (experimental wholesale market), 18, 72